The
Splendor
of
Creation

The Triumph of the Divine Will on Earth
and the Era of Peace in the Writings of the
Church Fathers, Doctors and Mystics

Rev. Joseph L. Iannuzzi

St. Andrew's Productions
Pittsburgh, PA

ISBN: 1-891903-33-0

Distributed by:
St. Andrew's Productions
P.O. Box 54204
Pittsburgh, PA 15244

Tel: 412-726-2217
Fax: 412-787-5024
Web: www.SaintAndrew.com

Printed in the United States of America

DEDICATION

This book is dedicated to the late Archbishop Fulton J. Sheen, whose devotion to the daily Holy Hour before the Eucharist, to the Blessed Virgin Mary and to the Papacy, inspired my vocation to the priesthood.

Archbishop Fulton J. Sheen's Prophecy on the Era of Peace

Our Lady told the children to tell the world that there would come a great era of peace to the world... and Russia would be converted...

As I stood there (at Fatima) on the altar, overlooking that great crowd of one million people... my mind left that white square and went to the red square of Moscow... Somehow I felt that on this day there was the great crisis between the white square of Fatima and the red square of Moscow... Then in my imagination I could see a great change coming over the hammer on the sickle. I could see that hammer that had beaten down so many homes and profaned so many sanctuaries. I could see it being held aloft by millions of men and looking now like a Cross. And that sickle, which the communists used to cut human life like unripened wheat, I now saw as changing its figure and its symbolism and becoming, as the Book of the Apocalypse said, "the moon under the Lady's feet."

† Archbishop Fulton J. Sheen

TABLE OF CONTENTS

Amidst the dark and turbulent times in which we are living, the prophetic voice of Pope John Paul II has assured us again and again that we are living in the pre-dawn darkness of a bright new day and has urged us to renew our hope in "the definitive coming of the Kingdom of God" *(Tertio Millenio Adveniente)*. Father Iannuzzi's magnificent book, *The Splendor of Creation,* will assist us greatly in doing just that. The fruit of exhaustive and painstaking research, it helps us peer into two thousand years of reflection on the prayer which the Lord Jesus commanded us to pray together with Him. And still more, it presents us with convincing evidence that the day when this prayer will be answered is near at hand.

+ Archbishop George Pearce,
Diocese of Providence, R.I.
16 October 2003

Father Iannuzzi, I have previewed your work entitled *The Splendor of Creation.* I am impressed with the exhaustive research of the literature you have made. You have included the Fathers of the Church, the classical and great theologians of the Church and the writings of the mystics who are saints of the Church. In addition you adhered carefully to the official teaching of the Church found in the Ecumenical Councils and the Magisterium.

In our day when people are grasping here and there for personal receptions of God's communications and searching unapproved private revelations for guidance, your work can offer sound directions for people of faith who sincerely desire to know the Will of God in their lives.

Thank you for your scholarship. May it bring hope to many, advance souls on the way of salvation and love, and so further the kingdom of heaven on earth.

+ Bishop James H. Garland
Diocese of Marquette, MI
1 February 2004

Magnificent! A masterful introduction! Reading *The Splendor of Creation* gave me a new awareness of the grandeur of God's plan for a New Heavens and a New Earth! It opened up a new vision, and gave me a greater desire for holiness. It opened up my mind, vision, heart and desire for the coming of the Lord's Kingdom and for the fulfillment of the plan of mercy. As a fruit of *The Splendor of Creation,* I want to be holy, a saint, a "Living Eucharist." My reaction to this book is W.O.W. (Wonder of Wonders)! I thank Fr. Joseph for being the wise scribe that brings out treasures old and new!

The triumph of the Divine Will and the Era of Peace are presented in an exciting way that gives us a new and great hope in our troubled world. May the light Fr. Joseph sheds on the Era of Peace and the Final Coming of Christ bless all the readers of this book.

+ Rev. George Kosicki, O.S.B.
Renowned author and preacher of the Divine Mercy
4 April 2004

INTRODUCTION

For several centuries eschatology, dubbed "the doctrine of the Last Things," appeared content to lead a quiet life, that is, until its academic revival caused it to advance to the very fore of theology. Although eschatology had merited theological attention, never had it approached the zenith of notoriety it presently enjoys.

In recent years the Archbishop of Indianapolis Daniel Buechlein commented on an "inadequate presentation of eschatology" in catechetical texts.[2] As publishers were prompted to include necessary changes, theologians articulated new insights into the mysteries of death, judgment, heaven, hell and the final state of perfection of the people of God. That which had once shaped the attitude of the early Christians (marana tha: Come, Lord Jesus), began once again to dominate the entire theological landscape.

The invasion of a new eschatological awareness sent a ripple effect through theological circles, overcoming, in part, the age-old impasse between patristic eschatology and millenarianism.[3] With a fresh and innovative outlook theologians began to present eschatology in a way that was accessible to all. Young men studying for the priesthood were encouraged to explore the new phenomenon. Theological seminaries and universities incorporated eschatology into their curricula, referring to it as the Christian view of the kingdom of God both now (nunc) and in the age-to-come (tunc). Seminarians soon learned to esteem a science that had at first appeared rather unconventional, as a result of the erroneous teachings that marred its past.

Initially, some academics opposed the revival of eschatology within Catholic universities in view of its potential misrepresentation to the faithful. They felt that Jesus' words on the end times were too often misconstrued and misused by prophets of doom. However, other academics allayed such concerns by presenting eschatology within the traditional framework of biblical and historical theology. In their view, Jesus' words on the end times, if understood in their biblio-historical setting, offer a much-needed summons to hope in the ongoing journey toward a "new heavens and new earth."

The many approved apparitions of Mary in modern times have evoked a similar range of responses. While many of the faithful have received the messages of La Salette, Fatima, Akita, Betania and Cuapa in a spirit of optimism and renewal, others have promoted them as oracles of "doom and gloom." The attitude of optimism and renewal is indeed more in harmony with the Church's vision, as it derives from the eschatological works of the early Church Fathers. Their vision of man's historic destiny, and of the New Jerusalem of peace and holiness, is best summed up in the central petition of the Our Father: "Thy kingdom come, thy will be done on earth as it is in heaven". In this prayer the Fathers and the early Christian community embraced the kingdom of God on earth now, and in its future universal manifestation.

I have attempted to describe this kingdom and its elucidation through the centuries by the early Church Fathers, Doctors, ecclesiastical writers and approved mystics. Their literature persuasively portrays a future era of peace and an exalted type of Christian holiness in the life of the Church, during which Satan is enchained and Christ's will triumphantly reigns in man. While these authors achieved new insights in "various ways"[4] their writings never depart from their point of origin, namely Christ, thus preserving the integral development of the teachings contained in the Church's deposit of faith.

Because there are so many conflicting currents in the field of eschatology, I deem it necessary to add a word of caution. The study of such topics as the Antichrist, the end of an era and the Final Judgment, may lead to sentiments of fear that distort one's vision of the God who created us out of love. Like the early Fathers we must never lose sight of God's ultimate triumph over Satan, sin and death—a triumph that is guaranteed by Sacred Scripture, by the apostolic Tradition and by the Magisterium. Happily, the more information we derive from these inspired sources, the more we are caught up in the mystery of God's love for each and every one of us—a love which, St. John the Apostle tells us, "casts out all fear."

Initially, this work was ready for release in 1999, but circumstances allowed it to mature on the shelf and in my heart over the course of several years. It was not until October of 2002 that the reason for its delay became evident: At a gathering in Corato, Italy, The Archbishop of Trani, H.E., Mons Giovanni Battista Pichierri encouraged me to incorporate into this book the writings of the Servant of God Luisa Piccarreta. I then knew that the time had come for its release.

This work is the fruit of many years of research in Rome and of dialogue with experts in the field of eschatology. However, the more I have pursued my research, the more convinced I became of man's inability to fully comprehend God's mysteries. By their very nature God's mysteries continuously reveal themselves to the created mind without becoming exhausted or fully assimilated by his children. The Mystical Doctor St. John of the Cross wrote of the mystery of God's revelations: "To want to limit them to our interpretation and to what our senses can apprehend is like wanting to grasp a handful of air that will escape the hand entirely, leaving only a particle of dust."[5]

In light of this, I commiserate whole-heartedly with the masters of Israel who admonished their pupils either to approach eschatology with extreme prudence and caution, or not at all. The Mishna treatise Chaghiga', states as an example:

> Better for him who meditates on these things not to have been born: what is above, what is below, what is before and what is behind.[6]

The Talmudic commentary speaks of several masters in Israel who, in attempting to resolve prophetic mysteries, suffered dire consequences: Ben 'Azzaj died, Ben Zoma' went crazy, Elisha' ben Avuja' became an apostate.[7] To occupy oneself with eschatology can indeed be unsettling. To avoid this pitfall, I have surveyed the eschatological landscape from a biblio-historic perspective, using the Church's traditional modus operandi—a method of study that presents the traditional teachings of the past to our modern era as an inspired development of the teachings of Christ.

If nothing else, I hope to have acquired from my many years of research a profound awareness of mankind's ignorance before the uncreated wisdom. May the many hours I've spent researching these materials increase your knowledge of the Last Things, and may the knowledge you derive from this work dispose you to a more intimate and loving union with God.

—Joseph L. Iannuzzi

Synopsis

Chapter 1: The Sons of God

Creation was made by God to be holy, free and immortal. God placed man within the Garden of Eden to be its cultivator and protector, but man misused God's gifts and upset the natural order of creation. He was removed from Eden and placed on this earth to restore the order of creation. Sadly, this earth is a far cry from the holiness, freedom and immortality of Eden. Yet it is our earth that we are called to cultivate and protect. For in so doing, we co-operate with God and one another in restoring the beauty of the creation that man once enjoyed. Once this is achieved through God's activity in man, the aging, suffering, sickness and death that characterize our present civilization will be forever removed.

In this chapter, St. Paul alludes to the great and long-anticipated day of creation's freedom in his letter to the Romans, and statements by Pope John Paul II and Cardinal Ratzinger introduce us to a theology of creation's restoration. Modern mystics and exemplars develop this theology through their insights and lessons in how to hasten the great day of creation's rebirth that will be more glorious than the Garden of Eden.

Chapter 2: Scripture and Tradition

The early Fathers conveyed the teachings of the Apostles, some of whom had frequented their company. They are custodians and guardians of the teachings Christ left to his Apostles. They are also witnesses from the earliest centuries of

Christianity to Christ's promise of a day when creation will be set free from the bondage of slavery. From man to beast, from galaxies to planets, all creation will experience its freedom from the present laws of aging, suffering, sickness and death after a period of the Church's history commonly referred to as the "era of peace." Besides the early Fathers, several Church Doctors and approved mystics assist in elucidating the teachings handed down by Christ on this subject. This number includes several nineteenth and twentieth century exemplars of holiness who will be revisited in greater depth in the book's culminating chapter 3.5.

As always, Satan dreads and detests the restoration of the creation God gave to man. He sows confusion and controversy where God has sown order and peace to obstruct God's plan of restoration. In particular, Satan has cleverly confused a number of Catholic authors who have wrongly imputed heresy to the early Church Fathers' teachings on creation's rebirth, and by doing so, diverted our attention from the great day of creation's liberation.

Chapter 3: The Era of Peace

3.1 Church Fathers

This chapter lays the doctrinal foundation for the era of creation's peace through the witness of the Apostolic Fathers and Early Ecclesiastical Writers of early Christian times. The Fathers' teachings on "the era" were written in *allegories*. They often used allegorical and symbolic language, as this literary style was common to their day as exemplified in a popular book of that epoch known as Revelation.

The Church furthermore esteems the Ecclesiastical Writers of antiquity whose literature reinforces the teachings of the Apostles and early Fathers.

The lay reader may find this chapter somewhat prolix on account of the monologues, terminology and quotations from the earliest documented sources on the era. Nevertheless, this material helps to provide the doctrinal foundation for all the succeeding chapters, where the reader will encounter greater simplicity in style and speech.

The chapter also provides a much-needed chronology of the world's future events in tabloid form.

3.2: The Church Doctors

The writings of the Church's Doctors are presented here for chronological reasons, after the Apostles, the early Fathers and various Ecclesiastical Writers. This sequence allows the reader to better appreciate the historic continuity of Christian thought on the era of peace.

This doctrine began with Christ, was passed on to the Apostles, and was carefully elaborated through the centuries by the early Church Fathers, Writers and Doctors. Because this traditional doctrine does not deviate from Christ's original teaching, the reader can be sure of its orthodoxy. Special attention is paid to St. Augustine's work, *The City of God*, which contains new, compelling insights into the era of peace.

The first resurrection described in the twentieth chapter of the Book of Revelation is examined in light of recent biblical scholarship. The characteristics of people and events in the era of peace are reported in full detail, to provide the reader with a portrait of what it will be like to live in the days when God's Divine Will reigns in the will of the human creature, and when all creation will be set free.

3.3: The Holy Spirit and Mary in the Era of Peace

The Church's approved mystics describe the future era as a new presence of the Holy Spirit in the human spirit that grows exponentially. In particular the writings of the Servant of God Luisa Piccarreta and Venerable Conchita Cabrera de Armida take up the thread of the theology of creation's restoration where the patristic narratives left them.

Scripture scholars affirm that the universal outpouring of grace upon the entire house of Israel prophesied in the Old Testament is a unique gift reserved by the Holy Spirit and Mary for the end times. St. Louis De Montfort, St. Maximillian Kolbe and Venerable Maria of Agreda elaborate on Mary's role as a formatrix of the great saints who will arise during this era.

St. Paul intimates the era of Christian holiness when describing the future Church that is presented to Christ in a "holy and immaculate" state before his final return in glory, and Pope John Paul II offers a commentary on Paul's words.

3.4: God's Eternal Activity in the Priesthood

This chapter theologically examines the nature and activity of the priesthood of Christ to which all Christians have been invited. Today's theologian is entrusted with the task of ensuring that the interpretation of God's Word remains faithful to its point of origin. He must also illuminate the gospel message with deeper insights that both reaffirm its past and direct its future. The theologian does this by continuously drawing from the treasure trove of the Church's three modes of the transmission of revelation, namely Sacred Scripture, Tradition and the Magisterium, without neglecting new insights from the Church's Doctors, saints and mystics.

The Church always fosters contemplation of her mysteries, meditation on Sacred Scripture and new experiences of God's activity. When combined, God and man's activity contribute to the process of divinization through which all men *fully* partake in the "eternal activity of the priesthood of Christ".

3.5: *The Church Mystics*

This chapter introduces the double activity of the Divine Will and human will in the human creature. In response to the controversy of recent years concerning the writings of the Servant of God Luisa Piccarreta, this chapter explains *how* the eternal activity that God imparts to all the baptized is subject to a multitude of variations and increase in states and degrees. The baptized may internally experience the eternal realities of heaven on earth by virtue of their participation in Christ's *eternal* priesthood, while advancing to the state of God's *"continuously eternal"* activity.

God's "continuously eternal" activity constitutes the hallmark and essence of the new gift of mystical union that God is offering to his Church today! It is here presented for the first time in a way that is accessible to theologians and laity alike. This union of wills emerges from the approved writings of mystics as recent as the late nineteenth and twentieth centuries.

Chapter 4: Man's Full Participation in God's Divine Will

This chapter summarizes all the elements of the new gift of mystical union, whereby the human creature *fully* acts in God's Divine Will. It is a chapter that will benefit readers of every class, rank or place in society. It provides a point-by-point listing of all the characteristics that the Church's approved mystics experienced while *entering into* and *Living in God's Divine Will*, for growth in holiness, and for knowledge and insight.

Also included are testimonies of God's ability to lift man, after he has fallen, to a state of glory that exceeds all previous states, which reaffirms the simplest of all gospel messages: Nothing is impossible with God.

Lastly, sorrow and sanctification are presented as two key components that are intimately linked: Just as the mystics had to cross the spiritual desert to enter the promised land, so we must endure many trials and sorrows if we are to possess the greatest mystical gift of all, namely, "Living in God's Divine Will."

Chapter 5: The Final Coming of Jesus

This chapter exposes the absurdity of the *millenarian* doctrine on Christ's final return. Following the Church's Tradition, Christ's final return will mark the end of time, history and the world, as we know it.

The New Jerusalem will come down from heaven as a bride adorned to meet her immaculate spouse and will take her place in the New Heavens and the New Earth. Unlike the era of peace that occurs *within* human history, the New Heavens and the New Earth mark *the end of history*, time, aging, suffering, sickness, disease and death forever. After describing the characteristics of the New Jerusalem and the New Heavens and New Earth, this chapter offers a timely treatment of such popular topics as the Parousia, the Rapture and the *beatific mode* of the saints in heaven.

Chapter 6: *The Four Easy Steps to Living in the Divine Will*

In response to misconceptions surrounding the gift of the Divine Will, this chapter provides the reader with a simple and easy method by which he or she may enter and Live in God's Divine Will.

Chapter 7: *Magisterium and Millenarianism*

This chapter is of great benefit to today's theologian. History shows that the failure to distinguish between the various elements of doctrine led some academics to associate the teachings of several early Church Fathers with the heresy of *millenarianism*. Here one discovers the underpinnings of the Church's official position on millenarianism, and the much-needed distinction between millenarianism and the orthodox writings of several early Church Fathers, Doctors and mystics.

Epilogue: *Prophecies of Roman Pontiffs on the Era of Peace*

O, Holy Spirit, beloved of my soul... I adore You.
Enlighten me, guide me, strengthen me, console me.
Tell me what I should do... give me your orders.
I promise to submit myself to all that You desire of me and to accept
all that You permit to happen to me.
Let me only know your Will.

—Cardinal Mercier

Chapter 1
THE SONS OF GOD

"Youth of the new millennium, do not misuse your freedom… Submit yourselves solely to Christ, who desires your good and authentic joy… In this way you will discover that *it is in adhering to the will of God alone that we can become the light of the world and the salt of the earth!* These realities, as sublime as challenging, can be understood and lived solely in a climate of constant prayer. This is the secret *to enter into and to live in the will of God.*"[8]

Pope John Paul II delivered this speech at a recent gathering with the youth of Rome. It is a speech on constant fidelity to prayer and to the will of God for a new millennium of Christian witness, and is traceable to his encyclicals. Indeed his encyclical dedicated to the third Christian millennium affirms that Christianity is on the threshold of a "new springtime," that brings with it "a rediscovery of the Church's holiness"[9] and "a new era in the life of the Church."[10] Cardinal Joseph Ratzinger acknowledges that the pontiff's words concerning a new millennium allude to St. Paul's Letter to the Romans:

> Creation groans with eager longing for the
> revelation of the sons of God… Creation itself

will be set free from its slavery to corruption and obtain the glorious freedom of the sons of God.[11]

Cardinal J. Ratzinger comments:

> And we hear today the groaning as no one has ever heard it before... The Pope does indeed cherish a great expectation that the millennium of divisions will be followed by a millennium of unifications.[12]

Similarly, the approved works of the Third Order Dominican mystic, the Servant of God Luisa Piccarreta[13] have described a future millennium of unity and holiness. This new millennium, Luisa affirms, will witness an explosion of mystical gifts, particularly that of "Living in the Divine Will," and is a process that restores creation to its original splendor through the activity of God's will in the human will. To Luisa Jesus reveals that the aim of man's existence is to live in God's Divine Will, and to restore creation to its original splendor by the assimilation of Jesus' *groans of love*:

> Therefore, the soul must transform herself into Me and become one likeness with Me, thus making My Life her own, My prayers her own, My groans of Love her own, My pains her own, My fiery heartbeats her own...[14]

> I desire, therefore, that My children enter My Humanity and copy what the Soul of My Humanity did in the Divine Will... Rising above every

creature, *they will restore the rights of Creation—* My own as well as those of creatures. *They will bring all things to the prime origin of Creation and to the purpose for which Creation came to be.*[15]

In My wounds, in My Blood is seen this seed that wants to transplant itself in the creature so that it may take possession of My Will and I may take possession of its will. *In this way the work of Creation may return to its beginning whence it came;* not only by means of My Humanity but also by means of the creature... *Thus I shall have the army of souls who will live in My Will, and in them, creation shall be reintegrated, all beautiful and fair as it came forth from my hands.*[16]

A more recent exemplar of total abandonment to the Divine Will is Rev. Walter Ciszek (1904-1984), a Jesuit priest convicted of being a "Vatican spy" by the Russian government during World War II. Fr. Ciszek spent 23 years in Soviet prisons, sounding the depths of the Spirit's groanings in creation. Before his cause of beatification was introduced, several of his writings were examined by theologians in Rome who found them to be both inspired and prophetic.[17] In one of his works, Fr. Ciszek describes *how* creation is transformed and set free from its slavery to corruption through the activity of God's will in man's will:

Christ's life and suffering were redemptive; his "apostolate" in the scheme of salvation was to restore the original order and harmony in all creation that had been destroyed by sin. His perfect obedience to the Father's will redeemed man's first and continuing disobedience to that will. "All creation," said St. Paul, "groans and labors up till now," awaiting Christ's redemptive efforts *to restore the proper relationship between God and his creation.* But Christ's redemptive act did not of itself restore all things, it simply made the work of redemption possible, it began our redemption.

Just as all men share in the disobedience of Adam, so all men must share in the obedience of Christ to the Father's will. Redemption will be complete only when all men share his obedience...

This simple truth, that the sole purpose of man's life on earth is to do the will of God, contains in it riches and resources enough for a lifetime... The notion that the human will, when united with the divine will, can play a part in Christ's work of redeeming all mankind is overpowering. The wonder of God's grace transforming worthless human actions into efficient means for spreading the kingdom of God here on earth astounds the mind and humbles it to the utmost, yet brings a peace and joy unknown to those who have never experienced it, unexplainable to those who will not believe.[18]

The aforementioned writings reveal *how* creation is transformed under the influence of God. It is not through one individual, but through mankind's obedience to God's will manifested in the humanity of Jesus Christ that creation emerges from its slavery to corruption and enters what St. Paul calls 'the glorious freedom of the sons of God.'

The Vatican II Council and the works of the early Church Fathers reinforce this teaching when presenting Christ's Incarnation as a grafting of man's human nature to his Divine Nature. The more man cooperates with God's grace the more the fruits of Christ's humanity and Redemption are rendered effective in him and, by him, in creation:

> Man was created in God's image and was commanded to conquer the earth with all it contains and to rule the world in justice and holiness: he was to acknowledge God as maker of all things and *relate himself and the totality of creation* to him, so that through the dominion of all things by man the name of God would be majestic in all the earth... When he works, not only does he transform matter and society, but he fulfills himself... Here then is the norm for human activity – to harmonize with authentic interests of the human race, in accordance with God's will and design, and to enable men as individuals and as members of society to pursue and fulfill their total vocation.[19]

> The mystery of the Incarnation lays the foundation... which... moves towards God himself, indeed towards the goal of divinization.[20] *This occurs through the grafting of the redeemed on to Christ and their*

admission into the intimacy of the Trinitarian life. The Fathers have laid great stress on this soteriological dimension of the mystery of the Incarnation.[21]

The early Fathers viewed the Incarnation as a mystery that is unfolding, until all things in heaven and on earth are restored in Christ, and through him, *fully* partake in the Trinitarian life.

Several Fathers present the first and last books of the Bible as a telltale sign of creation's future characterized by universal peace and holiness: from man to beast, galaxies to planets, all creation will experience its freedom from corruption in the period of the Church's history known as the "Sabbath Rest," or the "era of peace."[22] Their point of departure is the Genesis creation account that symbolizes the world's future: the seven days of creation symbolically represent the 7,000 years of the world's existence; and God's rest on the seventh day after all his works represents the world's Sabbath Rest in an allegory of 1,000 years. Inasmuch as the Fathers teachings are rooted in the Old and New Testament books, so too is their style. Their narrations of the "era of peace" are often couched in the Old Testament style of symbolisms and allegories, and expressed through the imagery of nature. One example is found in the Book of Isaiah:

> On this mountain the Lord of hosts will provide for all peoples. A feast of rich food and choice wines, juicy, rich food and pure, choice wines.[23]

The Church Fathers Saints Justin Martyr and Irenaeus affirm Isaiah's vision of a world replete with material provisions:

I and every other orthodox Christian feel certain
that there will be a resurrection of the flesh,
followed by a thousand years in the rebuilt,
embellished, and enlarged city of Jerusalem, as
was announced by the Prophets Ezekiel, Isaias
and others.[24]

So, the blessing foretold undoubtedly refers to
the time of His Kingdom, when the just will rule
on rising from the dead;[25] when creation, reborn
and freed from bondage, will yield an abundance
of food of all kinds from the heaven's dew and the
fertility of the earth... the Lord taught and spoke
about these times... Days will come when... all
the animals who use the products of the soil will
be at peace and in harmony with one another,
completely at man's beck and call.[26]

Of the numerous characteristics associated with the era
of peace, the most significant, from the theological point
of view, is the Holy Spirit's activity in man and in creation.
We find this reflected in the liturgy of the early Christian
community, which replaced the words of the Lord's Prayer
"Your kingdom come" with "May your Holy Spirit come upon
us and cleanse us."[27] Since what the Church prays reflects
what she believes (lex orandi, lex credendi), the invocation of
the Spirit's purifying action on the pilgrim Church reflected
the early Church's belief in her ultimate transformation. The
Spirit's transforming action in creation received renewed
attention centuries later in the Church's public worship
with the invocation: "Come Holy Spirit, fill the hearts of your

faithful and enkindle within them the fire of your love. Send forth your Spirit that we may be recreated, and you shall renew the face of the earth."[28] Since it is the Spirit's sanctifying action, merited by the Son, that purifies, illumines, unifies and divinizes creation, we, the sons of God for whom all creation groans with eager longings, are empowered to cry out, "*Abba, 'Father'... so that we may be glorified in him.*"[29]

Chapter 2
SCRIPTURE AND TRADITION

The use of Sacred Scripture is not only extremely useful but necessary for the presentation of Christ's teachings. Because the study of Scripture continuously develops and perfects theology, it has been called the "soul of theology." In many of its inspired books one encounters the theme of creation's divinization.

As the normative expression of God's revelation (*locus theologiae*), Scripture was often used in the past to refute heresies so that the truth might be rendered more accessible and comprehensible to all the faithful.[30] The early Fathers— who faithfully conveyed the teachings of the Apostles— not only used Scripture for the refutation of heresies, but to instruct and admonish those within the household of faith. Their presentation of God's inspired Word reflected the teaching method of the Apostles, and is hence known as the *apostolic Tradition* (*kèrygma ton apostolon*). If the Apostles preached Christ according to Scripture so too did the Fathers. For both of them, Christ not only fulfilled Scripture but endowed it with meaning. For both groups, Christ's message not only fulfilled the Old Testament prophecies but revealed the entire structure of God's plan of salvation.

Church Fathers

Ever since the early centuries of Christianity, the Fathers were considered men of great learning and holiness. The Church accepts the definition of St. Vincent of Lerins who distinguishes them in the following ways: 1) for common orthodox doctrine, which does not imply immunity from individual error; 2) for a holy life according to the standards of Christian antiquity; 3) for recognition by the Church, which need not be explicit but may be expressed by quotations from their writings; 4) for having lived in patristic times, that is, before the death of Isidore of Seville in the West or St. John Damascene in the East (about the middle of the 8th century).[31]

The theological and literary contributions influenced all ecclesiastical literatures that followed them. Schooled and educated by the finest teachers of classicism, they utilized both written and verbal expertise, ranging from rhetoric to apologetics to simple sermons. The result of their combined talents enriched the Church with a deeper understanding of herself and her mission through Councils, liturgy and institutions, and in all that pertains to her doctrine.

Their importance was noted when the bishops were gathered at the early Ecumenical Council of Chalcedon. They introduced their statements as follows, *"Following therefore the holy Fathers."* This statement identifies the bishops of Chalcedon not as innovators but as custodians of a faith handed down from the Apostles *and* the Fathers.[32] After all, the Apostles and Fathers both drew from the same inspired source of Sacred Scripture. As Clement of Rome put it: *"Christ comes with a message from*

God; the Apostles with a message from Christ",[33] and the Fathers, the Church adds, come with a message from the apostles:

> To ensure that the Gospel might remain always alive and whole within the Church, the Apostles left Bishops as their successors, and made over to them their own position of responsibility as teachers. What was handed on by the Apostles comprises all that makes for holy living among God's people and the increase of their faith... *The tradition received from the Apostles develops within the Church under the guiding presence of the Holy Spirit... The writings of the Holy Fathers of the Church testify to the life-giving presence of this tradition,* as its riches flow into the life and practice of the Church, in its belief and in its prayer. Through the same tradition the complete canon of the sacred books is made known, *and Holy Scripture itself is understood in greater depth and becomes continuously alive and active.*[34]

While Tradition is sometimes defined as that which is old, Tradition is hardly confinable to the past. The Church's *"living Tradition"* develops and grows throughout the centuries without, however, departing from its point of origin, namely Christ, the apostles and the early Fathers.

Scripture and Tradition, therefore, play an integral role in teaching us what Christ taught his Apostles and what the Holy Spirit continues to teach us through Christ's mystical body, the Church.[35] The *Dogmatic Constitution on Divine Revelation* of the

Second Vatican Council shows "how" Christ's teachings unfold throughout history:

> The tradition received from the apostles develops within the Church under the guiding presence of the Holy Spirit. Understanding of the realities and the words handed down grown through contemplation and study by the faithful as they ponder them in their hearts, through the deep insight into spiritual things that they come to experience, and through the preaching of those who, with succession in the episcopate, have received the sure charism of truth.[36]

The Holy Spirit, who reveals new insights, continuously unfolds the meaning and treasures of Scripture beyond that which has presently been grasped and understood. And it is in this sense that Tradition not only conveys God's pure and simple inspired Word (*kèrygma*), but contributes to its further development so that the gospel truth *is more accessible to us today than during the time of the Apostles:*

> Regarding its substance, faith does not grow with the passage of time, for whatever has been believed since the beginning was contained in the faith of the early Fathers. As regards its explication, however, the number of articles has increased, for we moderns explicitly believe what they believed implicitly.[37]

When the Apostles handed down their teachings to the Fathers and to their disciples, a change occurred in the order of priority. No longer were the Apostles the sole authoritative bearers of the Good News, but the Fathers as well. Therefore, when the Church has not yet made a definitive pronouncement on a matter of Christian faith, it defers the matter to the teachings of these learned men:

> If some new question should arise on which no such decision has been given, they should then have recourse to the opinions of the Holy Fathers, of those, at least, who, each in his own time and place, remaining in the unity of communion and the faith, were accepted as approved Masters; and whatsoever these may be found to have held, with one mind and one consent, this ought to be accounted the true and Catholic doctrine of the Church, without any doubt or scruple.[38]

The Fathers, who taught as a body of men in agreement, were seen as following in the line of Christ and the Apostles. Arising from the four Councils of Nicaea (325), Constantinople (381), Ephesus (431) and Chalcedon (451), the authority of their teachings continued to gain impetus. Pope Gregory the Great, at the end of the sixth century, considered these four councils as normative as the four gospels—a comparison which has held true to this day. Pope Leo XIII[39] and Blessed Cardinal John Henry Newman[40] also assign the same degree of authority to the universal teachings of the Fathers as to the teachings of the Apostles. Since it is the consensus of the Fathers that guarantees their orthodoxy on any point of doctrine, present-day scholars use this principle to evaluate their writings on the era of peace and to determine the proper place of that teaching in the Church's Tradition.

Church Doctors

In addition to the Apostles and Fathers, the Church extols her Doctors as renowned men and women who, by reason of their holiness, orthodoxy and eminence of knowledge, brought Christ's teachings into the modern era. They differ from the Church Fathers for three reasons: a) they may not have lived in ancient times; b) their education must be extraordinary so as to merit the praise of the *Doctor Optimus, Ecclesiae sanctae lumen* ("Excellent Doctor, light of the holy Church"); c) this title must be conferred on them in a sufficiently explicit way (through a solemn act of the Pope).[41] While not all Doctors are theologians, they are all experts in the *scientia amoris* (knowledge of love). Their intuitive knowledge of God's love is exemplified in the writings of the "Little Flower," Saint Therese of Lisieux, whom Pope John Paul II proclaimed a doctor and extolled as God's young veteran of love:

> Love is truly the "heart" of the Church, as was well understood by saint Therese of Lisieux, whom I proclaimed a doctor of the church precisely because she is an expert in the 'scientia amoris': "I understood that the Church had a heart and that this heart was aflame with Love. I understood that Love alone stirred the members of the Church to act... I understood that Love encompassed all vocations, that Love was everything."[42]

Not only are the Church Doctors faithful communicators of the teachings of Christ, the Apostles and Fathers, they are its developers as well:

There exists the Tradition of the Apostles, continued in the Church and impossible to separate from the Church's Tradition, developed through the centuries by the Councils, the Fathers, the liturgy and institutions, the teaching of the Magisterium and of *the Doctors*, the practice of the faithful and the entire exercise of the Christian life... and that all the truths necessary for salvation are contained in the canonical Scriptures... There is no doctrine of the Church based solely on Scripture independently of Tradition.[43]

The Tradition of the Apostles is, therefore, an ongoing development of the teachings of Christ that constitutes *"a deposit handed on, a living teaching authority and a transmission by succession."*[44]

The Church Doctor St. Augustine of Hippo recalls the Tradition of the Apostles and Fathers in his commentary on the 20th chapter of the Book of Revelation, when he describes creation's freedom from its slavery to corruption. In interpreting this 20th chapter, Augustine acknowledges the possibility of a future era of universal Christian holiness which he refers to as a *"seventh-day Sabbath"* and *"holy leisure following six thousand years since man was created,"* following Christ's birth and preceding his final return in the flesh:

Those who... have suspected ... by the number of a thousand years... that the saints should thus enjoy a kind of Sabbath-rest during that period, a holy leisure after the labors of six thousand years since man was created...(and) there should follow on the completion of six thousand years, as of six days, a kind of seventh-day Sabbath in the succeeding thousand years... This opinion would not be objectionable, if it were believed that the joys of the saints, in that Sabbath, shall be spiritual, and consequent on the presence of God...[45]

If indeed several Church Fathers and Doctors foretell a future epoch of universal peace, recent mystical literature attributes it to the Holy Spirit's action through a "new Pentecost."[46] In their Church-approved writings, recent mystics describe what one may call a new presence and activity of God in the human soul and in human history. With expressions of a *new divine indwelling,* identifiable with Jesus' *"real presence"* in the Eucharist and in the *"blessed in heaven,"*[47] a new stage of holiness exponentially emerges at the dawn of the third Christian millennium.

Before addressing the approved works of 20th century mystics, let us recall the words of Cardinal Joseph Ratzinger concerning the possibility of a future, historic and universal era of peace: *"The question is still open to free discussion, as the Holy See has not made any definitive pronouncement in this regard."*[48]

Church Mystics

Among the approved writings of recent exemplars that have internalized the holiness that will set the earth ablaze in the era of peace, worthy of mention are the Servant of God Luisa Piccarreta (1865-1947), Venerable Conchita de Armida (1862-1937), St. Hannibal di Francia (1851-1927), Blessed Elizabeth of the Trinity (1880-1906), Saint Padre Pio di Pietrelcina (1887-1969), the Servant of God Rev. Michael Sopoćko (1888-1976), St. Maximilian Kolbe (1894-1941), Blessed Dina Bélanger (1897-1929), the Servant of God Archbishop Luis Martinez (1881-1956), the Servant of God Sister Mary of the Holy Trinity (1901-1942), the Servant of God Marthe Robin (1902-1981), St. Faustina Kowlaska (1905-1938), Rev. Walter Ciszek (1904-1984), Blessed Mother Teresa of Calcutta (1910-1997) and Vera Grita (1923-1969).

These authors developed the spirituality of the preceding centuries through an increased experience and understanding of the effects their predecessors describe. This opens before us in their illustrations of man's "full" participation in the activity of the three divine Persons that culminates in a *new, eternal mode of being and operation*. What makes this indwelling "new" is not the *divine activity* that begins in Baptism and that developed in the lives of early century mystics.[49] What is new is *man's continuous participation in God's eternal activity* that enables him to exert a *transtemporal* influence upon the lives of all creatures of the past, present and future, and man's *corresponding awareness* of said influence. Here man's every thought, word and deed are not only rendered *divine*, they become participants in the same degree of *eternal* being and operation as the blessed in heaven, while exerting an eternal influence over every act of every creature. By the power of God, man fully partakes in God's eternal realities, penetrating more deeply than ever before into his eternal activity. The writings of the late 19th century Italian Servant of God Luisa

Piccarreta (1865-1947) and Polish mystic St. Faustina Kowalska (1905-1938) effectively convey this cardinal point.

Luisa writes:

> I found myself in Jesus. My little atom swam in the Eternal Will. Moreover, *since this Eternal Will is a single Act that contains together all the acts – past, present, and future – I, being in the Eternal Will, took part in that single Act which contains all acts, inasmuch as it is possible for a creature.* I even took part in the acts which do not yet exist, and which must exist, unto the end of centuries, and as long as God will be God. And also for this did I love Him, thank Him, bless Him, etc...

[Jesus said:]

> Have you seen what living in my Will is? It is to disappear. It is to enter into the ambience of Eternity. It is to penetrate into the Omnipotence of the Eternal, into the Uncreated Mind, and to take part in everything and in each Divine Act inasmuch as it is possible for a creature. It is to enjoy, while remaining on earth, all the Divine qualities. It is to hate evil in a Divine way. It is that expanding oneself to all without exhausting oneself, because the Will that animates this creature is Divine. It is the Sanctity not yet known, and which I will make known, which will set in place the last ornament, the most beautiful

and most brilliant among all the other sanctities, and will be the crown and completion of all the other sanctities.[50]

I Myself knew how many graces were necessary, having to work the greatest miracle that exists in the world, which is that of *living continuously in My Will*: the soul must assimilate everything of God in its act, so as to give it back again intact, just as the soul assimilated it, and then to assimilate it again.[51]

The same kind of mystical experience is described in the Diary of St. Mary Faustina Kowalska.[52] St. Faustina was a Polish sister endowed with many extraordinary visions and revelations, as well as the hidden stigmata, prophecy and the gift of reading human souls. In fact, she read her own soul through the optic of Jesus' real presence in the consecrated Host. In the mid 1930's, shortly before her transit to heaven, Mary Faustina experienced a mysterious presence of Jesus within her, which she found hard to describe. She then foresaw this very mystical presence enveloping the entire earth:

> Suddenly, when I had consented to the sacrifice with all my heart and all my will, God's presence pervaded me. My soul became immersed in God and was inundated with such happiness that I cannot put in writing even the smallest part of it. I was extraordinarily fused with God... *A great mystery took place... a mystery between the Lord and myself... At that moment I felt transconsecrated.*

THE SPLENDOR OF CREATION

> *My earthly body was the same, but my soul was different; God was now living in it with the totality of His delight.*[53]

> *The Divine Mercy will triumph over the whole world and will be worshipped by all souls...* Today, I saw the Sacred Host of Jesus, in the midst of a great brilliance. The rays were issuing forth from the wound [in his side] and spreading out over the entire world.[54]

Shortly before the dawn of the twentieth century, another mystic by the name of Sister Mary of the Divine Heart (1863-1899) had a *vision* of the new mystical presence that several 20th century mystics would *experience* and that would, eventually, fill the entire earth:

> *He will make a new light shine forth across the entire world... Interiorly, I seemed to see this light... this adorable Sun which will make its rays descend upon the earth, at first, from afar off, then increasing, and then finally illuminating the whole world.* Then He said: "From this light the peoples and the nations shall be illuminated, and from its ardor they shall all be warmed."[55]

As a final illustration, we find in the life of Vera Grita (1923-1969), a 20th century Italian mystic, a beautiful work entitled *The Living Tabernacles*.[56] In a manuscript bearing the 1989 *nihil obstat* of Bishop Giulio Sanguinetti, Jesus dictates to Vera the meaning of Living Tabernacles. On November 6th, 1969, Jesus told Vera that in order to enter more deeply into the mystery of his "real presence," she must offer to God her *Fiat*:

> I desire that My work be diffused among priests…
> They will know how to prepare other souls that
> live in the world but are not of the world to receive
> Me. These will bring Me to the streets, into homes
> and families that I may live close to souls that are
> far from Me so that they may feel My *continuous*
> *Eucharistic presence.* The rebellious will fall… My
> daughter, I know where to lead you! But I cannot
> if you do not adhere completely to My Will. I need
> your *Fiat*… so that My Design of Love may be
> accomplished in its fullness in your soul and in the
> souls of others.[57]

Jesus later assured Vera that her *Fiat* helped actualize in her soul the new mystical union:

> I am already a living tabernacle in this soul and
> she does not realize it. She must realize it because
> I want her to assent to My *eucharistic presence in*
> *her soul.* Have you not already given your soul
> to Me completely? Wherefore I, Jesus, am the
> Master of your soul. And the Master is free to
> give as much as he likes… If souls learned to at
> least seek Me in humility… they would discover
> My human-divine *real presence*: Me, Jesus.[58]

Mary relates to Vera the future era of peace that is characterized by the Eucharistic reign of Jesus in souls:

Jesus comes to you with immense grace, *that which has never been given before to mankind.* Your *Eucharistic Jesus* will descend upon you so that you may seek and save those that are lost. Then the world will be purified by a "visit" from God, and also I, your Mother, will be with you and with My Son, the Eucharistic Jesus, to receive together with you, God the Creator in the revelation of his love and of his justice…[59]

Jesus tells Vera:

Behold, I will return to the world, I will return in the midst of souls to speak to them, to draw closer to them, to address them directly until the veils fall and they recognize Me in every brother… Prepare the [Living] Tabernacles for this gift so that from this mystical union My coming in your midst may be revealed to the good… My Will will be done on earth as in heaven.[60]

Months before Vera's departure for heaven, Jesus prophesied an immanent era of peace when the human race would experience the new reality of "Living Tabernacles." As a woman who spent her life in Italy, Vera must have rejoiced on hearing Jesus speak of a future house in Rome, from which the new spirituality he had been dictating to her would set the earth ablaze:

I want a home all to Myself. It must stand in Rome as a light that will light up the whole world.

My home will accept all who are called to become
bearers of the eucharistic Jesus. This house will
be a place that will shelter the Living Tabernacles
for shifts of spiritual exercises all year long... Here
the spirituality of the Living Tabernacles will be
strengthened under the light of the gospel... This
will be the Mother House... Others will blossom
in Italy, then in Europe and then everywhere; and
they will have the same purpose: to prepare the
souls called to take Me in their soul...and bring
Me to all your brothers.[61]

Given the foregoing, it appears that in the new era, those
who experience the eucharistic presence of Jesus within
themselves will no longer be few in number. In the words of the
St. Maximilian Kolbe, they will comprise many of the earth's
inhabitants who had been trained and formed by Mary's 'fiat':
"When, oh when, will *the divinization of the world* in her and
through her come about?"[62] One may call these privileged souls
in whom Jesus' unique presence abounds the "sons of God" who
set the world free from its slavery to corruption.

When one considers the testimony in favor of a future
era of universal peace and holiness from the teachings of the
Apostles, Fathers, Doctors and mystics, the evidence in its favor
seems overwhelming. Yet stemming from the ancient heresy of
millenarianism, the novel notion that the early Church Fathers
and ecclesiastical writers believed in a *falsified* concept of the
kingdom of God on earth undermined the acceptance of their
teachings on the era of peace.[63] The primary source of this novel
notion was the fourth century *historian*, Eusebius of Caesarea.

He is the earliest recorded Church writer to have attributed the heresy of millenarianism to several early Church Fathers.

A Malaise to be Overcome

Eusebius of Caesarea, Church Historian (263—340 A.D.)

Eusebius Pamphilus of Caesarea belonged to the pre-Nicene period. He represented the tumultuous Constantinian epoch marked by antecedent Christian persecutions, which may have contributed to his anti-heretical literary style. Despite his strenuous efforts, Eusebius himself became a victim of the doctrinal errors he once opposed and was, subsequently, declared a "schismatic." The Church affirms that Eusebius became a follower of subordinationism; that he held semi-Arianistic views during the debates on the Arian heresy; that he took part in activities against the Nicene Creed and assisted in deposing St. Athanasius (the promoter of Christ's consubstantiality with the Father and of the Divinity of the Holy Spirit; Eusebius regarded St. Athanasius' doctrine as Sabellianism); that he attacked Bishop Marcellus of Ancyra, the defender of the Nicene faith in two dogmatic treatises; that he rejected the consubstantiality of the Father with the Son throughout his life; that he regarded the Holy Spirit as a creature; and that he condemned the veneration of images of Christ "so that we may not carry about our God in an image, like the pagans."[64]

While acknowledging his contribution as an historian, the Church distances herself from his theology: *"Despite his outstanding scholarship, Eusebius is not one of the great theologians; his lasting work is due to his work as the great historian."*[65]

Of his many adherents, the following are worthy of mention: Acacius of Caesarea (the leader of the Homoiousions), Eusebius of Emesa (a semi-Arian), Gelasius of Caesarea (Eusebius' second successor), Rufinus of Aquileia (translated Eusebius' writings and adapted them), Philip of Side, Philostorgius, Socrates of Constantinople (a Novatian sympathizer), Sozomen, and Theodoret of Cyrus. In the succeeding centuries, these instructors would perpetuate Eusebius' influence upon scores of prominent theologians. Unfortunately, Eusebius completely misinterpreted the Fathers' doctrines on the era of peace, as is evident in his historical work (Bk. III, Ch. 28), where he accuses St. Papias and other Church Fathers of preaching a falsified, carnal millennium:

> After the resurrection of human flesh, [they maintain] there is to be an earthly reign of Christ, during which period men traverse a thousand years in Jerusalem, dedicated to the wedding feast and liturgical celebrations, while remaining enslaved to the lusts of the flesh and inclinations to pleasure.

It is true that *carnal* millenarianism was widespread in the days of early Christianity among the early Jewish converts and that many instructors were equally engaged in fighting back this heresy. It is noteworthy that none of the Church Fathers and Doctors who speak of an era of peace condones the carnal *millenarianism* condemned by the Church.[66]

It is now generally understood that Eusebius often rejected the deeper allegorical sense of early century parchments. After acknowledging his inability to unearth Papias' completed works on the thousand years rest—which he henceforth refers to as *"fragments"*—Eusebius accuses Papias of being influenced by the Millenarians of his day. (This is one of the facts that never seems to appear in history books, although it is well documented). Consequently, the Church Father St. Papias became increasingly suspect for teaching *"a millennium after the resurrection from the dead, when the personal reign of Christ will be established on this earth,"* even though his works contain no such wording.[67]

Church Father and Doctor St. Jerome reveals that it was Eusebius (who died 80 years before) who denounced St. Papias and other Church Fathers for their millenarian doctrines:

> [It was] Eusebius who accused Papias of transmitting the heretical doctrine of Chiliasm to Irenaeus and other early churchmen.[68]

One wonders if Jerome was not here responding to Eusebius' dismissal of Papias as "a man of very little intelligence"—the same Papias whom the Apostles themselves had ordained Bishop of Hierapolis.[69] In any case, it is certain that Jerome corrected those who had mistakenly accepted Eusebius' theology as Church doctrine: "He [Papias] it is, *so they say*, who originated the Jewish tradition of the millennium... in which our Lord is to reign in the flesh with his saints."[70]

In attributing to the Church Fathers and Early Ecclesiastical Writers the heresy of millenarianism, several academics unfortunately advanced the opinion of Eusebius—the accepted *opinion* of their day, but not the Apostolic Tradition. By nature a very zealous man, Eusebius may have attempted to defend his opinion by *"severely edit[ing] Papias' text and preserv[ing] only short excerpts."* And it is precisely these short excerpts or fragments that led to the idea that Papias of Hierapolis, the Catholic Church Father, Bishop and Martyr, drew false information from "acquaintances" and not from the Apostles.

Chapter 3
THE ERA OF PEACE

3.1 THE CHURCH FATHERS

THE APOSTOLIC FATHERS

Since it is not possible to examine in these pages the entire breadth of the Fathers' teachings, I refer to the broader orientations of their thinking. It is important to recall that no one Father intended to write an exhaustive treatise on the era of peace, or Sabbath Rest, though we frequently encounter references to this theme in their writings, scattered and uncoordinated. The Fathers did preserve a common thread, however. It is the eschatological banquet of the Lamb that spans from the Sabbath Rest to the New Jerusalem and the New Heavens and New Earth.

St. Papias, Church Father (*floruit ca.* 130 A.D.)

St. Papias (70–155A.D.) was the Bishop of Phrygia from a city within Hierapolis, in the first half of the second century. He was said to have suffered martyrdom about 163 A.D. Having been a listener to St. John the Apostle and on intimate terms with many who had known the Lord and his disciples, Papias was acutely familiar with the apostle's teachings. His contribution lay in the profound knowledge and memory of Sacred Scripture, which he wove into his works and divided into five books.

In his work on eschatology, he speaks of a period of universal peace that was described *by the Apostles*:

> So far as you are concerned, I shall not hold back a single thing *I carefully learned from my seniors and carefully remember,* and shall thoroughly guarantee the truth of these matters. For I do not delight in wordy accounts, as many people do, but in accounts that tell the truth. Furthermore, I do not take delight in the commandments of anybody else, but in those mentioned as having been given by the Lord for our belief and which proceed from Truth itself. Whenever anyone came my way, who had been a follower of my seniors, I would ask for the accounts of our seniors: *what did Andrew or Peter say? Or Philip or Thomas or James or John or Matthew, or any other of the Lord's disciples?...* For, as I see it, it is not so much from books as from the living and permanent voice that I must draw profit.[71]

Clearly, Papias' *seniors*, some of whom he designates as "the Lord's disciples," are not mere *acquaintances* of the Apostles as Eusebius implies. The 2nd century apostolic Father and Saint, Irenaeus of Lyons, uses the same word as Papias, *presbyteri*, to denote faithful and authoritative witnesses entrusted with guarding the apostolic Tradition in its entirety and with governing the early Christian communities:

> His Kingdom, when the just will rule on rising from the dead; when creation, reborn and freed from bondage, will yield an abundance of food of all kind from the heaven's dew and the fertility of the earth, *just as the seniors recall.*[72]

Both Ss. Papias and Irenaeus refer to seniors, *presbyteri*, whom the Catholic Church esteems and recognizes as "leaders" of the early Christian community. Although *presbyteri* was a title given to both the Apostles and to a small group of wise leaders, Papias indicates the former when stating, *"What did Andrew or Peter... or Philip or Thomas or James say... the Lord's disciples?"*[73] Much like St. Mark who interpreted and faithfully penned Peter's recounts without ever having heard or followed the Lord, Papias conveyed with doctrinal accuracy St. John's teachings in the Book of Revelation on the "thousand years" of peace. This is perhaps best expressed by Irenaeus who reassures his listeners that Papias drew his information from St. John the Apostle, and in the Church's acknowledgement of Papias' faithful transmission of John's Gospel under his dictation:

> Papias by name, of Hierapolis, a disciple dear to John... copied the Gospel faithfully under John's dictation.[74]

Papias' contemporary, the apostolic Father and Saint Justin Martyr, reinforces the teaching that St. John the Apostle instructed his disciples on the era of peace:

A man among us named John, one of Christ's
Apostles, received and foretold that the followers
of Christ would dwell in Jerusalem for a thousand
years, and that afterwards the universal and, in
short, everlasting resurrection and judgment
would take place.[75]

It is understood that Papias adopted the allegorical style of St.
John the Apostle, which held the key to the mysteries of the faith
(*mystogogy*). In point of fact, several Fathers interpreted many
scriptural passages through what is known in theology as the
allegorical method of biblical exegesis. This method enabled them
to understand the obscure passages that are found in Scripture
and to incorporate their understanding into their writings on the
era of peace.

The Book of Sirach mentions the allegorical style in scriptural
parables: "The man who devotes himself to the study of the
law of the Most High explores the wisdom of the men of old
and occupies himself with prophecies; He treasures discourses
of famous men, and goes to the heart of involved sayings; *He
studies obscure parables, and is busied with the hidden meanings of
the sages.*"[76]

The *allegorical method* derives from the word "allegory."
Allegory in Greek signifies, "saying something other than
what one seems to say." When applied to Sacred Scripture,
the allegorical genre assumes that the text to be interpreted
says or intends something other than what its literal wording
suggests; it contains within it a deeper, mystical sense not
derivable from the words themselves.[77] Hence the allegorical

expressions of the Book of Revelation, penned by St. John the Apostle:

> I saw a woman seated on a scarlet beast that was covered with blasphemous names, with seven heads and ten horns.[78]

St. Justin Martyr, Church Father (100/110 — 165 A.D.)

St. Justin was martyred for the faith with six companions in Rome. He is considered the most important apologist of the second century. He wrote two apologies in defense of the Christian religion: *The Dialogue with Trypho,* and other writings that have been preserved only in minor fragments. It is in his long Dialogue – a two-day conversation with Trypho, a man of Jewish origin – that St. Justin mentions an era of peace while quoting the Prophet Isaiah and explaining the allegorical meaning of various parts of Scripture:

> "Sir," Trypho said... "do you really believe that this place Jerusalem shall be rebuilt, and do you actually expect that you Christians will one day congregate there to live joyfully with Christ, together with the patriarchs, the prophets, the saints of our people and those who became proselytes before your Christ arrived?"

> "Trypho," I replied... "I have declared to you earlier that I, with many others, feel that such an event will take place. However, I did point out

that there are many pure and pious Christians who do not share our opinion. Moreover, I also informed you that there are some who are Christians by name, but in reality are godless and impious heretics whose doctrines are entirely blasphemous... If you ever encountered any so-called Christians who do not admit this doctrine [of the universal era of peace]... do not consider them to be real Christians... *But I and every other orthodox Christian feel certain that there will be a resurrection of the flesh followed by a thousand years in the rebuilt, embellished, and enlarged city of Jerusalem, as was announced by the Prophets Ezekiel, Isaias and others."*

These are the words of Isaias concerning the millennium: "...For, behold... I shall rejoice over Jerusalem, and be glad over My people. And the voice of weeping shall no more be heard in her... Then the wolves and lambs shall feed together, and the lion shall eat like the ox, and the serpent shall eat earth like bread..." (Is 65:17-25). Now... *we understand that a period of one thousand years is indicated in symbolic language.* When it was said of Adam that "in the day that he eateth of the tree, in that he shall die," we knew he was not a thousand years old [Adam lived to be 930 [79]]. We also believe that the words, "The day of the Lord is a thousand years," also led some to the same conclusion. Moreover, *a man among us named John, one of Christ's Apostles, received and*

foretold that the followers of Christ would dwell in
Jerusalem for a thousand years, and that afterwards
the universal and, in short, everlasting resurrection
and judgment would take place.[80]

In this lengthy discussion at Ephesus, St. Justin impresses upon Trypho the necessity of remaining faithful to what had been handed down to them. Much like St. Justin, St. Papias refers to St. John the Apostle as the source of his teachings on the era of peace. He uses the allegorical method when quoting Isaiah and John the Apostle, thus qualifying the 1,000 years rest in its symbolic sense. Not only were Justin and Papias born one generation after the Apostles, they both insist on the unmodified influence of their teachings.

St. Irenaeus of Lyons, Church Father (140 — 202 A.D.)

The works of St. Irenaeus stand out for their treatment of Jesus *(Logos)* and his activity in revelation; there is one and the same Word of God presiding over the revelation of the Old and New Testament. It is this Word, the Son of God made man, who teaches men to know God, *"The Son, who is from the beginning with the Father, reveals from the beginning."*[81] Irenaeus admires the marvelous progress of God's plan of revelation in his Son and compares it to a nursing mother:

> Just as a mother cannot give a perfect nourishment
> to her child because the child is not yet capable of
> supporting this solid nourishment, the same thing
> is true of God; *He could have offered perfection to*

> *man from the very beginning, but man would have*
> *been incapable of supporting it... God prepares man*
> *for the vision of Himself by a constant increase in the*
> *activity and presence of his Word among men.*[82]

The revelation of the Father through the Word takes place *progressively*. Like a good teacher concerned for his students, God slowly weans, educates and leads humanity to the full stature of Jesus Christ. The idea of God's progressive revelation may be called the leitmotif of St. Irenaeus, whom many theologians have labeled the "illustrious and renowned Father of Catholic Dogmatics."

St. Polycarp of Smyrna (69-156 A.D.), the apostolic Father who saw and listened to the Apostle John and who was later consecrated Bishop of Smyrna, schooled St. Irenaeus in his youth. His formidable education proved successful when Irenaeus penned what would become one of the greatest of all refutations, *Adversus Haereses*. This masterly work against the Gnostic heresy is divided into two principal parts. The second part contains five books, the last of which addresses the era of peace. Like his predecessors Irenaeus avails himself of the allegorical genre of his day in his commentaries on Sacred Scripture:

> Scripture says: "And God rested upon the seventh day from all His works"... And in six days created things were completed; it is evident, therefore, that they will come to an end in the six thousandth year... But when Antichrist shall have devastated all things in this world, he will reign for three years and six months... And then the Lord will come from Heaven in the clouds...

sending this man and those who follow him into the lake of fire; *but bringing in for the righteous the times of the kingdom, that is, the rest, the hallowed seventh day... These are to take place in the times of the kingdom, that is, upon the seventh day... the true sabbath of the righteous.*[83]

So, the blessing foretold undoubtedly refers to the time of His Kingdom, when the just will rule on rising from the dead; when *creation, reborn and freed from bondage*, will yield an abundance of food of all kinds from the heaven's dew and the fertility of the earth, just as the seniors recall. *Those who saw John, the Lord's disciple, [tell us] that they heard from him how the Lord taught and spoke about these times...* Days will come when vines will grow each with ten thousand shoots, and on each shoot ten thousand branches, and on each branch ten thousand twigs... ten thousand clusters... ten thousand grains... And other fruits and seeds, and grass... And *all the animals who use the products of the soil will be at peace and in harmony with one another, completely at man's beck and call.*[84]

Irenaeus' use of the expression "ten thousand" to indicate God's divine intervention in salvation history reflects the allegorical usage of biblical writers. We find the same expression in the psalmist and in the author of Samuel:

A thousand may fall... ten thousand fall at your right.[85]

Let our barns be filled to overflowing with crops
of every kind; our sheep increasing by thousands,
by tens of thousands in our fields, may our oxen
be well fattened.[86]

The chariots of God were ten thousand; thousands
of them that rejoice.[87]

The woman played and sang: "Saul has slain his
thousands, and David his ten thousands".[88]

That Irenaeus was faithful to the allegorical method of
the Apostles is evident from the annals of one of the Church's
greatest exegetes, Archbishop Andrew of Caesarea. In his
acclaimed *Preface of the Apocalypse* Andrew comments on the
Book of Revelation:

I do not think to linger any more on the inspiration
of the Book of Revelation, since Saints Gregory
and Cyril have born witness to its genuineness.
In addition, the ancients Papias, Irenaeus,
Methodius and Hippolytus add their testimony
on this point.[89]

If this eminent archbishop regarded the interpretations of Ss.
Papias, Irenaeus, Methodius and Hippolytus (the writings of the
latter two are present below) as dissident (*millenarian*), certainly
he would not have recommended them to anyone for the proper
interpretation of a book so couched in mystical and symbolic
language as that of Revelation. Other scholars, whose lives and

contributions are simply too extensive to list in this book, added their approvals and endorsements to the works of this sixth century scholar and chronicler archbishop.

EARLY ECCLESIASTICAL WRITERS

The Author of the Epistle of Barnabas (130-131)

The Epistle of Barnabas contains no clue to its author or to those for whom it was intended. Its aim is to impart to its readers the exact knowledge of God's plan of salvation. It is made up of two parts. The first part addresses the evil days that are at hand in which the end of the world and the Judgment shall appear, as well as freedom from the bonds of the Jewish ceremonial laws. The second part sets out to comprehend the nature of the Old Testament, which helped free Christians through Mosaic regulations. In short, the ordinances of the law are to be understood as referring *allegorically* to the Christian virtues and institutions, while prefiguring the law of Christ and his Church.

The author of the *Epistle of Barnabas* was contemporaneous to the *Didache* (the teaching of the twelve Apostles) and extremely similar in its structure. It refers to the idea of the world enduring for 7,000 years as an analogical reference to the seven days of creation:

> Concerning the Sabbath He (God) speaks at the beginning of creation: "And God made in six days the works of His hands, and on the seventh day He ended, and rested on it and sanctified it." Note, children, what "He ended in six days" means.

It means this: that the Lord will make an end of everything in six thousand years. And He Himself is my witness, saying: "Behold the Day of the Lord shall be a thousand years." So, then, children, in six days, that is in six thousand years, everything will be ended. "And He rested on the seventh day." This means: when His Son will come and destroy the time of the lawless one and judge the godless, and change the sun and the moon and the stars—then He shall indeed rest on the seventh day... Furthermore, He says to them: "I will not abide your new moons and your Sabbaths." You see what He means: The present Sabbaths are not acceptable to Me, but that Sabbath which I have made, in which, after giving rest to all things, I will make the beginning of the eighth day, that is, the beginning of another world.[90]

Barnabas vision of God's Sabbath rest with creation reechoes St. Papias' vision of creation "reborn and freed from bondage", St. Justin's Martyr's vision of a millennium of peace and harmony, and St. Iranaeus' vision of the "true sabbath of the righteous."

Admittedly, theologians maintain that the author of the Epistle of Barnabas was not the Apostle who frequented the company of St. Paul. His namesake, St. Barnabas, accompanied Paul in his first voyage to Galatia, where they encountered what was perhaps the greatest opposition to their ministry. The early Jewish converts insisted on circumcision, abstinence from certain foods and, by way of contradiction, sought to expel them from Galatia. After they left the Galatian territory, they reported all they had experienced to the Council of Jerusalem. It was in response to this experience that Paul addressed his famous Letter to the Galatians.

Interestingly, chapters 1-17 of this Epistle of Barnabas recall that the *"value and importance of the Old Testament directives on sacrifice, circumcision and food were meant in a higher, spiritual sense... The Jews... had perverted the will of God and understood the fulfillment of the Law in the literal sense."*[91] As for the resistance Paul and Barnabas encountered in Galatia, it appears to have been a question of poor biblical interpretation. In fact, St. Paul alludes to this in his Letter to the Corinthians. Paul distinguishes two spiritualities, "fleshly" and "spiritual" (1 Cor 3:1). The former are likened to infants who cannot be spoken to in spiritual terms, as they are insistent on the letter of the law and therefore incapable of understanding its deeper meaning. The latter are likened to adults who are able to understand the deeper meaning of the Mosaic law, for they have learned "to die to self in order that Christ may live in them."

Tertullian (155 — 240 A.D.)[92]

Tertullian was a convert since 197. He was the first great ecclesiastical writer in Latin who lived during the age of Christian dogmatic discovery, when the persons and natures of Christ were not yet defined. In his pioneering efforts to assist the Church in her discovery of the truths rooted in Scripture and Tradition, his rigorous *moral* beliefs failed to win the Church's favor. For this reason, the Church's ordinary Magisterium esteems his *development of eschatology* in the apostolic Tradition

as "*part of the stock of the Christian teaching*," but refrains from
endorsing the moral doctrines he received from the Montanists,
such as forbidding second marriages to the widowed; flight from
persecution (the Christian soldier is always obliged to die for his
faith); and imposed rigorous fasts.[93]

The Church's esteem for Tertullian may be summarized in the
following statement: "*On the whole... his interests were scholarly
rather than speculative. Tertullian, it is said, may very well have been
the most learned man of his day. This was certainly the opinion of
St. Jerome, a man of immense erudition himself...*"[94] In his treatise
Against Marcion, Tertullian recalls the teachings of Ss. John,
Papias, Justin Martyr, Irenaeus and Barnabas on the era of peace:

> *We do confess that a kingdom is promised to us upon
> the earth*, although before heaven, only in another
> state of existence; inasmuch as it will be after
> the [first] resurrection *for a thousand years in the
> divinely built city of Jerusalem...* We say that this
> city has been provided by God for receiving the
> saints on their resurrection,[95] and refreshing them
> with the abundance of all really spiritual blessings,
> as a recompense for those which in the world we
> have either despised or lost...[96] *Of the heavenly
> kingdom this is the process. After its thousand years
> are over*, within which period is completed the
> resurrection of the saints, who rise sooner or later
> according to their deserts [merits], *there will ensue
> the destruction of the world and the conflagration of
> all things at the judgment*: we shall then be changed
> in a moment into the *substance of* angels, even by

the investiture of an incorruptible nature, and so
be removed to that kingdom in Heaven [the New
Jerusalem].[97]

In his work entitled the *Apology*, Tertullian illustrates the
final two stages of the kingdom of God: the kingdom's historic
era of peace—allegorically expressed as "a millennial interspace"
lasting figuratively 1,000 years—followed by the eternal kingdom
in which the human race is raised forever:

> When, therefore, the boundary and limit, that
> millennial interspace, has passed when even
> the outward fashion of the world itself... passes
> away, then the whole human race shall be raised
> again, to have its dues meted out according
> as it has merited in the period of good or evil,
> and thereafter to have these paid out through
> the immeasurable ages of eternity... But the
> profane... in like manner shall be consigned to
> the punishment of everlasting fire.[98]

St. Hippolytus of Rome (170 – 235 A.D.)

Another martyr, saint and scholar who wrote of the era of
peace is the Bishop and Greek author, Hippolytus of Rome.
Hippolytus lived in the turbulent period of the newborn Church,
when Rome was just emerging as the universal center of the faith.
His bona fide efforts to keep the Church free of nationalism, it
appears, met with slippery slope results. Unfortunately almost
all the information on the person of St. Hippolytus is so cryptic

that what little evidence historians have compiled suggests little more than speculation. Doubts surface as to whether or not this Hippolytus is the reputed controversialist who, bearing the same name, criticized Popes Zephyrinus and Callistus I for laxity in discipline and modalism in Christology. What is ascertainable from documents is the testimony of St. Jerome, who made reference to St. Hippolytus as a prolific writer and bishop. Following Jerome's lead, theologians address Saint Hippolytus as a leading intellectual of the early Roman Church who was martyred in defense of the true faith. He is considered a disciple of Irenaeus and contemporary of Origen, as well as one of the last western Church scholars to write in Greek.

Among his works that have survived is his treatise on *The Refutation of All Heresies*, *The Extant Works and Fragments*, and *The Fragments from Commentaries on Various Books of Scripture*, which is divided into two parts. The first part offers commentaries on the books of Sacred Scripture, while the second addresses dogmatic and historical questions. The first part foretells an era of universal peace, which both he and the author of the Letter to the Hebrews call God's "Sabbath Rest" with creation. His proficiency with the exegetes and rhetoricians of his day is evident in the blending of their literary genre with his own hermeneutic style. Here emerges once again the allegorical method as the tool for interpreting the eschatological works of the Apostles and early Fathers. In his exegetical work on the Book of Daniel, preserved only in part, he reassures his listeners of the coming era:

> For the first appearance of our Lord in the flesh
> took place in Bethlehem... and He suffered in

the thirty-third year. *And 6,000 years must needs be accomplished, in order that the Sabbath may come, the rest, the holy day "on which God rested from all His works." For the Sabbath is the type and emblem of the future kingdom of the saints...* as John says in his Apocalypse: for "a day with the Lord is as a thousand years." Since, then, in six days God made all things, it follows that 6, 000 years must be fulfilled. And they are not yet fulfilled.[99]

Origen (185-253/4 A.D.) [100]

Born in 185, Origen was barely seventeen when a bloody persecution of the Church of Alexandria broke out. When his father Leonides was cast into prison, Origen wrote an ardent letter exhorting him to persevere courageously. After his father was martyred and his fortune confiscated by the imperial authorities, Origen labored to support himself, his mother, and his six younger brothers. This he successfully accomplished by opening a school of grammar at the age of eighteen, by selling his manuscripts, and through the generous aid of a rich benefactress who admired his talents. He attended catechetical school, frequented the philosophical schools, devoted himself to the study of the philosophers, particularly Plato and the Stoics, and learned Hebrew. It is reported that in his excessive zeal he took Matthew 19.12 literally and mutilated himself.

The course of his work at Alexandria was interrupted by five journeys. When he journeyed into Greece, he passed through Caesarea where Theoctistus, Bishop of that city, raised him to the priesthood. On his return to Alexandria, Origen learned that he had been banished by Bishop Demetrius, who called two synods to censure his ordination as illicit. St. Jerome declares expressly that he was not condemned on a point of doctrine.

After having been expelled from Alexandria, Origen settled in Caesarea, Palestine, with his protector and friend Theoctistus and, having founded a new school there, resumed his "Commentary on St. John." He was soon surrounded by pupils, the most distinguished of which was St. Gregory Thaumaturgus. When he was over sixty he wrote "Contra Celsum" and a "Commentary on St. Matthew," which were interrupted due to the persecution of Decius. During this persecution Origen was imprisoned and barbarously tortured, but his courage was unshaken, as is evidenced in his prison letters breathing the spirit of the martyrs. He died at sixty-nine and was buried with honor as a Confessor of the Faith. St. Jerome assures us that the list of Origen's writings drawn up by St. Pamphilus contain around two thousand titles.

Many of the early Fathers' symbolic writings were later codified by Origen (185-253/4 A.D.) in his classical exegesis known as the *Hexapla*. Origen's exegetical labors comprised three series of works: The *Scholia, Commentaries* and *Homilies*. He believed that Scripture offers the reader three diverse senses that are superimposed one upon the other: the *historical sense,* the *moral sense* and the *spiritual* or *allegorical sense*. Much like the early Fathers he believed that all Sacred Scripture is a great allegory that has to be interpreted, explained and clarified, lest one remain bereft of the sense and meaning the inspired author sought to convey. Origen maintained that beneath the letter of

Scripture lies a deeper meaning to be uncovered, and that history demonstrates that this exegetical method was indeed familiar to all the Fathers, even if not in its codified Origenian form.

The third century Bishop of Alexandria Saint Dionysius applied Origen's allegorical sense to his commentaries on the Book of Revelation. In his work entitled *On The Promises*, Dionysius provides *allegorical* or *mystical interpretations* to such symbols as trees, leaves and water in order to convey the mysteries of God's plan of the universal restoration of all creation. Obviously, such allegories were not intended in the literal sense, but symbolically. Nor was the use of allegories unusual when it came to expressing certain mysteries of the faith that required symbols, often the only tool that effectively conveyed their deeper meaning.

St. Methodius of Olympus (d. 300 A.D.)

St. Methodius of Olympus, a reputed bishop and martyr, was the third century Greek author of several Christian works. He had a comprehensive philosophical education, was a learned theologian and a prolific author. His works, written in the third and fourth centuries, exercised great influence in the field of theology. They treat the topics of virginity, free will, the Resurrection, the lives of Simeon and Anna, the Psalms, the Passion of Christ, and other themes preserved only in part.

In his work *The Symposium* or *The Banquet of the Ten Virgins*, Methodius speaks of the eight ages of the world: Five are the ages of the old law, the sixth age is the institutional Church, the seventh is the triumph of holiness, which he calls the "great resurrection-day," and the eighth is the eternity of heaven:[101]

Here we have two striking confirmations of the reality of a future era of peace and of the allegorical interpretation of Scripture:

> God, when He appointed to the true Israelites the legal rite of the true feast of the tabernacles, directed, in Leviticus, how they should keep and do honour to the feast; above all things, saying that each one should adorn his tabernacle with chastity…

> Here the Jews, fluttering about the bare letter of Scripture… fully believe that these words and ordinances were spoken concerning such a tabernacle as they erect; as if God delighted in those trivial adornments which they, preparing, fabricate from trees, not perceiving the wealth of good things to come…

> For since in six days God made the heaven and the earth, and finished the whole world, and rested on the seventh day from all His works which He had made, and blessed the seventh day and sanctified it, *so by a figure in the seventh month, when the fruits of the earth have been gathered in, we are commanded to keep the feast to the Lord…* When the appointed times shall have been accomplished, and God shall have ceased to form this creation, *in the seventh month, the great resurrection-day it is commanded that the Feast of our Tabernacles shall be "celebrated" to the Lord.*[102]

St. Methodius shows the importance of going beyond the nude and crude letter of Scripture to unmask its deeper, spiritual meaning and to apprehend what God wishes to reveal in us.

Caecilius Firmianus Lactantius (250 – 317 A.D.)

A teacher of Latin rhetoric, L. Caecilius Firmianus Lactantius is known for his mastery of literary form and for his steadfast witness during the time of the Christian persecutions. Coined the "Christian Cicero" due to the nature of his sublime literature, Lactantius composed seven books, the last of which addresses the Last Things. His book, *The Divine Institutes*, depicts the unfolding of this world's six thousand years in an eschatological framework. At the end of the six thousandth year, there will arise the great rebellion of the lawless one, whom St. John the Apostle and several Fathers identify as the incarnate "spirit of antichrist." Lactantius ascribes a two-fold reprisal and defeat to this spirit accompanied by a two-fold "judgment": the first occurs *before* the universal era of peace, and the second at its *terminating point*. He concurs with chapters 19 and 20 of St. John's Book of Revelation, envisioning a "great judgment" and condemnation of "the prince of devils," followed by the completion of "the thousand years," the devil's final defeat and the "last judgment." Lactantius' chronology reflects the Book of Revelation inasmuch as it identifies the defeat of evil *before* the era with the defeat of "the false prophet and the beast," and identifies the final defeat of evil and the Last Judgment *after* the era with the defeat of Gog and Magog. Lactantius writes in chapters 14 and 24:

Since all the works of God were completed in six days, the world must continue in its present state through six ages, that is, six thousand years. For the great Day of God is limited by a circle of a thousand years, as the prophet shows, who says: "In Thy sight, O Lord, a thousand years are as one day" (Ps. 89:4). And as God labored during those six days in creating such great works, so His religion and truth must labor during these six thousand years, while wickedness prevails and bears rule. *And again, since God, having finished His works, rested on the seventh day and blessed it, at the end of the six thousandth year all wickedness must be abolished from the earth, and righteousness reign for a thousand years;* and there must be tranquility and rest from the labors which the world now long has endured.[103]

Therefore, the Son of the most high and mighty God shall come... But He, when He shall have destroyed unrighteousness, and executed His *great judgment,* and shall have recalled to life the righteous, who have lived from the beginning, *will be engaged among men a thousand years,* and will rule them with most just command... Then they who shall be alive in their bodies shall not die,[104] but during those thousand years shall produce an infinite multitude, and their offspring shall be holy and beloved by God... About the same time *also the prince of devils, who is the contriver of all evils, shall be bound with chains, and shall be imprisoned during the thousand years of the heavenly rule in which righteousness shall reign in the world, so that he may contrive no evil against the people of God...* The earth will open its fruitfulness and bring forth most abundant fruits of its own accord; the rocky mountains shall drip with honey; streams of wine shall run down, and rivers flow with milk; in short the world itself shall rejoice, and all nature exult, being rescued and set free from the dominion of evil and impiety, and guilt and error. Throughout this time beasts shall not be nourished by blood, nor birds by prey; but all things shall be peaceful and tranquil. *Before the end of the thousand years the devil shall be loosed afresh and shall assemble all the pagan nations to make war against the holy city. He shall besiege and surround it.* "Then the last anger of God shall come upon the nations, and shall utterly destroy them" *and the world shall go down in a great conflagration.* The people of God will be concealed in the caves of the earth during the three days of destruction, until the anger of God against the nations and *the last judgment* shall be ended. "Then the righteous shall go forth from their hiding places, and shall find all things covered with carcasses and bones... *But when the thousand years shall be completed, the world shall be renewed by God, and the heavens shall be folded together, and the earth shall be changed, and God shall transform men into the similitude of angels,* and they shall be white as snow; and they shall always be employed in the sight of the Almighty, and shall

make offerings to their Lord, and serve Him forever.
At the same time shall take place that second and
public resurrection of all, in which the unrighteous
shall be raised to everlasting punishments".[105]

Here we have what is perhaps the finest exposition on the
universal era of peace in early Tradition. Lactantius' expression
"He [Christ] will be engaged among men a thousand years" is a far
cry from the millenarian vision, which teaches that Christ will
come visibly and physically to reign on earth within human
history. When read in the context of the early Fathers' allegories,
Christ's being "engaged among men a thousand years" principally
signifies an interior and spiritual reign in souls.

In his development of the era of peace, Lactantius introduces
us to the most comprehensive eschatological vision beyond that
which has been disclosed thus far. It extends from a judgment, to
Satan's imprisonment to the era of peace, and from Satan's final
reprisal to the Final Judgment. Lactantius' chronology provides
a summary of the vision of several early Fathers, which I here
present in tabloid form.

- God pronounces judgment on nonbelievers, vanquishes
  atheism and enchains Satan.

- He spiritually recalls to life those that have died in Christ.

- Christ establishes the universal reign of his Divine Will in
  the souls of men for a prolonged period in human history,
  symbolized by the expression "one thousand years."

- All creation rejoices in God's gifts of universal peace, holiness
  and justice.

- Shortly before the end of the era, Satan is released. He assembles all the pagan nations to wage war on God's holy city.

- The pagan nations surround the holy city, "then the last anger of God shall come upon the nations, and shall utterly destroy them" and the world shall go down in a great conflagration.

- Christ returns for the final resurrection and the General Judgment of the living and the dead, in which the righteous will be raised to eternal happiness and the unrighteous to everlasting punishments.

- God renews the universe: the heavens are folded up, God creates New heavens and a New Earth, and men are transformed "into the similitude of angels" and rejoice in God's beatific vision for all eternity.

Since Lactantius presents two judgments, *before* and *after* the era of peace, a review of the patristic concept of "judgment" will help us understand his chronology of world events. Although some Fathers address two eschatological judgments, they are not for that matter unrelated. The *first judgment* occurs before the universal era of peace, which is pronounced on all the nonbelievers that are alive on earth. The *second judgment* occurs shortly before the end of the universal era, which involves all the dead who await the Final Judgment. It is not my aim to here present an exhaustive treatise on judgment or on the figure of Antichrist; I have devoted a book entitled *Antichrist and the End Times* to these topics. It is my concern to distinguish the relationship between the two judgments.

The first judgment is a Particular Judgment insofar as it neither occurs at the end of human history nor merits public pronouncement, whereas, the second judgment is a General Judgment that confirms the Particular in the resurrected bodies of all the dead. The Church reinforces this teaching when acknowledging the invariability of the sentences pronounced at the Last or General Judgment and those of the Particular:

> The Last Judgment will hold no surprises for us, as far as our own fate is concerned. We shall have already undergone our own Particular Judgment; our souls already will be in heaven or hell. The purpose of the Last Judgment is primarily to give glory to God... whose wisdom and power, love and mercy and justice have been at work through the whole of life.[106]

> This General Judgment is already begun at death... We cannot speak of a time, in our sense, between death — the Particular Judgment — and judgment on the Last Day (the General Judgment). We simply cannot know how this can be...[107]

When speaking of the General Judgment, the Council of Trent mentions three principal signs that precede it: a) the preaching of the gospel throughout the world, b) a falling away from the faith, c) the coming of Antichrist. It also adds, "'This Gospel of the kingdom,' says the Lord, 'shall be preached *in the whole world,* for a testimony *to all nations,* and then shall the consummation come'".[108] Admittedly, the Council does not use the term "era of peace," though it is certainly implied. "The preaching of the gospel throughout the world" indicates an era of gospel universality, or what the Church has called an historic "period of triumphant Christianity." One has only to consult the magisterial statements in its favor. Published in 1952 by a theological commission of qualified experts, *The Teachings of the Catholic Church* states that it is *not* contrary to Catholic teaching to believe or profess "a hope in some mighty triumph of Christ here on earth *before* the final consummation of all things":

> This wise counsel of the Church's ordinary Magisterium, is not contrary to Catholic teaching to believe or profess "a hope in some mighty triumph of Christ here on earth before the final consummation of all things. *Such an occurrence is not excluded, is not impossible, it is not all certain that there will not be a prolonged period of triumphant Christianity before the end.*"[109]

> The point of division between the legitimate aspirations of such devout believers and… false millenarism is this: the Chiliasts—as believers in the millennium are called, from the Greek word for a thousand—seem to expect *a coming of Christ and a presence of him in glory and majesty on this earth which would not be the consummation of all things but would still be a portion of the history of mankind. This is not consonant Catholic dogma...* The coming of Christ in the second Advent... is the consummation of all things, the end of human history. *If before that final end there is to be a period, more or less prolonged, of triumphant sanctity, such a result will be brought about, not by the apparition of the Person of Christ in Majesty but by the operation of*

> *those powers of sanctification which are now at work,*
> *the Holy Ghost and the Sacraments of the Church.*
> The Chiliasts of all times... and there are many to
> be found even to date, seem to despair, not only of
> the world, but even of that dispensation of grace
> which was inaugurated at Pentecost; they expect
> from the visible presence of Christ a complete
> conversion of the world, as if such a happy result
> could not be otherwise brought about.[110]

Insofar as the gospel shall become a testimony to all
nations for a prolonged period of *"triumphant Christianity"* and
"triumphant sanctity" before the consummation of the world,[111]
it intimates the early Fathers' teachings of an historic era of
peace. Here the Church affirms that only through the works of
sanctification—namely, those actions the Holy Church Councils
have "appropriated" to the Third Person of the Blessed Trinity—
will a "more or less prolonged period of triumphant sanctity"
occur.[112] The work of sanctification is not simply the work of the
Son or that of the Father, but also and more appropriately the
work of the Holy Spirit who *"renews the face of the earth."*

In his commentary on Rom 8:19-20, J.A. Fitzmyer relates that
Paul envisions *"the physical created universe... groaning in hope,*
expectation and in pain" as it awaits its transformation through
the work of *"the Holy Spirit".*[113] The Church's traditional prayer to
the Holy Spirit expresses this conviction. In her rule of belief, the
Church invokes the Spirit as the Sanctifier of creation: *"Come,*
Holy Spirit fill the hearts of Thy faithful and kindle within them the
fire of Thy Love. Send forth Thy Spirit that we may be recreated and
Thou shalt renew the face of the earth."[114]

In the early Church's liturgy, in particular during the third century, the Holy Spirit played an eminent role in her life of worship. He was often invoked as the one who cleanses, sanctifies and prepares us for the Father. And so do we find in the Lord's prayer several early Fathers, including Gregory of Nyssa, using the words, *"May your Holy Spirit come upon us and cleanse us,"* as a substitute for the petition, *"Your Kingdom come"*; the same prayer that became *"the centre of daily and liturgical prayer... solemnly entrusted (traditio) to the catechumen as the expression of his new birth."*[115] This early practice of the Church was an affirmation of the Tradition handed down by the Apostles and faithfully transmitted by Ss. Papias, Irenaeus and Justin Martyr to the early Christians.[116] These Fathers foresaw that the kingdom of universal peace and holiness would not come solely from man's efforts, but above all, from the Holy Spirit's sanctifying action. In the same tradition, Pope John Paul II recalls the primacy of the Holy Spirit's action:

> During this important time... unity among all Christians of the various confessions will increase until they reach full communion... We are all aware, however, that the attainment of this goal cannot be the fruit of human efforts alone, vital as they are. Unity, after all, is a gift of the Holy Spirit.[117]

Allegorical Extremes

While St. John the Apostle and several early Fathers wrote in Greek, both the New Testament writers and Greek Fathers did not write in classical Greek, but in Koiné—a common, almost colloquial tongue. This language was popular throughout the Hellenistic world from the third century B.C. to the end of ancient Christianity, that is, until the beginning of the fourth century A.D. Its versatile flavor and rich vocabulary allowed several Fathers to relate allegories in a way that shrouded their meaning from the uninitiated (newcomers to the faith). St. Anastasius of Sinai (d.700), a Palestinian monk and exegete who fought against the Monophysites, acknowledges the early Fathers' use of the allegorical method:

> The famous Papias of Hierapolis, the disciple of John the Evangelist... took a *spiritualistic view* of the passages of Paradise and referred them to Christ's Church.[118]

Though most modern readers would find such allegories perplexing, not so the scholar, who should never look to the past through modern lenses, or misinterpret an early century allegory in a modern key. Unfortunately, several later historians and philologists misinterpreted the allegories of the early Fathers, which led to their being labeled "millenarian." In later centuries, the Fathers' works were not only viewed with suspicion, but openly criticized by scores of theologians, who interpreted the writings of Papias, Justin, and other eminent Church Fathers in the *literal sense* only. Eventually, these literalisms gave rise to a distorted interpretation of their teachings, which would later become enmeshed with the heresy of *millenarianism*.

Since the Fathers and early Church writers' teachings on the era of peace are couched in allegories, it will be helpful to review the extremes often associated with allegorical language. Of the allegories the Fathers employed, none resembled the unpolished metaphors that accompanied the poor method of *"exaggerated allegorism."* In the early centuries there were in circulation a variety of hackneyed opinions concerning the Last Things that were clearly opposed to the apostolic preaching on the 'doctrine of faith' (*fides quo*). While the *apostolic allegorical method* was careful to preserve the historical interpretation of many scriptural passages, the *exaggerated allegorism* assumed an innovative approach. It substituted the historic and objective truth with an illusory and capricious understanding, which devolved into the error of the later Alexandrian School that applied a purely symbolic sense to the whole of Scripture. The Fathers avoided this extreme by distinguishing the literal from the allegorical meanings of the sacred texts and diligently applying them to their respective parts.

With paralleled intensity there arose yet another extreme in the opposite direction known as *"exaggerated literalism."* It sprouted among the early Jewish converts who were dependent on an oral tradition. It is likely that the information they received was first spoken extempore and written down afterwards, as this might explain their dependency on oral tradition and literal recall. Hence, as *exaggerated allegorism* suffered from a too broadly symbolic vision of Scripture, *exaggerated literalism* labored under a vision that was excessively narrow and literal.

In the face of these two extremes, one indisputable fact remains: There is no evidence to suggest that the Fathers were unfaithful to the teachings of the Apostles on the Last Things (*fides qua*). Naturally, one is compelled to ask why academics had attributed errors to the Fathers in the first place. While we have answered this question in part, a more complete answer can be found in the history of interpretations of the era of peace.

Early Jewish converts to Christianity ushered in a heretical doctrine known as *Chiliasm*: this heresy professed belief that Christ would come down to *earth* to reign in the *flesh* with his saints for *literally* 1,000 years amid *immoderate carnal banquets*, furnished with an amount of meat and drink such as to surpass the measure of credulity itself. The author of the Epistle of Barnabas acknowledges this when he affirms that early Jewish converts lacked the necessary tools for the correct interpretation of Scripture:

> But how can the Jews understand or comprehend these things? At any rate we, *rightly recognizing them*, announce the commandments as the Lord intended. For this reason, he circumcised our hearing and hearts that we should understand these things.[119]

3.2 THE CHURCH DOCTORS

St. Cyril of Jerusalem, Church Father and Doctor (315 – 386 A.D.)

St. Cyril lived during the reign of Constantius, the son of Constantine the Great, in 340. His formidable and pious education led him to the priesthood. His learning attracted the attention of his bishop St. Maximus who entrusted him with the instruction of catechumens. At the death of the Patriarch of Jerusalem, Cyril succeeded him in 350 as the bishop of Jerusalem and fought for the dogmas of the Apostles and early Fathers. However, Akakios the Arian, who held the throne of Ceasaria-in-Palestine, tyrannically banished Cyril from Jerusalem.

Eleven years later, Cyril was allowed to go back only to find Jerusalem ravaged by heresy and strife. He attended the Council at Constantinople in 381 where the Nicene Creed and orthodoxy triumphed and Arianism was finally condemned. Cyril was rehabilitated at the same Council which cleared him of all previous rumors and commended him for fighting "a good fight in various places against the Arians." Sixteen of his thirty-five years as bishop he spent in exile.

The works of St. Cyril include a sermon on *The Pool of Bethsada*, a *Letter to the Emperor Constantius*, three small fragments and the famous *Catecheses*. The *Catecheses* contains numerous catechetical lectures, which are among the most precious remains of Christian antiquity. They include an introductory address, eighteen instructions delivered in Lent and five in Easter to those preparing for Baptism. It is in this work that St. Cyril alludes to three comings of Christ:

> We do not preach only one coming of Christ, but a second as well, much more glorious than the first. The first coming was marked by patience; the second will bring the crown of a divine kingdom.

> In General, what relates to our Lord Jesus Christ has two aspects. *There is a birth* from God before

the ages, and a birth from a virgin at the fullness of time. *There is a hidden coming,* like that of rain on fleece, *and a coming before all eyes, still in the future...*he will come again in glory to judge the living and the dead, and his kingdom will have no end. Our Lord Jesus Christ will therefore come from heaven. He will come at the end of the world, in glory, at the last day. For there will be an end to this world, and the created world will be made new.[120]

The Church Father and Doctor St. Cyril provides us with the expression, "the hidden coming," that would be interpreted in the middle ages as the period that spans "from the first coming of Christ to the end of the world." Cyril's "hidden coming" would later be interpreted only as the intermediary time of the institutional Church, and is rediscovered in the writings of the Church Doctor St. Bernard of Clairvaux.

St. Bernard of Clairvaux, Church Doctor (1090 – 1153 A.D.)

St. Bernard, Abbot and Doctor, was an exponent of what many modern scholars call monastic theology, which "aims at a clear, orderly, warm exposition of the truth, such as will serve to dispose the soul to prayer and contemplation."[121] Bernard's theology does not share the fanciful novelties speculative theologies profess, but develops the teachings of the Apostles and Fathers in fluid and sublime prose. In fact, the Church bestowed upon him the title of "Mellifluous Doctor," in honor of his warm and extraordinary style. His doctrines are "not distinguished by the discovery of new modes of thought or the achievement of new conclusions... Bernard's sources were principally the Scriptures, then the Fathers of the Church."[122] Bernard reiterates Cyril's nomenclature concerning the "hidden coming" of Christ:

> We know that there are three comings of the Lord. The third lies between the other two. It is invisible, while the other two are visible. In the first coming, He was seen on earth, dwelling among men; He Himself testifies that they saw Him and hated Him. In the final coming, "all flesh will see the salvation of our God, and they will look upon Him whom they pierced." The intermediate coming is a hidden one; in it only the elect see the Lord within their own selves, and they are saved. In his first coming, our Lord came in our flesh and in our weakness; in this middle coming, He is our rest and consolation.
>
> In case someone should think that this middle coming is sheer invention, listen to what our Lord Himself says: "If anyone loves me, he will keep my word, and my Father will love him, and we will come to him."[123]

While some maintain that Ss. Cyril or Bernard's "hidden coming" was not intended to be associated with the era of universal peace, but with the period of the Church that spans from Christ's Incarnation to his final coming,[124] the writings of several early Fathers and saints provide the Church with the doctrinal foundation of the "hidden coming" and the "era of peace."

Moreover, St. Cyril's contemporary, the Church Father, Doctor and Saint Augustine of Hippo, reveals another sense in which one may interpret the intermediary time of the institutional Church. He refers to it as God's Sabbath Rest: "a kind of Sabbath-rest... a holy leisure after the labors of six thousand years since man was created... there should follow on the completion of six thousand years, as of six days, *a kind of seventh-day Sabbath in the succeeding thousand years.*"

While Ss. Cyril and Bernard refer to Christ's hidden coming as an interior advent of conversion and perseverance to God's saving action of grace, St. Augustine and other Church Fathers interpret it in a broader sense. This opens before us as we read the three periods of the Church's history in his writings. St. Augustine maintains the early Church Fathers' belief that all mankind will worship God together with the risen saints is indeed valid. Augustine refers to this epoch as a "spiritual" and "holy leisure after the labors of six thousand years since man was created" and "a kind of seventh-day Sabbath in the succeeding thousand years." It is noteworthy that on St. Augustine's authority, the Council of Ephesus (431) condemned belief in *millenarianism* as a superstitious aberration, while implicitly upholding his teachings on the future, historic seventh-day Sabbath.

St. Augustine of Hippo, Church Father and Doctor (354 – 430 A.D.)

St. Augustine (*Doctor gratiae*) was the bishop of Hippo for 35 years (395-430). He was Born in Tagaste, N. Africa, and after a conversion from Manichaeism, became a strong defender against its heretical teachings, and opposed the heresies of Donatism and Pelagianism. His writings include the autobiographical *Confessions*, *City of God*, treatises on the Trinity, grace, and passages from the Bible. Through his writings, St. Augustine became a dominant influence in Christian thought for centuries.

In the *City of God* Augustine defends the patristic doctrine on the era of peace while denouncing the bizarre doctrines of *millenarianism*. Augustine's writings on the era have been meticulously studied throughout the centuries by scores of renowned theologians.[125] Admitting the complexity and ambiguity of Augustine's treatise, scholars have arrived at varying interpretations and conclusions. Of the leading scholarly reviews, no one article appears to discredit Augustine's historic era of peace, which he biblically refers to as a Sabbath Rest. In 1956 G. Folliet discovered Augustine's three-fold typology in his presentation of a "Sabbath" to indicate three distinct periods of the Church's history.[126] Based on Augustine's vast knowledge of the biblical senses familiar to the early Fathers, he refers to the three periods as three interpretations of the thousand years rest of the Book of Revelation 20:4-7. Augustine's Sabbath Rest typology presents the following schema:

1) In the first period, Augustine interprets the Sabbath Rest according to the Fathers' biblical method. This rest *allegorically* represents a thousand years, and occurs at the end of the six thousand years of man's existence, when the saints experience a *spiritual* resurrection in Christ (Rev 20:4-7, "the first resurrection").

> Those who, on the strength of this passage [of Revelation 20:1-6], have suspected that the first

resurrection is future and bodily, have been moved, among other things, specially by the number of a thousand years, as if it were a fit thing that *the saints should thus enjoy a kind of Sabbath-rest during that period, a holy leisure after the labors of six thousand years since man was created...*(and) there should follow on the completion of six thousand years, as of six days, *a kind of seventh-day Sabbath in the succeeding thousand years;* and that it is for this purpose the saints rise, viz., to celebrate this Sabbath. *And this opinion would not be objectionable, if it were believed that the joys of the saints, in that Sabbath, shall be spiritual, and consequent on the presence of God...* But as they [carnal millenarians] assert that those who then rise again shall enjoy the leisure of immoderate carnal banquets, furnished with an amount of meat and drink such as not only to shock the feeling of the temperate, but even to surpass the measure of credulity itself, such assertions can be believed only by the carnal. They who believe them are called by the spiritual Chiliasts, which we may reproduce by the name of Millenarians...[127]

2) The second Augustinian interpretation portrays the Sabbath Rest as the spiritual and historical depiction of the various stages of spiritual life leading to the final stage of perfection. These stages encompass all souls, from personages of the Old Testament to those at the threshold of the world's consummation. The

Sabbath day of rest represents the soul's quest for union with God and its final achievement, continuous rest in him.

> He the Apostle saw in the Apocalypse "an Angel coming down from heaven... And he laid hold of the dragon... and bound him a thousand years"... *Now the thousand years may be understood in two ways, so far as occurs to me:* because these things happen [the Angel chaining the dragon] in the sixth thousand of years... he calls the last part of the millennium the part that is which had yet to expire before the end of the world — a thousand years... [the Sabbath rest] or he used the thousand years *as an equivalent for the whole duration of this world.*[128]

3) Finally, the Sabbath Rest marks the end of the Old Testament covenant and law. With Jesus' Incarnation there begins Israel's rest from toil and slavery. Thus the Sabbath or 1,000 years rest symbolically represents the Church, beginning with Christ's Incarnation and ending with his final coming in glory.

> The devil, then, is not bound during the whole time which this book [of Revelation] embraces — that is, *from the first coming of Christ to the end of the world* — not bound in this sense, that during this interval, which goes by the name of a thousand years, he shall not seduce the Church.[129]

It is noteworthy that only Augustine's third and final presentation of the Sabbath Rest was adopted by the medieval church no less than 800 years later, while the former two presentations were excluded. Why this exclusion? One must bear in mind the medieval culture in which Augustine's works were meticulously dissected. This culture produced the Inquisition in which heretics were hunted and punished, and theologians were ordered to remove from Catholic literature all materials that might undermine the *Credo* – the *Credo* was then viewed as a summary of the articles of faith Catholics were obliged to uphold under the penalty of excommunication and possible physical torture. The Inquisition was a creature of its time when crimes against faith were regarded as crimes against the state. Pope John Paul II's recent *mea culpa's* recall the unconscionable measures taken against alleged heretics that, some affirm, led to the dismantling of Augustine's three-fold Sabbath typology: two of Augustine's presentations of the three-fold Sabbath typology were dropped and only one preserved, namely the third and final one. In their efforts to repel the erroneous teachings of *millenarianism* and to safeguard the faithful from all breaches of faith, it is said that the inquisitors carelessly discarded Augustine's first two interpretations of the Sabbath Rest. Subsequently, the third interpretation of the Sabbath Rest was used exclusively for centuries to follow, and it spanned from Christ's Incarnation to his final coming in glory. The end result? As "*the Sabbath Rest*" grew into the promotional nomenclature that best defined its medieval heritage, Augustine's first and foremost interpretation of the Sabbath Rest fell into obscurity.

For a long time, many academics chose to avoid discussing the possibility of an historic era of peace for fear of preaching what others might perceive as *millenarianism*. After all, why engage in debate on a topic impregnated with cryptic overtones when it can be avoided? Although the Church had never condemned the apostolic Fathers' doctrines on the era of peace, she did condemn *"even modified forms of this falsification of the kingdom to come under the name of millenarianism, especially the 'intrinsically perverse' political form of secular messianism."*[130] So, unless the professor was abreast of patristic doctrines and their allegorical methods, any talk of an era of peace would have been met by complete, instant and automatic certainty that he was a lunatic. To go against the inquisition would have proven equally disastrous, for any slipshod remark might quite conceivably have placed him on par with Apollinaris, whose novel doctrines on the Sabbath Rest resulted in his ecclesiastical deposition and condemnation.[131] In short, tacit conformity was the discipline most professors preferred.

Let us here recall the Talmudic commentary that listed the dangers of dabbling in eschatology. Several of the masters in Israel, in attempting to resolve prophetic mysteries, suffered dire consequences. Ben Zoma' went crazy and Elisha' ben Avuja' became an apostate. To occupy oneself with eschatology was, therefore, quite unaccommodating. Two means of providing closure to so irritating a topic are arguably exemplified in the editing of Papias' fragments by Eusebius of Cesarea, and in the exclusion of Augustine's three-fold Sabbath typology. Here we encounter a brief affirmation of the latter mentality:

> On account of these words, as Augustine relates (De Civitate Dei XX, 7), certain heretics asserted that there will be a first resurrection of the dead that they may [physically] reign with Christ on earth for a thousand years; whence they were called chiliasts or millenarians. Hence Augustine

says (De Civitate Dei XX, 7) that these words are to be understood otherwise, namely of the 'spiritual' resurrection, whereby men shall rise again from their sins to the gift of grace: while the second resurrection is of bodies. *The reign of Christ denotes the Church* wherein not only martyrs but also the other elect reign, the part denoting the whole; or they reign with Christ in glory as regards all, special mention being made of the martyrs, because they especially reign after death who fought for the truth, even unto death.[132]

If this statement was the byproduct of a maturing spirituality in need of refinement, more needs to be said in its favor. As earlier mentioned, some early converts from Judaism accepted false doctrines concerning the Sabbath Rest, known as *millenarianism*, which resulted in an overly literal reading of Scripture. These erroneous doctrines heightened the concerns of prelates who feared its influence within their dioceses:

> For there are also many rebels, idle talkers and deceivers, especially the Jewish Christians. It is imperative to silence them, as they are upsetting whole families by teaching for sordid gain what they should not... Therefore, admonish them sharply, so that they may be sound in faith, instead of paying attention to Jewish myths and regulations of people who have repudiated the faith.[133]

This notwithstanding, the expression of a future and universal Sabbath Rest continued to advance. The medieval exclusion of Augustine's three-fold interpretation of the Sabbath Rest did not dishearten its many lively debates in the academia nor the timelessness of its character. As Cardinal Joseph Ratzinger alluded earlier, the first presentation of St. Augustine's Sabbath Rest was *never* officially rejected nor condemned by the Church.

Despite the temporary setback of Augustine's treatise, G. Folliet and other contemporary theologians have helped resurface its place in theology. The very title of his work, *City of God*, conveys a theocratic system of religion and government. One must bear in mind the age in which Augustine lived. It was an age in which the Church and state were politically united, but marked by intolerance, wars and strife. His work was geared to the establishment of an historic city in which the Church and state are at peace; in which God's authority is recognized at every level of human existence. He saw God as the one authority of a theocratic system of government, inspiring its religious, social, legal, political and economic structures and the diversity of the Spirit's gifts ordered to the universal enrichment of minds and hearts. The conditionings of culture, race and language would serve as vehicles of the Holy Spirit's action to purify, illuminate and unify man's imperfect visions and relations. Only in such a world could peace, holiness and justice truly reign. Augustine's presentation on the Sabbath Rest, therefore, may be viewed as a telltale of the world's conversion and the establishment of God's kingdom on earth.

It must be noted that Augustine and the early Fathers were not the originators of the idea of an era of universal peace. They simply drew their information from the books of the Old and New Testaments and from the Tradition of the Apostles. The books of the major and minor prophets, 2 Peter, the Gospels of Matthew and Mark, Revelation and other sources provided them with abundant descriptions of the earth's transformation and renewal. Rather than delve into all of the vivid biblical depictions they afford, I limit myself to Matthew's portrayal of the present earth challenged by "the sword":

> Do not think that I have come to bring peace upon the earth. I have come to bring not peace but the sword. For I have come to set man against his father, a daughter against her mother, and a daughter-in-law against her mother-in-law; and one's enemies will be those of his household.[134]

The present earth under the tyranny of the sword is not the theater of the universal peace and holiness the Fathers envisioned. The patristic vision is characterized by the Holy Spirit's presence who, "renewing the face of the earth," removes the sword of division thereof. They respectively refer to the world's transformation and renewal as the Sabbath Rest/era of peace, and the New Jerusalem/ New Heavens and Earth. The Sabbath Rest/era of peace is "an historic period of triumphant Christianity and sanctity" on earth; the New Jerusalem/New Heavens and Earth, is not an historic period, but the eternal establishment of God's reign on earth and throughout the entire cosmos.

It is only on a purified and transformed earth that the words of Jesus assume new meaning, *"Holy Father, keep them in your name that you have given me, so that they may be one just as we are one."*[135] The Jesus that came to bring a sword and sow division on earth fervently implored its unification on a transformed earth. This opens before us in the Book of Revelation and again in the Letter to the Hebrews:

> Then I saw an angel come down from heaven, holding in his hand the key to the abyss, and a heavy chain. *He seized the dragon, the ancient serpent, which is the Devil or Satan, and tied it up for a thousand years, and threw it into the abyss, which he locked over it and sealed, so that it could no longer lead the nations astray until the thousand years are completed.* After this, it is to be released for a short time... I saw the souls of those who had been beheaded for their witness to Jesus and for the word of God, and who had not worshipped the beast or its image nor had accepted its mark... *They came to life and they reigned with Christ for a thousand years.*[136]

> *In reference to the seventh day,* Scripture somewhere says, "And God rested from all his work on the seventh day"; and again, in the place we have referred to, God says, "They shall never enter into my rest." Therefore, since *it remains for some to enter, and those to whom it was first announced did not because of unbelief,* God once more set a day, "today," when long afterward he spoke through David the words we have quoted: "Today, if you should hear his voice, harden not your hearts." Now, if Joshua had led them into the place of rest, God would have not spoken afterward of another day. *Therefore, a Sabbath rest still remains for the people of God. And he who enters into God's rest,*

rests from his own work as God did from his. Let us strive to enter into that rest, so that no one may fall, in imitation of the example of Israel's unbelief.[137]

The First Resurrection

When commenting on the 20th chapter of the Book of Revelation and its millennium of peace, several early Fathers give considerable importance to those saints for whom it is reserved. To this era, St. John links the reappearance of the many martyrs who were put to death for having refused Satan worship: *"[Those] who had not worshipped the beast nor accepted the mark on their foreheads or hands... came to life and reigned with Christ for a thousand years... This is the first resurrection"* (Rev. 20:4-5). Biblical parallels portray the martyred as an allegorical rendering of God's elect.[138] They appear in St. John's writings as an elect group that returns to life to reign with Christ for one thousand years. Scripture and Patristic allegories further suggest that these martyred will *not* return to definitively reign on earth in the flesh, but will *"appear"* throughout the era to instruct the remnant of Israel, much like the visions and apparitions of the saints of the past.[139] The idea that the righteous that enter the era of peace will witness an explosion of apparitions of the martyred that "had not worshipped the beast" finds its corollary in the Book of Acts and in the Gospel of Matthew. Both Acts and Matthew present an explosion of the apparitions of Christ and his elect to the newborn Church shortly after his resurrection from the dead:

> He presented himself alive to them by many proofs after he had suffered, "appearing" to them forty days and speaking about the kingdom of God.[140]

And behold, the veil of the sanctuary was torn in two from top to bottom. The earth quaked, rocks were split, tombs were opened, and the bodies of many saints who had fallen asleep were raised. And coming forth from their tombs after the resurrection, they entered the holy city and "appeared" to many.[141]

If biblical events repeat themselves as several Scripture scholars maintain, this would bolster the idea that Christ and his martyrs will re-appear throughout the era of peace to peoples of various nations.

The first resurrection assumes another connotation when applied to those that live on earth in the state of grace during the era. St. Augustine refers to it as a spiritual resurrection, and not a *definitive* resurrection in the body, which rejoins the soul only at the end of history and at the Final Judgment:

> On account of these words, as Augustine relates (De Civitate Dei XX, 7), certain heretics asserted that there will be a first resurrection of the dead that they may [physically] reign with Christ on earth for a thousand years; whence they were called chiliasts or millenarians. Hence Augustine says (De Civitate Dei XX, 7) that *these words are to be understood otherwise, namely of the spiritual resurrection, whereby men shall rise again from their sins to the gift of grace*: while the second resurrection is of bodies.[142]

Allegories from the writings of the early Fathers also suggest a period when the just will rise to *a new life of grace* during the millennium of peace:

> So, the blessing foretold undoubtedly refers to the time of His Kingdom, when *the just will rule on rising from the dead.*[143]

> We say that this city has been provided by God for receiving the saints on their resurrection, and *refreshing them with the abundance of all really spiritual blessings.*[144]

> But He, when He shall have destroyed unrighteousness, and executed His great judgment, and shall have *recalled to life the righteous,* who have lived from the beginning, will be engaged among men a thousand years, and will rule them with most just command.[145]

More forcefully, the renowned theologian Jean Daniélou affirms that the Church awaits an era in which only those that are saints will remain on earth:

> The doctrine underlies the various developments to be found in the Revelation of John. The essential affirmation is of *an intermediate stage in which the risen saints are still on earth and have not yet entered their final stage,* for this is one of the aspects of the mystery of the last days *which has yet to be revealed.*[146]

One can speculate endlessly as to what the future holds for the "first resurrection." Whether there might be apparitions of the martyred to instruct the faithful remnant on earth or a rebirth of all Christians to a new life of grace, is far less meaningful than our obedience to the Church's final decision in this regard. When stripped of all non-essentials, all that God requires of us is to remain faithful to Christ and to the Church for which he shed his Blood.

Characteristics of the Era of Peace

The excerpts I have thus far presented from Sacred Scripture, the Apostolic Tradition and the Magisterium on God's triumph in human history introduce us to the teachings of an historic and universal era of peace and holiness. As presented in the opening chapters, several early Church Fathers describe the Incarnation as a mystery that is continuously unfolding, to a point at which all things in heaven and on earth will rediscover their original splendor through God's divine action in man's activity. From man to beast, from galaxies to planets, all creation will experience an outpouring of grace, a "new Pentecost," that will set it free from its slavery to corruption. The Fathers Ss. Papias, Justin Martyr and Irenaeus provide its first illustrations, which the ecclesiastical writers Tertullian, St. Methodius, Hippolytus, Lactantius and Doctor St. Augustine later adopt and develop.

Of the various interpolations associated with their writings on the eschatological era, I limit myself to the following extracts from Sacred Scripture, Tradition and the Magisterium, presented here in tabloid form. These sources of the Christian faith lay the foundation for a theology on the era of universal peace.

- Modification of Evil [147]

> The beasts of the earth you need not dread. You shall be in league with the stones of the field and *the wild beasts shall be at peace with you.*[148]

> And it is right that when creation is restored, *all the animals should obey and be in subjection to man, and revert to the food originally given by God... that is, the productions of the earth.*[149]

> At the end of the six thousandth year *all wickedness must be abolished from the earth,* and righteousness reign for a thousand years.[150]

> All who are alert to do evil will be cut off...[151]

- Begetting of Children

> There shall no more be an infant of days there, nor an old man that shall not fill up his days; for the child shall die a hundred years old... For as the days of the tree of life, so shall be the days of My people, and the works of their hands shall be multiplied. My elect shall not labor in vain, nor bring forth children for a curse; for they shall be a righteous seed blessed by the Lord, and their posterity with them.[152]

> Also there shall not be any immature one, nor an old man who does not fulfill his time; for the youth shall be of a hundred years old...[153]

Raise a glad cry, you barren one who did not bear, break forth in jubilant song, you who were not in labor, for more numerous are the children of the deserted wife than the children of her who has a husband...[154]

As the years of a tree, so the years of my people... They shall not toil in vain nor beget children for sudden destruction; for a race blessed by the Lord are they and their offspring.[155]

See, I come to you... I will settle crowds of men upon you... cities shall be repeopled, and ruins rebuilt. I will settle crowds of men and beasts upon you, to multiply and be fruitful. I will repeople you as in the past, and be more generous to you than in the beginning; thus you shall know that I am the Lord.[156]

- *Creation's Rebirth*

  The coast shall belong to the remnant of the house of Judah... for the Lord their God shall visit them and bring about their restoration.[157]

  ...that the mountains may yield their bounty for the people and the hills great abundance.[158]

  Her deserts he shall make like Eden, her wasteland like the garden of the Lord.[159]

As for you, mountains of Israel, you shall grow branches and bear fruit for my people Israel, for they shall soon return.[160]

"This desolate land has been made into a garden of Eden," they shall say.[161]

Creation, reborn and freed from bondage, will yield an abundance of food of all kind from the heaven's dew and the fertility of the earth.[162]

The earth will open its fruitfulness and bring forth most abundant fruits of its own accord; the rocky mountains shall drip with honey; streams of wine shall run down, and rivers flow with milk; in short the world itself shall rejoice, and all nature exult, being rescued and set free from the dominion of evil and impiety, and guilt and error.[163]

The earth shall yield its fruit, for God, our God, has blessed us.[164]

- *Rule of Righteousness*

My chosen ones shall inherit the land.[165]
We will be made just and holy.[166]

No longer shall the sound of weeping be heard there, or the sound of crying.[167]

I will turn their mourning into joy, I will console and gladden them after their sorrows. I will lavish choice portions upon the priests, and my people shall be filled with my blessings, says the Lord.[168]

Old men and old women, each with staff in hand because of old age, shall again sit in the streets of Jerusalem. The city shall be filled with boys and girls playing in her streets... I will whistle for them to come together and when I redeem them they will be as numerous as before.[169]

- *Physical Endowments*

  He [the Lord] will renew your strength and you shall be like watered gardens.[170]

  The weakling among them shall be like David on that day.[171]

  Strengthen the hands that are feeble, make firm the knees that are weak... Then will the eyes of the blind be opened, the ears of the deaf be cleared; Then the lame will leap like a stag, then the tongue of the dumb will sing.[172]

  I will lead the blind on their journey... I will turn darkness into light before them, and make crooked ways straight.[173]

- *World Praise*

> Then the Lord's name will be declared on Zion, the praise of God in Jerusalem, when all peoples and kingdoms gather to worship the Lord.[174]

> I come to gather nations of every language; they shall come and see my glory.[175]

> In those days ten men of every nation, speaking in different tongues, shall take hold, yes, take hold of every Jew by the edge of his garment and say, "Let us go with you, for we have heard that God is with you."[176]

> From one new moon to another, and from one Sabbath to another, all mankind shall come to worship before me, says the Lord.[177]

- *Divine Light* [178]

> The sun will become seven times brighter than it is now.[179]

> The light of the moon will be like that of the sun and the light of the sun will be seven times greater...[180]
> I will turn darkness into light before them.[181]

- *Agrarian Society*

> And they shall build houses and inhabit them; and they shall plant vineyards, and eat the fruits of them, and drink the wine... and the works of their hands shall be multiplied. My elect shall not labor in vain.[182]

> He will give rain for the seed that you sow in the ground, and the wheat that the soil produces shall be rich and abundant. On that Day your cattle will graze in spacious meadows; the oxen and the asses that till the ground will eat silage tossed to them with shovel and pitchfork. Upon every high mountain and lofty hill there will be streams of running water.[183]

> They shall live in the houses they build, and eat the fruit of the vineyards they plant... and my chosen ones shall long enjoy the produce of their hands. They shall not toil in vain.[184]

> At that time, says the Lord, I will be the God of all the tribes of Israel, and they shall be my people. Thus says the Lord: The people that escaped the sword have found favor in the desert. As Israel comes forward to be given his rest, the Lord appears to him from afar: with age-old love I have loved you; so I have kept my mercy toward you. Again I will restore you, and you shall be rebuilt, o virgin Israel; Carrying your

festive tambourines; you shall go forth dancing with the merrymakers. Again you shall plant vineyards on the mountains of Samaria; those who plant them shall enjoy the fruits. Yes, a day will come when the watchmen will call out on Mount Ephraim: 'Rise up, let us go to Zion, to the Lord, our God.[185]

They shall rebuild and inhabit their ruined cities, plant vineyards and drink the wine, set out gardens and eat the fruits.[186]

• *Royal Priesthood*

You yourselves shall be named priests of the Lord, ministers of our God you shall be called.[187]

...Like living stones, let yourselves be built up into a spiritual house to be a holy priesthood to offer spiritual sacrifices acceptable to God through Jesus Christ.[188]

...You are "a chosen race, a royal priesthood, a holy nation, a people of his own, so that you may announce the praises" of him who called you out of darkness into his wonderful light.[189]
You made them a kingdom and priests for our God, and they will reign on earth.[190]

Blessed and holy is the one who shares in the first resurrection. The second death has no

power over these; they will be priests of God
and of Christ and they will reign with him for
the thousand years.[191]

3.3 THE HOLY SPIRIT AND MARY

The Holy Spirit in the Human Spirit

"Parousia" is the Greek word whose English equivalent
denotes *presence, coming* or *return.* The teachings of the
Magisterium define it as, *"the return of Christ, as Judge of the living
and the dead, at the end of the world."*[192] Christ's return "at the
end of the world" may, in part, explain why the Fathers refrain
from using the word Parousia when referring to the era of peace.
Whenever the Church Fathers speak of a Sabbath rest or era of
peace, they do not foretell a return of Jesus in the flesh nor the
end of human history, rather they accentuate the Holy Spirit's
transforming power in the sacraments that perfects the Church,
so that Christ may present her to himself as an immaculate bride
upon his final return.

Several Church Fathers and Early Ecclesiastical Writers
describe the era as a coming of the Spirit of Jesus, otherwise
known as a *"pneumatic coming."* The word "pneumatic"
derives from the Greek *pneuma*, meaning "spirit", which finds
its recent embodiment in the lives and approved writings of
contemporary mystics. The internal experiences of several
20th century mystics describe the pneumatic coming as a
new presence of the Holy Spirit in the human spirit revealed
exponentially at the threshold of the third millennium. The

writings of the Servant of God Luisa Piccarreta and Venerable Conchita Cabrera de Armida take up the thread where the patristic narratives left them.

Jesus tells Luisa:

> Ah, my daughter, the creature always races more into evil. How many machinations of ruin they are preparing! They will go so far as to exhaust themselves in evil. But while they occupy themselves in going their way, I will occupy Myself with the completion and fulfillment of my *Fiat Voluntas Tua* so that my Will reign on earth – but in an all-new manner. *I will occupy Myself to prepare the Era of the Third Fiat*, in which my Love will be demonstrated in a marvelous and unheard-of manner. Ah yes, I want to confound man in Love! Therefore, be attentive. I want you with Me to prepare this Era of Celestial and Divine Love, and we will work together.[193]

> When my *Fiat Voluntas Tua* has its fulfillment "on earth, as It is in Heaven", then the second part of the Pater Noster will be fulfilled, that is, "Give us today our daily bread."[194]

> If Creation is attributed to the Father—the Divine Persons always being united in their works—Redemption is ascribed to the Son, and *the Fiat Voluntas Tua will be attributed to the Holy Spirit. It is precisely in the Fiat Voluntas Tua where the work of the Holy Spirit will overflow.*[195]

Jesus tells Venerable Conchita:[196]

> *The time has come to exalt the Holy Spirit in the world...* I desire that this last epoch be consecrated in a very special way to this Holy Spirit... It is his turn, it is his epoch, it is the triumph of love in My Church, *in the whole universe.*[197]

> Once this transformation into Jesus is brought about in a soul, *the Holy Spirit also becomes the spirit of the creature... the Holy Spirit absorbs the creature's spirit* in the course of transformation and fills it with this so pure love which is Himself. Then, it is with this same love that he loves the divine Word...

> Loving with the Holy spirit is the grace of graces... the creature no longer acts, for *it is the Holy Spirit who acts... who lives in it and loves in it and wholly surrounds it... it is a union of the same nature as that of the union in heaven."*[198]

It can be gleaned from the works of recent mystics that in the era of peace, the Holy Spirit's full possession of the human spirit will restore man to God's likeness. Once the Holy Spirit's activity becomes the motive force of the human spirit, man is no longer under the dominating influence of lust, but is raised to the level in which he can gaze upon God within himself in perfect truth and liberty. Pope John Paul II reaffirms this teaching in *The Theology of the Body:*

> Biblical lust indicates the state of the human spirit
> removed from its original simplicity and fullness of
> values... lust is explained as a lack which has its roots
> in the depths of the human spirit...[199]

In the Encyclical *Redemptoris Mater* and in his General
Audience speech, the Holy Father presents the action of the
Holy Spirit in Mary and her corresponding "fiat" through a
"very firm decision" an integral to her having become "the
archetype of all those in the Church" who have chosen to
serve the Lord:

> At the Annunciation Mary entrusted herself
> to God completely, with the "full submission of
> intellect and will"... This *fiat* of Mary – "let it
> be to me" – was decisive... the mystery of the
> Incarnation was accomplished when Mary
> uttered her *fiat*."[200]

> How powerful too is the action of grace in her
> soul, how all-pervading is the influence of the
> Holy Spirit and of his light and power!... Her
> pilgrimage is interior: it is... a pilgrimage in
> the Holy Spirit... It is precisely in this ecclesial
> journey... and even more through the history of
> souls, that Mary is present...[201]
> It is clearly apparent from her question to the
> angel at the time of the Annunciation that she
> had come to *a very firm decision*... The grace which
> prepared her for virginal motherhood certainly
> influenced the whole growth of her personality,

while the Holy Spirit did not fail to inspire in her, from her earliest years, the desire for total union with God… By her *decision* however she becomes the archetype of all those in the Church who have chosen to serve the Lord… [202]

Furthermore St. Maximillian Kolbe presents Mary as the prototype of the Spirit's full possession of the human spirit:

The Holy Spirit is her spirit. Far from being alienated in her personality because of the dominance of the Holy Spirit, she is on the contrary more than any other creature in full possession of herself… *She lives in a state of divine synergy with the Holy Spirit.*[203]

Mary, Model of the Church's Holiness

In presenting the future Church as a holy and immaculate bride before Christ, St. Paul chose the Greek word "immaculate" to best describe her positive quality of pure and perfect obedience to God's will. St. Jerome brought this word into the Vulgate as "immaculatus" and attributed it to the Blessed Virgin Mary, as if to designate Mary as the prototype of the future Church. The New Testament develops this theme in two notable passages from the Gospel of Luke and the Book of Acts. In Gabriel's greeting to Mary, "Hail, full of grace,"[204] St. Luke reechoes the Old Testament prophetic salutation addressed to the reborn Jerusalem, the daughter of Zion. In Luke 1:28, Mary's greeting by the angel Gabriel, "Hail," was not a simple salutation, but an exultation: "Exult! Rejoice, full of grace!" Such an exultant greeting assumes incredible proportions in that it echoes the oracles of the Old Testament prophets Zephaniah, Joel and Zechariah, who triumphantly addressed the daughter of Zion, Jerusalem, the religious center of Israel: "Rejoice exceedingly, daughter of Zion... See, your king shall come to you, a just Savior is he".[205] The Greek Fathers commonly taught that Luke's narration of Mary's angelic salutation re-echoed the Old Testament salutation to the *entire house* of Israel. The king in this passage has been traditionally regarded as the Messiah, while the daughter of Zion represents the *induction* of Jerusalem at the eschatological age of universal peace, and Israel's new religious center of the Hebrews and Gentiles gathered within her walls.

This cross-reference is a key-point to the mystery of Luke's passage. According to the Scripture scholar Aristide Serra, Luke foresees in the Holy Spirit's overshadowing of Mary, the prototype of universal holiness in the era to come. When the Holy Spirit overshadowed Mary, he revealed the manner by which he will overshadow the reborn Jerusalem, the daughter of Zion. Hence Vatican II presents Mary as the model and type of the Church's future state of holiness:

> The Mother of Jesus... is the image and beginning of the Church as it is perfected in the world to come.[206]

> *The Blessed Virgin... is a type (typus) of the Church in the order of faith, charity, and perfect union with Christ.*[207]

One may foresee in the Holy Spirit's overshadowing of Mary a marvelous sign of the "new Pentecost" when he overshadows the entire house of Israel at the dawn of the eschatological era.[208] Scripture scholars affirm that the Old Testament prophecies of a universal outpouring of grace upon the entire house of Israel signify a unique gift reserved by the Holy Spirit *and* Mary.

In one of the leading biblical journals composed by a theological commission, *Parola, Spirito e Vita*, a relationship is drawn between the Holy Spirit, Mary and the eschatological Church.[209] Since Mary's maternity came by the power of the Holy Spirit for the purpose of generating and forming the Son of God, the Church bestows upon her the title "Mother of the Church" to illustrate the continuity of her mission of generating and forming other sons of God. St. Louis de Montfort reaffirms this prerogative of hers during the eschatological era:

> She [Mary] will consequently produce the marvels which will be seen in the latter times. *The formation and education of the great saints who will come at the end of the world are reserved to her.*[210]

> Towards the end of the world... Almighty God and his holy Mother are to raise up great saints who will surpass in holiness most other saints as much as the cedars of Lebanon tower above little shrubs.[211]

> In the second coming of Jesus Christ, Mary must be known and openly revealed by the Holy Spirit

so that Jesus may be known, loved and served through her.[212]

She [Mary] will extend the Kingdom of Christ over the idolaters and Muslems, and there will come a glorious era when Mary is the Ruler and Queen of Hearts.[213]

Mary's privileged role in the end times is reinforced in the writings of Blessed Mary of Agreda and Saint Maximilian Kolbe:[214]

It was revealed to me that through the intercession of the Mother of God all heresies will disappear... Mary will extend the reign of Christ over the heathens and the Muslims, and it will be a time of great joy when Mary is enthroned as Mistress and Queen of hearts.[215]

The image of the Immaculate will one day replace the large red star over the Kremlin, but only after a great and bloody trial.[216]

If St. Maximilian Kolbe speaks of the *holiness of Mary* that will eclipse Christians in the end times,[217] it is because she was immaculately conceived for the very purpose of generating all of God's children into the perfect likeness of her divine Son. Her prerogative of generating her sons into her divine Son draws its strength from her Son's holiness that is more purely reflected in her than in any other creature. St.

Maximilian refers to Mary as the "Immaculata" to emphasize this truth. The expression "Immaculata" accentuates the dignity of Mary's office as Mother of the Son of God, whose eternal holiness that eclipsed her entire being, empowers her to continuously generate God's children into the holiness she received. Indeed Maximilian speaks of a future era when all Christians will approach the holiness of Mary more closely than ever before.[218] It will be an era of the triumph of the "Immaculata," or, in the words of our Lady of Fatima, "the Triumph of her Immaculate Heart."

Only after the Last Judgment will Mary rest;
from now until then, she is much too busy with
her children.

— St. John Vianney

The Immaculate Church

When St. Paul wrote from his prison cell the letter to the Church in Ephesus,[219] it was not intended for Ephesians only, but for the purpose of making God's plan of universal salvation known to all.[220] It was clearly a letter intended to reveal the Holy Spirit's world mission to the Church. Paul's efforts in Ephesus, which lasted well over two years,[221] emphasized the unity that would come about for both Jews and Gentiles within the triune God.[222] This opens before us when we read his description of the future Church that is presented to Christ in a *"holy and immaculate"* state before his final return in glory. If the Church will be presented before

Christ in a "holy and immaculate" state, then something will have to provide for her holiness and immaculacy. In his Letter to the Ephesians Paul indicates that it is the groom who seeks to *"sanctify and cleanse"* his Church *"by the bath of water"* in order *"to present the Church to himself in splendor without spot or wrinkle or any such thing, that she might be holy and without blemish (immaculate)."*[223] In commenting on this passage Pope John Paul II affirms:

> "The washing of water" serves, on the part of the groom "to present the Church to himself in splendor without spot or wrinkle..." The text quoted indicates that the Christ-spouse himself takes care to adorn the spouse-Church. He is concerned that she should be beautiful with the beauty of grace...*Baptism is only the beginning from which the figure of the glorious Church will emerge.*[224]

The Pope attributes to Christ the work of preparing and adorning the Church through the action of grace. Admittedly, the bride's cleansing and sanctification proceed from the Church's sacramental graces. The sacraments are certainly an indispensable means for the attainment of Church's beauty. However, since grace is directly mediated to the Church through the merits of Jesus Christ and by the power of the Holy Spirit,[225] Christ is said to effect the work of grace in the sacraments. In this sense, it is Christ who "presents the Church to himself" through his *glorified Spirit* and the *sacraments*. The Immaculate Church during the era of universal peace will, therefore, proceed from the power of

Christ's glorified Spirit and the sacraments:

> *If before that final end there is to be a period,*
> *more or less prolonged, of triumphant sanctity,*
> *such a result will be brought about,* not by the
> apparition of the Person of Christ in Majesty but
> *by the operation of those powers of sanctification*
> *which are now at work, the Holy Ghost and the*
> *Sacraments of the Church.*[226]

Paul further describes the Church's sanctification as the
fruit of the "charisms" or "gifts" that the Spirit imparts. The
charisms serve "to equip the holy ones for the work of ministry,
for building up the body of Christ, *until we all attain to the unity*
of faith and knowledge of the Son of God... to the full stature of
Christ."[227] If the "unity of faith" and "knowledge in the Son of
God" are wrought by the Holy Spirit's power at work in the
sacraments and through his charisms, it advances the teaching
that they are the means by which the Church approaches her
state of Immaculacy.

That the Church will experience a universal unity of faith
in the Son of God is rooted in the event of Christ's virgin
birth. Just as Christ was unable to come to earth save through
the immaculate womb of his mother, he can neither return
to earth without his expectant Immaculate Church. St. Peter
alludes to this nuptial encounter in his first letter when he
assures her of her promised "inheritance that is imperishable,
undefiled and unfading, kept in heaven... for a salvation
ready to be revealed in the last days,"[228] and St. John bolsters
this idea when presenting the Church as a community of holy

ones dressed in white garments who arise after the days of Christian persecution.[229]

3.4 GOD'S ETERNAL ACTIVITY IN THE PRIESTHOOD

The Priesthood and the Divine Will

Since man's activity was impaired through the sin of Adam, who sinned through the use of his free will, reparation was required to correct its impairment. Hence a sacrificial offering made in the Person of Christ Jesus who, through a perfect act of free will, reordered man in his disfigured and wounded state. Since Adam's failure to do God's will resulted in his expulsion from the Garden of Eden, it is understood that even before he sinned, he was required to sacrifice his gift of free will to God who accompanied his every thought, word and action. By this offering of self to God, Adam exercised the sacrificial character of the office of priest: "every high priest is appointed to offer gifts *and* sacrifices."[230]

It is noteworthy that in Adam's state of innocence, sacrifice was not associated with the expiation or atonement of sin; that would come later through original sin. Sin did not enter into the economy of God's creation until Adam voluntarily juxtaposed his own will with that of his creator. Hence division ensued, whereby he and his partner were removed from the garden and stripped of their preternatural gifts. From this expulsion, Adam and Eve's priesthood underwent a radical change in character; sacrifice was no longer simply largesse, or a free offering, but one of atonement. Sacrifice eventually became an offering of "the blood of goats and bulls" in atonement for the division of sin that entered the world.[231] Only through a gradual reordering of a fallen world did sin and division become reversible and conquerable once and for all.

Since Jesus was above and outside the fallen world and lived in a paradisiacal state of innocence similar to that of Adam and Eve before the fall, he would be the first fruit of its reordering. By assuming our human nature, Jesus reproduced the perfect state of innocence in which a pure sacrifice of praise was offered through the perfect submission of the human will to the Father's will: "I do not seek my own will but the Will of the One who sent me."[232] By assuming the frailty of our human condition, he "learned obedience from what he suffered."[233] Unlike the sacrifice of the high priests who "offer sacrifice day after day,"[234] Jesus' sacrifice was founded upon "a new covenant" of which he is the mediator.[235] Therefore, "when he speaks of a 'new' covenant, he declares the old one obsolete,"[236] and where a sacrifice is offered in his memory, there is no invention of atonement for sins, for Jesus "did that once for all when he offered himself."[237]

The new covenant, ratified and consummated through the blood of Christ and in the power of the Spirit, was a pledge of the world's reordering that would come through the primacy of the God's will in man's will. The perpetuation of the unbloody sacrifice of Christ upon the altar is, therefore, celebrated in thanksgiving to the Father, through the Son and in the Holy Spirit for the reordering of this world.

In spite of the walls of division that separate wounded humanity from God, Christ's total submission to the Father caused these walls of division to crumble. Jesus, whose mission was to reconcile all things to himself in the Father, demonstrated his saving power, as a man outside the world of sin, by mastering the laws of nature. He calmed the tempestuous winds, walked on the waters, cured the lame, healed the deaf, and restored sight to the blind. By this means, he began the world's reordering and established the reign of God's kingdom on earth, a kingdom of steady and exponential increase and expansion.

When the Fathers and Early Ecclesiastical Writers associate God's kingdom with a universal outpouring of the Spirit, they describe what the Eastern Fathers call man's recovery of God's "likeness," or the "full" participation in God's Trinitarian life, through the process of *"divinization."* We initially encounter God's likeness in Adam. After Adam sinned, we encounter it anew in Jesus the eternal Priest. As God-man, our Lord was peculiarly adapted to be a priest, a spotless intermediary between God and man whose divinity empowered his humanity to perform perfect priestly acts.

The Eternal Priesthood of Christ

It is in the Priesthood of Christ that we discover God's likeness and the *typus* of holiness that man possessed before sin. Christ's priesthood is tangibly perpetuated in the dispensers of the sacraments, the ministerial priests. As Creator and cause of all supernatural life and holiness, Christ procures grace through the operation of secondary causes of supernatural grace, his ordained priests who administer the sacraments. Since the priests administer the sacraments Christ entrusted to them for the sanctification of others, the administrators of the sacraments (*mysterion*) receive an indelible spiritual mark upon ordination called a "character" that guarantees its validity (*ex opere operato*). This eternal character is a participation in the ministerial *power* of Christ who "is a priest forever." The priests are, therefore, the aqueducts, the channels of grace that enable divine life to flow into the Church, and into the souls of the laity who can nonetheless condition the effects of this influx by their disposition. This divine mechanism is what is called in theology "the sacramental economy."[238]

We find the benefits of this priestly power in Scripture through a body of men, *sharing in Christ's own priestly power* and continuing his ministry in the world. This sharing is particularly manifest in the marvelous transformation of bread and wine into the Body and Blood of Christ at the consecration of Mass. It is an action of Christ (*in persona Christi*), not the priest, not the action of man, which brings about transubstantiation. It is an action of the saving reality of the Risen Christ, a life-giving action. And it is on this basis that the timeless action of worship in the gift of the priest can be approached. Because it is an action of Christ, man cannot offer perfect sacrifice to God himself, he cannot redeem himself and he cannot sanctify himself. Christ, who is present as the glorified Lord, no longer existing in the conditions of earthly existence, performs an *eternal act* in the priest. The Letter to the Hebrews expresses this eternal action through the power of the Holy Spirit: "Christ, who through the power of *the eternal Spirit*, offered himself unblemished to God."[239] It is the function of the Spirit to bring about a reality in the bodily existence of the Risen Christ.

In defining the way Christ acts in his ordained ministers, the Second Vatican Council speaks of a "special grace" they receive, that enables them to better pursue the very perfection of Christ and share in his priestly and *eternal activity*:

> Every priestly ministry shares *in the fullness of the mission entrusted by Christ*... For the priesthood of Christ, of which priests have been really made sharers, is necessarily *directed to all peoples and all times, and is not confined by any bounds*...

> "Be perfect as your heavenly Father is perfect" (Mt. 5:48)... Priests are bound by *a special reason* to acquire this perfection. They are consecrated to God in *a new way* in their ordination and are made the *living instruments of Christ the eternal priest*... Since every priest in his own way assumes the person of Christ, he is endowed with *a special grace*. By this grace the priest...*is able the better to pursue the perfection of Christ*...

> Priests are able, *in the holiness with which they have been enriched in Christ*, to make progress towards the perfect man... Priests as ministers of the sacred mysteries, especially in the sacrifice of the Mass, *act in a special way in the person of Christ*... So when priests unite themselves *with the act of Christ* the Priest, they daily offer themselves completely to God... In the same way they *are united with the intention and charity of Christ* when they administer the sacraments... For the whole mission of Christ is dedicated *to the service of the new humanity* which Christ, the victor over death, raises up in the world.[240]

The powers Christ imparted to his priests at ordination are a sharing in his singular office. Vatican II qualifies this sharing by "a special reason" and "a special grace," in order to enable priests to "act with the intention of Christ" for the sake of a "new humanity."

I call special attention to the relationship between the ministerial priesthood and the common priesthood. While the ordained ministers may be privy to Christ's priestly *"powers,"* in particular that of consecration and absolution (ministerial priesthood), his priestly *"activity"* extends to all individuals (common priesthood).

When St. Paul states that we are "...predestined to be conformed to the image of his Son, so that he might be the firstborn among many brothers,"[241] he implies a sharing in Christ's priestly office that extends beyond the ministerial priesthood. It is in the 'image' to which Paul refers that all become sharers in Christ's office, so that "though we bear the image of the earthly one, we shall also bear the image of the heavenly one."[242] In distinguishing the office of Christ's ministerial priesthood from its common exercise and sharing of the faithful, Vatican II accentuates their commonality:

> Though they differ essentially and not only in degree, *the common priesthood of the faithful and the ministerial or hierarchical priesthood are nonetheless ordered one to another; each in its own proper way shares in the one priesthood of Christ.* The ministerial priest, by the sacred *power* that

he has... effects the Eucharistic sacrifice and offers it to God in the name of all the people. The faithful indeed, by virtue of their royal priesthood, participate in the offering of the Eucharist. They *exercise* that priesthood too, by the reception of the sacraments, prayer and thanksgiving, by the witness of a holy life, abnegation and active charity.[243]

The ministerial and common priesthoods are thus ordered to one another through their activity that originates in baptism. Because this activity is an empowerment of the same Spirit that empowered Christ in the exercise of his eternal priesthood, it is a *sharing in his eternal activity*. But things do not end here; the sharing continues to increase exponentially throughout the Christian's spiritual journey,[244] particularly through the actions of the ordained ministers who administer the sacraments.[245] The Servant of God Luisa Piccarreta and Venerable Conchita de Armida reveal that the Holy Spirit imparts the unique gift of Jesus' eternal activity to the world by means of his priests, who will be the first fruits of its reordering:

I have placed close to you *the vigilant assistance of my ministers* as cooperators, guardians and depositories of the knowledge, goods and prodigies that My Will contains. Because It wants to establish Its Kingdom in the midst of people, I want, by your means, to deposit in My ministers this celestial doctrine, as to new apostles, *in order to "first" form with them the link with My Will, so that they may in turn, transmit it to the people.* If this were not the case, or had not been the case, I would not have insisted so much in making you write; nor would I have permitted the daily visits of the Priests, but would have reserved this entire work of Mine up to you and Me.[246]

The time has arrived for My priests to shake off from themselves all pusillanimity and, with warlike atmosphere and without fear... fight and vanquish hell... The Holy Spirit is the great motive force of the Church, its being and its life that enlivens the hearts of those who surrender themselves to him. My priests who do this... will fulfill the purpose... for the salvation of the world... All depends on their correspondence with what I ask, and everything depends upon their fidelity and love toward Me... by making his will one with My Will.[247]

Moreover, in describing their ability to influence the lives of *all creatures*, the Servant of God Luisa Piccarreta and Blessed Dina Bélanger[248] respectively suggest a *full* sharing in the eternal priesthood of Christ that is *"directed to all peoples and all times, and is not confined by any bounds"*:

I found myself in Jesus. My little atom swam in the Eternal Will. Moreover, since this Eternal Will is a single Act that contains together all the acts of the *past, present, and future*, I, being in the Eternal Will, took part in that single Act which contains all acts, inasmuch as it is possible for a

creature. I even took part in the acts which do not yet exist, and which must exist, unto the end of centuries, and as long as God will be God.[249]
It was my desire to utilize the merits of Jesus and the infinite means he places at our disposal… *for all creatures past, present and future*, in the measure they are capable of profiting by them.[250]

The Theologian's Task in Relation to Public and Private Revelation

Private revelations differ from the public revelations (*revelatio pubblica*) in that the latter is the general norm of faith and has universal and perpetual significance, whereas the former alone relate to the concrete historical context that becomes its *Sitz im Leben*. Insofar as Jesus' private revelations to his chosen mystics on the gift of "Living in the Divine Will" are seen through the lens of the Church's sacramental economy, they illuminate her doctrine and reveal its *locus* in the deposit of faith. In this sense private revelations complement what the Church has always taught on man's participation in Christ's eternal priesthood, in his eternal priestly acts and in his eternal mode of operation. The approved private revelations of the aforementioned mystics can therefore be seen as an integral and internal development of the traditional teachings of Jesus' eternal priesthood. Still, because the impoverished form, style and speech of several mystics may shroud their intended meaning, it is the theologian's duty to uncover the substance or doctrine contained therein, without prejudicing their intentions or words, so as to illuminate the teachings contained in the Church's deposit.[251]

One of the challenges offered to the idea of a new era of peace and holiness is that nothing *new* may be added to the Church's public deposit of faith:

> What was handed on by the apostles comprises everything that serves to make the People of God live their lives in holiness and increase their faith... He [Jesus] himself... completed and perfected Revelation and confirmed it with divine guarantees... No new public revelation is to be expected before the glorious manifestation of our Lord, Jesus Christ.[252]

According to several scholars, however, in particular, Yves Congar, O.P., God's dispensation of mystical gifts extends beyond the death of the last Apostle and Ascension of Jesus Christ, otherwise known as the "deposit of faith" (*depositum fidei*).[253] If God, having said all that he had to tell us in Jesus Christ, no longer intervenes in the world by a new public revelation, he expects to see his people "more thoroughly understand" and "grow in insight" into the Word it has received.[254] However, his people are not waiting for it, expectant and inactive, but are advancing through time down every path and every direction imaginable. Throughout time there are constantly unfolding new expressions, new editions and rediscoveries of the unique message of Jesus Christ. The challenge in all this lies in trying to ensure that the interpretation of God's Word remains faithful to its point of origin, Jesus Christ. Hence the theologian's task is to revisit the gospel message, and to emerge with deeper insights that both reaffirm its past and direct its future.

He does this by continuously drawing from the treasure trove of the Church's three modes of the transmission of revelation, namely Sacred Scripture, the apostolic Tradition and the Magisterium, without neglecting new insights from the Church's doctors, saints and mystics. There are and always will be in the Church a contemplation of the mysteries, a meditation of Sacred Scripture and new experiences of God's presence and activity. In this sense, the good scholar in the kingdom of heaven is one who brings forth from his treasure trove new things as well as old.[255] The old sap, still living, brings life to a new tree. Likewise, the theologian's delivery of the gospel message is not simply a repetition of the old, like a new impression of an old recording, but an original expression, clothed in a new vocabulary. The old belongs to eternity and is indeed repeated, but not in its former state. With the task to reply to new problems, it uses new resources drawn from a given period and fashioned by human activity. The revered theologian Hans Urs von Balthasar brings this truth to the fore:

> To remain faithful herself to her mission, the Church has continually to make an effort of creative invention. Faced with the gentiles who were to enter the Church, successor to the Synagogue, Paul was forced to invent. The same happened to the Greek Fathers, faced with Hellenic culture, and to St. Thomas, faced with Arab philosophy and science. We have no alternative, faced with the problems of today.[256]

The deposit of faith is the Church's heritage of the faith contained in Sacred Scripture and Tradition, handed down in the

Church from the time of the Apostles, from which the Magisterium (*mysterium salutis*) draws all that it proposes for belief as being divinely revealed. This sacred deposit is comprised of two equally vital aspects, one of conservation and one of development. There is a sort of dialectic between purity and totality, neither of which should be sacrificed. The Magisterium, whose chief mission is to keep and transmit a deposit, is more concerned with purity, and that should be its duty. However, faced with time's challenges, the Church must react in obedience to the mission Jesus entrusted her with, by displaying the gospel as extensively as possible to mankind, both quantitatively and internally. It is no coincidence that the expression "living Tradition" was first used during the Jansenistic debate to counter their false concept of Tradition as purely documentary, historical and static. In fact, the dogmas of Mary's Immaculate Conception and Assumption can hardly be passed off as the simple explanation of a formal statement of Scripture. And yet these dogmas have strong ties with Scripture, which, when placed in the context of a living Tradition, makes possible the "analogy of faith." This expression, taken from St. Paul's letter to the Romans,[257] signifies in theology, the relationship between the different statements or articles that have been revealed, such that new statements, not made *explicitly* in the documents of Scripture, appear possible and even necessary. St. Thomas Aquinas affirms:

> Regarding its substance, faith does not grow with the passage of time, for whatever has been believed since the beginning was contained in the faith of the early Fathers. *As regards its explication, however, the number of articles has increased, for we moderns explicitly believe what they believed implicitly.*[258]

Moreover, the Church possesses other sources of knowledge besides mere documents. Many theologians, in particular Maurice Blondel, acknowledge that it is precisely here where the theologian must discern; it is here where the synthesis is realized between historical transmission of the gospel and today's challenges, which, when combined, help direct the Church's future. The deposit of faith in the Church's living Tradition is an historical journey. It earns interest, as it were, during the centuries, which is added to its capital foundation. What was handed down to her once and for all has yet to be "filled with all the fullness of God."²⁵⁹ This earning of interest, or development of doctrine, is what is known as "positive theology," for it takes as the foundation of its contemplation the richest possible material of Tradition and attempts to include in its knowledge all that has already been said by the doctors, saints and mystics who have lived and contemplated their faith before us.

Yet not all appreciate the contributions of the mystics. Many regard mysticism as merely a variety of psychological experience, or among the extraordinary graces and favors that are catalogued by St. Paul, as the *gratia gratis data*, that do not sanctify *the individual*, but are "purely" ordered to the spiritual welfare *of others*. Yet mystical experiences are infusions of purifying and sanctifying grace that one cannot dismiss as psychological fancies or as falling in a category other than the Church's deposit of faith. There are numerous mystical authors who, without recourse to theological argument, show themselves unwilling to allow that mystical gifts have any intimate connection with personal achievement, and who are more willing to allow that mystical perfection is the highest form of Christian excellence. Theologians justify this position by regarding the mystical life as an "extension" or "prolongation" of the life of Christian virtue begun at baptism, and the goal and crown of the active life. Its authority, adopted by all theologians, mystical as well as dogmatic, divides all believers into three classes: sinful, practicing, and contemplatives. While some gifts of the Spirit are not due to the merit of the individual nor *directly* ordered to his/her sanctification, but to the good of the entire Church, some are in a form that is indeed ordered to *directly* sanctify the individual *(gratia gratum faciens)*. And yet the gifts that are directly ordered to the good of the entire Church do not pass by without leaving a sanctifying *effect* on the individual. Inasmuch as all graces are ordered, directly or indirectly, to benefit the entire Church or to sanctify the individual, there is no basis to the notion that certain graces are "purely" ordered to the entire Church. All graces exercise an influence on the individual and the entire community of believers simultaneously; they lead the recipient to the total service of Christ in the Church that he has helped to perfect in holiness.

Moreover, every action of every agent is performed with the direct assistance of God, who not only bestows the power to act, but also concurs with the action in such a way that if he withdrew his aid the action would cease. Despite this assistance the human being remains always free to accept or to refuse the end for which God has ordained each human act. Such is the case in a person who is baptized. Despite the theological "infused" virtues of faith, hope and love, he remains free to commit deliberate sins. All of the powers God has bestowed on his soul–which are aspects of one great power of love poured into it by the Holy

Spirit through Jesus Christ—are rendered ineffective without the consent of his free will. Thus he stands in need of God's uncreated and ancillary activity by which he may grow and approach God more intimately, provided he acts with *His* divine help. As he approaches God, sanctifying grace communicates divine life to his soul exponentially, whereby it increases union, but as leaven that must work upon the whole mass. As the leaven works, he approaches still higher forms of God's action in his soul through the dispensation of God's mystical gifts. Thus the more he cooperates with these gifts, the more completely does he see with *God's* sight and act by *His* activity. The mystical graces enable knowledge and love to be infused in his soul in unending degrees so that it is possible for God to flood it with greater expressions of his uncreated love. In all of this, the new and higher forms of grace, which are needed by his soul if there are to be no gaps and imperfections in its vision, raise the human action to a divine action, then to a continuously divine action, to finally God's continuously eternal Act. In this way, the stages of Baptism, Spiritual Betrothal, Spiritual Marriage and Living in God's Divine Will unfold within the framework of the Church's mystical tradition.

Christian Tradition and medieval theology have described these mystical graces in terms of the "Gifts" of the Holy Spirit. These gifts come to the soul at Baptism, along with the theological and cardinal virtues that serve to enlighten the mind to a deeper appreciation of the truths of the faith, while empowering the soul to attain to the *fullness* of divine-human cooperation. The truths of the faith such as the divinity of Christ or the absolute sinlessness of the Mother of God are indeed "mystical," for they come to the mind without any discursive reasoning and cannot be fully communicated to others. Nevertheless, the recipient has no kind of mystical "experience," and the light that is received illuminates a truth that is, to some degree, already known and expressed in words. When, however, the influence of these truths reveal the gifts in a more pronounced manner, and the soul realizes that the divine things it receives are different from its past experience, the entrance to the mystical way has taken place.

Of the many gifts the Church bestows upon her members, we often encounter in the approved writings of the mystics those gifts that are called "mystical." Mystical gifts are not imparted to all in the same way, shape or size, but are imparted *"unequally."* This unequal distribution is a prerogative of God alone, who freely imparts his gifts to those whom he chooses according to his good pleasure. In other words, while all the baptized have an *equal* share in the life of the three divine Persons through the infusion of the three theological gifts, *not all share equally in the mystical gifts* God selectively grants to certain souls. This teaching on the unequal distribution of God's mystical gifts can be found in the writings of Vatican II and of the mystical Doctor St. John of the Cross:

> It is not only through the sacraments and the ministrations of the Church that the Holy Spirit makes holy the people, leads them, and enriches them with his virtues, allotting his gifts according *as he wills,* (Cor. 12:11) He also distributes special graces among the faithful of every rank.[260]

> God calls us all to this intimate union with him, even if the special graces or extraordinary signs

of this mystical life are granted *only to some* for the sake of manifesting the gratuitous gifts given to all.[261]

God does not bring to contemplation all those who purposefully exercise themselves in the way of the spirit, nor even half. Why? He best knows.[262]

St. Faustina Kowalska's insights reinforce John's doctrine concerning God's election of certain souls:

When I had stepped into the chapel for a moment, the Lord gave me to know that, *among His chosen ones, there are some who are especially chosen, and whom He calls to a higher form of holiness, to exceptional union with Him.* These are seraphic souls, from whom God demands greater love than He does from others (entry 1556)... Such a soul understands this call, because God makes this known to it interiorly, but the soul may either follow this call or not... The soul that is especially marked by God will be distinguished everywhere, whether in heaven or in purgatory or in hell. *In heaven, it will be distinguished from other souls by greater glory and radiance and deeper knowledge of God.* In purgatory, by greater pain, because it knows God more profoundly and desires Him more vehemently. In hell, it will suffer more profoundly than other souls, because it knows more fully whom it had lost. This indelible mark of God's exclusive love, in the soul, will not be obliterated.[263]

We must allow the words and the actions of the mystics to be put in evidence before we roundly pronounce, even upon such a matter as the degree to which souls may aspire to union with God. It is easy for those far outside the pale of contemplative prayer to judge this and that to be silly or unpractical of God. For God's dealings with us, who often have just enough light to see our own infirmities, are often out of our ken and nearly impossible to predict.

Through the Church-approved works of recent exemplars of holiness, it is now possible to unveil the greatest of all mystical gifts, namely the gift of God's continuously eternal activity in souls. Their writings (reported in section 3.5 and chapter 4), articulate a new consciousness of God's activity, frequently referred to as *Living in the Divine Will; the Mystical Incarnation; the New Indwelling; the Divine Substitution; Living Hosts* and *Living Tabernacles*. While all the baptized are empowered by God's Spirit to *pursue* this unique mystical "gift," only God determines when and in whom it will be actualized. Even if, let us say, a saint of the 16th century had attained to the state of perfection and were absolutely disposed to embrace this gift, if God chose not to grant it, that saint could not receive it, and yet would remain no less holy and faithful than before. No saint, no matter how exceedingly holy or brilliant, can *acquire* God's mystical gifts as one might acquire virtues, lest the gift cease to be a gift altogether.

It is well established among Catholic spiritual masters that at the heights of mystical union it is God who does all in the soul, while the soul, having reached the point of being utterly disposed, accepts and receives whatever God wishes to give and to do in it. No saint would feel as if he had failed, or be doubtful of God's generosity, if he were to discover that God had given a gift to someone else that he did not receive. At the height of mystical union, all that has ever mattered is that the soul remain totally open to receive whatever God might wish to give it or respond to whatever he might ask of it. It is not a slight to the saints, therefore, to suppose that God, according to his own good will and pleasure, reserved the gift of the fullness of his activity in us for our times. Jesus reveals to the Servant of God Luisa Piccarreta and to other mystics that it does not depend upon the creature, but upon God's good pleasure to grant the extraordinary grace described as *Living in the Divine Will*:

> If Creation is attributed to the Father – although the Divine Persons are always united in their works – Redemption is ascribed to the Son, and the *Fiat Voluntas Tua* will be attributed to the Holy Spirit. It is precisely in the *Fiat Voluntas Tua* where the work of the Holy Spirit will overflow. You do this when, coming before the Supreme Majesty, you say: "I come to lovingly correspond with everything the Sanctifier does... Sanctifying Spirit, I beg and implore You to do it quickly: make your Will known to all so that, knowing It, they may love It and receive your first act, which constitutes Your most holy Will and their complete sanctification!"[264]

> This point which leads to union, even more, to unity, is the point of perfection which most approaches the Trinity... *The creature left to itself*

would be incapable of attaining this degree without the most powerful aid of Him who is the inexhaustible Source of graces, the Holy Spirit.[265]

In fact, the approved works of several recent mystics tell us that God reserved the fullness of this gift until the late 20th century, although he could have given it, in its fullness, as early as the first centuries of Christianity. Their writings further testify to the universality of this gift that is neither apportioned to one nor to a select few, but is given to the entire Church.[266] St. John of the Cross testifies to the ongoing actualization of God's gifts and to the human creature's virtually endless potential for holiness:

> However are the mysteries and marvels that the holy doctors have discovered and saintly souls understood in this earthly life, *all the more is yet to be said and understood.* There is much to fathom in Christ, for he is like an abundant mine with many recesses of treasures, so that however deep individuals may go they never reach the end or bottom, but rather *in every recess find new veins with new riches everywhere.* On this account St. Paul said of Christ: "In Christ dwells hidden all treasures and wisdom" (Col. 2:3).[267]

Arrival at the state of full and continuous participation in God's eternal activity does not signify the end of growth, but the beginning of endless degrees of greater union. Yet in order that the human creature may arrive at the *continuous* state of God's eternal activity, it must traverse the traditional stages of purgation, illumination, unification and divinization, so as to be trained to greater comprehend, appreciate and remain continuously faithful to God's gift. These stages help dispose the soul by freeing it from its slightest inordinate attachments, illuminating its vision of the here and hereafter, and divinizing its faculties in operation while uniting them more intimately to the three divine Persons.

The Church and the Kingdom

Ss. Augustine and Thomas confer upon the People of God two successive states, *nunc et tunc*: the provisional and definitive states. While the Church's ordained ministers may be "set apart from the common class of people," both priests and laity are equally called to progressive and unending degrees of union with God. Cardinal Journet illustrates this point through the redimensioning act of Jesus' Incarnation that raised all peoples to the level where they can participate in the "qualitative onward":

> We do not believe that one can refuse to identify the Church and the kingdom. We have two concepts here, but only one reality. The Church is the kingdom; the kingdom is the Church. The concept kingdom refers to eschatology. *But it is precisely with Jesus that eschatology, which belongs above all to the qualitative onward, has broken into time. From the time of Christ onward, the whole Church has entered the end time, she is eschatological.*[268]

This "breaking into time" is the work of God who intends to raise the human race to the fullness of his divine and eternal activity. From the moment Christ became human, the human race became divine, though not all arrive at the fullness of the kingdom. St. Augustine affirms that "sacramentally" the Church has neither arrived at the *fullness* of the kingdom nor at its definitive realization.[269] Assuredly, the nature of the sacrament belongs to the pilgrim Church, not to the perfected kingdom outside of time, for it lies in her relationship to the world. That God's eternal activity outside of time brings with it the fullness of the kingdom is made evident in the writings of recent mystics, which we shall explore in the next chapter. Their experiences and approved works present God's continuously eternal activity as the hallmark of the holiness and the fullness of the eschatological Church.

The relationship of the pilgrim Church to the world, moreover, allows Christ to call people to himself that they may participate in his eternal priestly activity in a variety of ways. An outstanding example is found in the actions of the priest. At the consecration of Mass, during absolution and in every sacrament, the divine and eternal activity of Christ is present. Although the priest is the chosen vessel of Christ's eternal action in the sacraments, the priest need not be in the state of grace for the sacrament to be valid. This does not mean that the priest forces Christ to act each time he performs the ceremony of a sacrament on his own personal initiative. If one views the sacrament as the carrying out of a mere ceremony, Christ's eternal activity is not freely communicated. If, on the other hand, one were to consider that Christ, by instituting the sacraments, had decided of his own to be constrained to give of himself in the sacrament, under certain conditions of validity, such activity would then be freely communicated.

Just as Christ's eternal action blends with the actions of the priest and gives life to the sacraments, so the free response of every Christian to Christ's free gift enables them to partake of Christ's one eternal Act.

Each person, in the measure that he freely receives and responds to God's grace, *shares* in the mission and action Christ entrusted to his Church.[270] Through the Holy Spirit's power in the sacraments, God's gifts and graces dispose the soul to more easily relate itself "to the totality of creation," to look upon its own work "as a prolongation of the work of the creator... and contribute to the fulfillment of history."[271] Yet in order that the soul may arrive at the *continuous state* of Jesus' eternal activity, or, as the mystics put it, its "possession," it freely desires to embrace the process of "divinization." As evidenced in the writings of Ss. Gregory of Nyssa, Augustine and Maximus the Confessor, divinization is the expectant stage for the reception of the *continuous state* of Christ's eternal activity. At this stage the soul does not demand from God the gifts, rather it passively awaits whatever graces God wishes to grant it. This penultimate level of divinization is beautifully articulated in the writings of Maximus the Confessor.

Divinization and the Divine Will

Maximus the Confessor (580-662)[272]

The process of divinization principally involves two dimensions of the human will: the *natural* and the *personal*. The "*natural will*" (logos) is the rational will which is created by God and resides in each human being. It is informed of God's natural law and is the "essential element" of the human will. By its very essence, it makes the will *human* and not the will of some other created being, and yet it is a part of all human beings.

However, the natural will cannot be considered apart from its personal dimension. The *"personal will"* (*tropos*) brings individuality in different ways. The personal will is the way (mode) in which persons will what is specific to each of them uniquely; it is a person's manner of conforming his natural will with the will of God, or, in other words, the mode of his *personal hypostasis*. It may be influenced, in particular, by God's grace and gifts (i.e., Baptism and Confirmation). The distinction between the human and personal will consists in the former being beyond human influence and the latter being wholly within each person's power to develop and to construct a *personal hypostasis*.

Each person's choices suffer from certain *"inclinations"* as to which choice it might make. Ideally, the personal will always freely chooses that which is good and in accord with God's will. But the result of the fall of Adam has corrupted our perception of good and obscured our vision of God's will. Humanity is not always able to see the true good which it ought to choose. This "inclination" that often keeps each person at odds with the good is what Maximus calls the *gnome*. It is a disposition or willful habit that is part of humanity wounded by sin. The *gnome* condition is a far cry from perfection, yet it is the situation of wounded humanity. It is the result of original sin, but not without hope.

In Jesus Christ there is both the *natural* and *personal will*. The Council of Chalcedon affirmed this teaching against the monothelitist heresy in the fifth century. Christ was fully human, but also fully divine. In virtue of Christ's human and divine natures, he possesses a human and Divine Will. Here we have two complementary truths. On the one hand, Christ possessed a human will, and on the other, he did not possess a peccable will. Christ's Divine Will empowered him to overcome the human inclination toward sin (*gnome*) and, for this reason, there was no deprivation of knowledge of the good in him. This deprivation, inherent to our wounded human condition, was overcome only in the Person of Christ. According to Maximus, Christ possessed the *"full natural will"* in his divine Person, that is, without its *inclination (gnome)*. In Christ's hypostatic union, therefore, there is reflected the way in which the human will and Divine Will produce two activities in such perfect accord that they result in one action, otherwise known as *divine synergy*.

Let us recall that in Jesus there was no *evil inclination (gnome)* due to the fact that his *personal will (Tropos)* was perfectly united to his *natural will (Logos)*. And in all humans conceived in original sin, the *personal will* is not so fortunate as to be so perfectly united to the *natural will* that it escapes all *evil inclinations*. Thus all men are conceived with a *gnomic will*. However, by the Holy Spirit's assuming full control of the human spirit, Maximus reveals that it is indeed possible for the *personal will* and *natural will* to recover the original, continuous and inseparable unity that Adam once enjoyed. Otherwise put, the *gnomic will* has conserved all the properties, characteristics and divinizing potencies that can restore God's likeness. The restoration of God's likeness in man occurs when the Holy Spirit takes *full* possession of the human spirit, whereby the *inclinations* may no longer exercise the active psychosomatic influence with the intensity that strained and scarred its past.[273] The result is a new *personal hypostasis*, similar to the hypostatic union enjoyed by Christ.

From this perspective, St. Maximus presents Jesus' state of holiness as that which man strives to attain by merging the two dimensions of his will through the process of *divinization*. Although both St. Augustine and St. Maximus never affirm that anyone had actually achieved this continuous state of the Holy Spirit's full possession of the human spirit since Adam, they acknowledge man's ontological potency to attain it, a potency whose actualization is entirely dependant upon God's gratuitous grace. In the process of divinization, God's grace, coupled with man's cooperation, *disposes* him to overcome his evil inclinations (*gnomic will*) and to recover his *full natural will*.[274] Although man may be properly disposed to recover his full natural will, unless God decides to grant him this gift, he cannot attain it. It remains God's prerogative to grant this gift to whomever he wills, whenever he wills.

That God has indeed granted the extraordinary gift of the full natural will, or Christ's *continuously eternal* activity in man, is evident in the lives of several contemporary mystics whose writings have been approved by the Church. In their writings Jesus accentuates the role of his divinizing power in overcoming the gnomic influence in the human creature. He tells the Servant of God Luisa Piccarreta:

> My Divinity, united to My Humanity, could have worked prodigies at every step, with words and works. And yet, I voluntarily restricted Myself in My Humanity by becoming

the poorest, and went so far as to mingle with sinners themselves... I wanted to exercise Myself in a variety of different actions in order *that man might be completely renewed and divinized even in his smallest works.* For such works, carried out by Me, who am God and Man, received new splendor and the seal of the Divine...[275] The power of My Will, without exempting you from original sin, *suppresses and holds Itself firm over the fomes of sin, so that they not produce their corrupting effects.*[276]

Other traces of God's power to actualize in man a union of wills so intimate that it resembles the union of Christ's divinity and humanity are found in the lives of the Servant of God Archbishop of Mexico Luis Maria Martinez[277] and Blessed Dina:

The soul gives to the Word that which he does not have: a new human nature, the capacity for pain and immolation. And the Word divinizes the soul, *uniting himself to it in a most intimate way (by union of wills) that imitates the hypostatic union.*[278]

During my thanksgiving after Communion, I was concentrating on remaining closely united with him... I was taken by surprise... He said: *"I want to deify you in the same way as I united My humanity with My divinity... The degree of holiness that I want for you, is the infinite plentitude of my own holiness, it is the holiness of my Father* brought about in you through me."[279]

The writings of the modern mystics confirm God's power to maintain man in the *continuous state* of a new union of wills. Jesus tells Luisa Piccarreta:

> Whoever lives in my Will finds himself already in this single Act. As the heart always palpitates in human nature and constitutes its life, so my Will palpitates *continually* in the depth of the soul, but with a single palpitation. As It palpitates, It gives it beauty, sanctity, strength, love, goodness, wisdom… This palpitation encloses Heaven and earth… This single Act, this palpitation of the soul, reigns completely, it has full vigor and is *a continuous prodigy that only a God can perform.* Therefore, new Heavens are unveiled in it, new abysses of graces, and surprising truths.[280]

Blessed Dina affirms:

> I need a perpetual and very powerful grace to *maintain me in this blessed state*: I am enjoying perfect beatitude… *It is truly eternity!*[281]

That it is above all through an act of "willing" that man fully reestablishes himself in Christ is brought out in the writings of Ss. Gregory of Nyssa, Augustine, and Maximus the Confessor. We also find the primacy of the will in the writings of Pico of Mirandola:[282]

> If Adam willingly listened to the seducer, if he looked and ate with his will, then it is primarily the will in

us that has suffered damage. If this is so, and if the Logos [the Word of God] had not assumed the will in his Incarnation, as they [the Monothelites] assert, then I have not got free from sin, and thus I am not redeemed either, for that which was not assumed [by Christ] has not been redeemed.[283]

More recently, Cardinal Archbishop Christoph Schönborn reinforces the tradition of the primacy of the will in man's reestablishing himself in Christ:

If it is clear that the fall was caused by a perversion of the human will, then it follows that the reestablishment must affect above all the act of human willing.[284]

Similar experiences of the sublime union of man's will and God's will are traceable to the writings of the spiritual daughter of Archbishop Luis Martinez, Venerable Conchita de Armida:

To speak of the Mystical Incarnation is then to consider the soul as entering into a phase of graces of transformation which will bring it, if it corresponds, to *the identification of its will with Mine... in order that its union with God come to the most perfect likeness possible.* Such is the gift of the Mystical Incarnation which the Holy Spirit gives as a gift to certain souls.[285]

In this loving act of supreme abandonment to the will of my Father there is perfection, the highest and complete sanctity.[286]

3.5   THE CHURCH MYSTICS

If several Church Fathers, Doctors and writers speak of a future era in which all creation will magnify God's greatness, the approved works of the 20th century mystics and exemplars describe its actualization in man. Earlier I referred to these mystics by name. Their approved writings characterize the new mystical union of wills[287] through the following expressions: "Living in the Divine Will" (Luisa Piccarreta and St. Hannibal di Francia[288]), "the Mystical Incarnation" (Venerable Conchita de Armida and the Servant of God Archbishop Luis Martinez), "the New Indwelling" (Blessed Elizabeth of the Trinity), "the Assumption of Souls in Love" (St. Maximilian Kolbe), "the Divine Substitution" (Blessed Dina Bélanger), "the Divine Will" and "Living Hosts" (Ss. Padre Pio and Faustina Kowalska, Mary-Rose Ferron,[289] Blessed Mother Teresa of Calcutta, the Servants of God Rev. Michael Sopoćko and Marthe Robin, Sister Mary of the Holy Trinity and Rev. Walter Ciszek) and "Living Tabernacles" (Vera Grita).

Until their literature appeared on bookshelves, little, if anything had been said of their extraordinary experiences. In their writings, one can identify the characteristic note that sets this new gift apart from all others, namely, *"the continuous participation in God's eternal activity."* Summarizing their approved works, one discovers God's motive for reserving this gift for our modern times: *that in showering his graces upon a world steeped in sin God's grace may abound all the more;*[290] *by inviting all on earth to partake in his eternal realities God may dispose the world for the era of universal peace and holiness, and actualize it through the Holy Spirit who will renew the face of the earth with a new Pentecost.*

God's Grace

Because God's triune essence was materialized in the act of the creation of man, God infused within him a supernatural aptitude to participate in his uncreated Nature. This supernatural aptitude is called *grace*.[291] Grace reflects man's infinite aptitude for holiness: *finitum capax retinendi infinitum* (the finite is capable of holding the infinite). Since man's nature remains essentially finite, the Holy Spirit adapts himself to the creature, expressing his uncreated activity through created grace in the faculties of his soul: in the will, the intellect and the memory. At Baptism, as in creation, God communicates to man the ability to *participate* in his uncreated, eternal activity. This participation is, however, the *beginning* of God's activity. In order for the soul to participate in the *fullness* of God's eternal activity, it must continuously aspire to higher forms of that holiness to which Adam had been called from the beginning:

> O Adam... you are equally free to be reborn *in higher divine forms* through your own decision.[292]

Thus the soul's perfecting is not something confinable to the past, but an ongoing journey during its pilgrim state on earth. After Baptism, the Holy Spirit invites the soul into the process of divinization, whereby it may partake more intimately in the knowledge and activity of the eternal priesthood of Christ. Let us recall that in Baptism, the soul is at once admitted to the common priesthood, whereby it may "profess faith in Christ publicly and as it were officially (*quasi ex officio*)," and perform the three-fold function of priest, prophet and king.[293] It is not, however, until the soul becomes more conformed to Christ through the four aforementioned levels of spiritual growth that it approaches the state of God's *likeness* that Adam possessed.

The Human and Divine Modes of Holiness

As the soul matures in its spiritual journey to God, it gradually leaves its human ways of thinking, praying and acting behind (*modo humano*) and enters the divine ways of thinking, acting and praying (*modo divino*). In the writings of St. Teresa of Avila, we find that in its spiritual journey, the soul must pass through seven mansions in order to be divinized and attain to the state of Spiritual Marriage. Noteworthy is the way in which Teresa presents this spiritual evolution. As the soul enters the fourth mansion, its thinking, acting and praying become divine, thus admitting it to the early stages of the *divine mode*, in which it perseveres through the succeeding mansions. It is not until the soul enters the seventh mansion that the divine mode, only by a "special" or "signal grace," divinizes the creature and admits it to the *"uninterrupted"* and *"habitual"* participation in God's *divine activity*.[294] The mystical theologian Fr. Dubay elaborates on the distinction between these two traditional modes:

> How does one pray in the third mansions? Consistently with her whole approach, Teresa says very little about the question, because the prayer is *modo humano*, still somewhat discursive… The last four mansions take up about 70 percent of the text… It is at this stage of development that "the natural is united with the supernatural" and… the mingling between the *human and divine modes*

of praying…When God wishes us to give up our *human mode* of praying, He illumines in *His mode* and leads us into an absorption in Himself.[295]

In the seventh mansion, St. Teresa describes God's *continuously divine activity* in the soul in the advanced stages of the *divine mode*:

> St. Teresa's descriptions of this continuous awareness are similar to those of St. John of the Cross. She expresses her mind in several ways: "The soul is almost continuously near His Majesty… *the three divine Persons are very habitually present in my soul… The presence is not merely 'almost continual' but also uninterrupted: The soul is always aware that it is experiencing this companionship…* they have become like two who cannot be separated from one another."[296]

> The soul always remains in its centre with its God… the soul itself is never moved from this centre… *they possess him continually in their souls.*[297]

Admittedly, it is only after the Holy Spirit equips the baptized with justifying and sanctifying graces that an additional "gift" or "special grace" is required in order that Christ may act *divinely* in the soul in an *habitual* and *continuous* manner. If the soul remains faithful to God's inspirations and graces, it progresses from the *human mode* to the *divine mode* to the *continuously divine mode* of holiness.

The New and Eternal Mode of the Holiness

Up to this point, no mystic has recounted an experience of being so totally absorbed in God as to exert an *"eternal,"* *"continuous"* and *"commensurate"* influence on *"every act"* of every creature. To suppose such an experience would suggest that God should elevate the creature beyond the *continuously divine mode* into his own *eternal mode (modo aeterno)* of operation. But have any mystics in recent times recounted such an experience? The answer is found in the approved writings of the aforementioned late 19th and 20th century mystics, who describe in full detail God's *"continuously eternal activity"* in the soul of the human creature. Indeed there were many saints before the 20th century that "experienced" some of the effects of this eternal mode, but, according to their approved works, not in its continuous state.

We find in the writings of the great mystical Doctor St. John of the Cross that the soul's participation in God's eternal activity, as enjoyed by the blessed in heaven, is *not continuous* in its lofty state of Spiritual Marriage:

> Even though a soul attains to as lofty a state of perfection in this mortal life as that which we are discussing, it neither can nor does reach the perfect state of glory, although *in a passing way* God might grant it some similar favor... *These experiences are rare.*[298]

In another work entitled the *Spiritual Canticle*, John further describes the soul in the state of Spiritual Marriage as not possessing as open and manifest a degree of union as that experienced by the blessed in heaven:

> Since the soul in this state of spiritual marriage knows something of the "what," she desires to say something about it… In the transformation that the soul possesses in this life, the same spiration passes from God to the soul and from the soul to God with notable frequency and blissful love, *although not in the open and manifest degree proper to the next life.*[299]

St. Teresa of Avila confirms John's experience:

> In heaven… all love him there and the soul's concern is to love him, nor can it cease to love him because it knows him. And this is how we should love him on earth, though *we cannot do so with the same perfection and continuity*; still, if we knew him, we should love him very differently than the way we do now.[300]

The Servant of God Luisa Piccarreta, on the other hand, sounds the distinctive note of the new mystical indwelling that God has recently imparted to the Church. It is a *continuous* and *eternal* participation in what St. John calls "the perfect state of the glory" that is "proper to the next life." Jesus tells Luisa:

> *The souls that have given themselves completely to Me and that I love, I don't want them to wait to go in the beatific state when they go to Heaven, I want it to begin on earth. I want to fill those souls*

not only with a Heavenly happiness, but also with the goodness, sufferings, and virtue that my Humanity had on earth. I therefore divest them not only of material desires, but also of the spiritual ones to refill them with all my goodness, and give them the beginning of true Beatitude.[301]

The soul who is still wandering unifies herself with my Will in such a way as to *never separate herself from It.* Her life is of Heaven, and I receive from her the same glory that I receive from the Blessed. Further, *I take more pleasure and satisfaction in her.* This is because what the Blessed do in Heaven they do without sacrifice, and with delight.[302]

Luisa relates:

I found myself in Jesus. My little atom swam in the Eternal Will. Moreover, *since this Eternal Will is a single Act that contains together all the acts- past, present, and future, I, being in the Eternal Will, took part in that single Act which contains all acts, inasmuch as it is possible for a creature. I even took part in the acts which do not yet exist, and which must exist, unto the end of centuries, and as long as God will be God...* (And Jesus said): "Have you seen what living in my Will is? It is to disappear. It is to enter into the ambience of Eternity. *It is to penetrate into the Omnipotence of the Eternal, into the Uncreated Mind, and to take part in everything and in each Divine Act inasmuch as it is possible for a creature. It is to enjoy, while remaining on earth, all the Divine qualities… It is the Sanctity not yet known, and which I will make known, which will set in place the last ornament, the most beautiful and most brilliant among all the other sanctities, and will be the crown and completion of all the other sanctities.*"[303]

I Myself knew how many graces were necessary, having to work the greatest miracle that exists in the world, which is that of *living continuously in My Will*: the soul must assimilate everything of God in its act, so as to give it back again intact, just as the soul assimilated it, and then to assimilate it again.[304]

The approved writings of Blessed Dina also affirm the continuously eternal character of the "eternal mode" of mystical union that God has imparted to his Church in recent years:

This morning, I received *a special grace* that I find difficult to describe. I felt taken up into God, as if in *the "eternal mode,"* that is in *a permanent, unchanging state…* *I feel I am continually in the presence of the adorable Trinity.* My soul, annihilated in the Heart of the Indivisible unity, contemplates it with greater suavity, in a purer light, and I am more aware of the power that pervades me… *Beginning with the grace of last January 25, my soul can dwell in heaven, live there without any backward glance toward earth, and yet continue to animate my material being.*[305]

My offering is far more active than in the
preceding dwellings where the love of my
sovereign Substitute led me... In this *new divine
indwelling*, what strikes me... is the power, the
greatness, the immensity of God's attributes.[306]

To illustrate that God's eternal mode of activity in the soul
of the human creature is the same interior state enjoyed by the
blessed in heaven–and which St. John of the Cross "experienced
in passing" only—Jesus tells Blessed Dina:

You will not possess me any more completely in
heaven... because I have absorbed you totally.[307]

In dialogue with Jesus, Saint Faustina Kowalska affirms:

The veils of mystery hinder me not at all; *I love
You as do Your chosen ones in heaven.*[308]

My whole being is plunged in You, and *I live Your
divine life as do the elect in heaven,* and the reality of
this life will not cease, though I be laid in the grave.[309]

That this new, continuously eternal activity brings
with it a deeper participation in the activity of
the three divine Persons of the Blessed Trinity,
is evident in Jesus' words to the Servant of God
Luisa and to Venerable Conchita de Armida:
All three Divine Persons descended from Heaven;
and then, after a few days, we took possession of
your heart and took our *perpetual residence* there.

We took the reins of your intelligence, your heart, all of you. Everything you did was an outlet of our creative Will in you. It was a confirmation that *your will was animated by an Eternal Will.*[310] Living in my Will is the apex of sanctity, and it bestows continuous growth in Grace.[311]

Do not think that in the mystical incarnation of the Word it is I who act, but the Trinity of the Divine Persons do so, each one of them operating according to His attributes, the Father, as Father, engendering: the Word as Son, being born; the Holy Spirit making fertile this divine action in the soul.[312]

That the *eternal mode* surpasses the *divine mode* of Spiritual Marriage is verified in the words of our Blessed Lord to Conchita. When Conchita asked our Lord if the new state she was experiencing was that of Spiritual Marriage as described by Ss. Teresa of Avila and John of the Cross, Jesus reassured her of its supremacy:

I dare say to him [Jesus]: 'Lord, what you had promised me, what you had asked of me, was it (spiritual) marriage... would it be my Jesus, spiritual marriage? "Much more than that... the grace of incarnating Me, of Me living and growing in your soul, never to leave it, of possessing you and of being possessed by you as in one and the same substance... is the grace of graces."[313]

The eminent theologian Hans Urs Von Balthasar further illustrates the new activity of God in the soul of Blessed Elizabeth of the Trinity, that is unique and unlike the common life of sanctity in the Church:

> Her whole mission is governed by the Third Person, by the spirituality proper to him, distinct from the Father and the Son, *rather than by his action through the "seven gifts" which is common to all life of sanctity within the Church.*[314]

The participation of Luisa Piccarreta and other recent mystics in the new gift of God's *eternal mode* intimates man's full admission to God's likeness and the recovery of the gifts that he lost in Eden.[315] Inasmuch as Eden was never infected with sin, as was man, one may envision the new outpouring of God's mystical gift as a symbol of its restitution. Speculatively, as the death of Christ opened the doors of heaven, so the new outpouring of God's mystical gift opens the doors of Eden and admits man to the gifts he once possessed, though in an imperfect environment.

From a less speculative angle, the new gift of God's *eternal mode* hardly demeans the virtues or holiness of the great saints of the past, whose cooperation with the will of God enabled them to attain perfection on earth. That Christian virtue is essential for the attainment of the gift of living in God's divine and eternal will is beautifully portrayed by Luisa Piccarreta's spiritual director St. Hannibal di Francia:[316]

> In order to form, with this new science, saints who may surpass those of the past, the new Saints

> *must* also have all the virtues, and in heroic
> degree, of ancient Saints – of the Confessors, of
> the Penitents, of the Martyrs, of the Anachorists,
> of the Virgins, etc.[317]

Since the gifts God freely bestows are not the direct result of man's virtues or holiness, but that of God's pure favor—which he grants when he wills and to whom he wills—his gifts are not the result of human achievement. Therefore, it is futile to make comparisons between the holiness of the Servant of God Luisa Piccarreta and Saint Teresa of Avila, or Saints Padre Pio and John of the Cross. It is safe to assert that one form of holiness is "greater" than another, when its greatness is determined by the intrinsic nature of the "gift" and not by the response of the recipient. Conversely, the recipient's personal holiness is not so much gauged by the loftiness of the gifts received, as by his or her faithful correspondence – which correspondence God *alone* beholds – to whatever graces God may wish to grant.

Though internally, the *eternal mode* may be identifiable with the same interior state as the *"beatific mode"* enjoyed by the saints in heaven, it does not confer upon the soul the qualities of the beatific vision, absolute impeccability and the inability to obtain merit; these qualities are experienced only in heaven.[318]

Analogical Stages of Spiritual Growth

As an illustration of the contrast between God's *divine mode* and God's *eternal mode*, consider the symbol of the early Christian community, a fish and its environment. Let the *divine mode* represent the three mystical levels of Baptism, Spiritual

Betrothal and Spiritual Marriage, analogously depicted in a fresh-water fish. And let God's *eternal mode* represent the ulterior stage of mystical union referred to as "Living in the Divine Will," analogously depicted in a salt-water fish. Let us now place these fish in their respective environments: in an aquarium (representing Baptism), in a pond (Spiritual Betrothal), in an ocean-fed lake (Spiritual Marriage), and finally in the ocean itself (Living in the Divine Will).

While the wellsprings of *Baptism* confer on the soul all that is necessary for a life of genuine piety and salvation, it is but "the beginning" of the Christian's spiritual journey to greater stages of mystical union with God. Likewise the waters that fill an *aquarium* contain that which is necessary for the life of the fresh-water fish. Hence, the *human mode* of the infant soul's thinking, acting and praying in the early stages of its spiritual journey.

In *a pond*, the fish can move with greater speed and mobility and achieve greater depths. The pond represents the soul that has advanced to the *divine mode* of mystical union through the gift of *Spiritual Betrothal*. Yet, since the pond is short and shallow, the fish is incapable of achieving its maximum speed.

In an ocean-fed *lake*, the fresh-water fish can reach greater depths, travel farther distances and attain speeds that rival its potential, though *rarely* experiencing the ocean's salt waters. In the case of the fresh-water salmon, they are by nature, salt-water fish that spawn in fresh water, and most of these are landlocked and adapted to fresh-waters only. Should these fresh-water salmon enter the ocean's salt waters and remain there for any considerable length, they would eventually die;

they do not have the talent–or better, the gift–to "live" in the ocean waters. Hence, the fresh-water salmon in an ocean-fed lake represents the soul that has advanced from *Spiritual Betrothal* and from the alternating human and divine modes of thinking, praying and acting to the *continuously divine mode* of *Spiritual Marriage*. Although the soul is here fed by the ocean of God's interminable love, only rarely does it experience his *eternal mode* of being and operation.

The *salt-water salmon,* on the other hand, can "live" in both fresh and salt-waters. Since the ocean is made up of vast expanses, containing all the necessary salts and minerals, it provides the ideal environment where it might thrive and travel, uninhibited by *space,* to the greatest length, depth and speed. The more the salmon remains in and adapts itself to the new realities of the ocean's unlimited food supplies, the more it converts them into energy. Accordingly, one may say that the ocean is continuously engaged in the life of the salmon and vice-versa. This is further illustrated in the salmon's life cycle. After the salt-water salmon spawns in streams or lakes and dies, its remains fertilize and enrich the environment of *all* fresh-water fish. All the nutrients, minerals and salts that the salmon acquired, now serve to enrich the lives of all fresh-water fish. In a word, the salt-water salmon vicariously influences the lives of all fresh-water fish, much as those that live in the *eternal mode* can commensurately influence the lives of all creatures of the past, present and future. Hence, the soul that receives the gift of advancing from the *divine modes* of Baptism, to Spiritual Betrothal, to Spiritual Marriage, and finally to the *eternal mode* of Living in God's Divine Will, experiences the most profound level of mystical union. As for the difference between the stages of Spiritual Marriage and Living in the Divine Will, the difference is literally eternal.

Theologically, in the soul that has entered the eternal mode of mystical union, knowledge and love are in greater and greater degree increased, and in purer and purer form, such that the more fully they are experienced, the less is it possible to give them expression in thoughts and words. For this reason, the Servant of God Luisa Piccarreta and Saint Faustina Kowalska describe the gift of God's *eternal mode* as indescribable. Jesus tells Luisa:

> I see your will working in mine with the same Creative Power which wishes to give Me everything and compensate for everyone... This is how I wanted the first man... *You cannot comprehend it.* The order of Creation is restored to Me, and its harmonies and joys occur without interruption. I see your human will working in Me in the light of the sun, in the waves of the sea, in the sparkle of the stars, in everything.[319]

St. Faustina affirms:

> I am at a loss to describe this, because in writing I am making use of the sense; but there, in that union, the senses are not active; there is a merging of God and the soul; and the life of God to which the soul is admitted is so great that the human tongue cannot express it... Souls united to God in this way are few, fewer than we think.[320]

The Effects of God's Pre-Existent Gifts

A timely analogy of the effects of God's eternal mode emerges from the effects of the sacraments in the lives of the Old Testament saints. While they were deprived of the gift of Baptism without which no one can be saved, salvation was nonetheless held out to them. They were justified, sanctified and saved by God's grace *even before* Christ instituted the justifying and sanctifying graces through the *sacrament* of Baptism, by virtue of an upright life known to them through the dictate of their conscience.[321]

In the words of the author of the Letter to the Hebrews, "By a single offering he [Jesus] has perfected *for all time* those who are sanctified."[322] The New Testament, in fact, throws light on the Person of Christ as the pre-existent head of the entire human race. In his book entitled *God in Creation and Evolution*, the Scripture scholar A. Hulsbosch, O.S.A. reveals that the expressions *"the first born of all creation"*[323] and *"the beginning of God's creation,"*[324] are synonymous titles for Jesus the Son of God. The Son, who belongs to creation, of which he is the first born, also transcends all of creation. Thus the title "first born" expresses Jesus' eternal presence before all worlds came to be in time and space.[325] As the *effects* of the future merits of Christ's Incarnation, Passion, death and Resurrection were applied to the personages of the Old Testament for their salvation, so the *effects* of the new stage of God's *eternal mode* of activity were analogously applied to the saints of the past. Jesus' words to Venerable Conchita de Armida illustrate this point:

> Many of My saints experienced the Mystical Incarnation without knowing it, inasmuch as they experienced in themselves the effects of this grace.[326]

Of the modern saints that experienced the effects of God's eternal activity, worthy of mention are Ven. Anne Catherine Emmerich,[327] St. Joseph Marello,[328] St. Thérèse de Lisieux[329] and a score of other exemplars in whose writings these effects are markedly present. By personal experience these saintly souls obtained a *general* intuitive knowledge of God's eternal operations, with respect to the *particular* knowledge that is found in the writings of the late 19th and 20th century mystics and that defines the Church's holiness during the era of peace.

Chapter 4

MAN'S FULL PARTICIPATION IN GOD'S DIVINE WILL

Man's Admission to God's Eternal Mode

1. Immediate Entry

That anyone in the state of grace[330] can *immediately* experience God's eternal mode of activity is abundantly clear in the writings of contemporary Church mystics.

Jesus tells Luisa:

> My daughter, only the word "Will of God" contains the Creative Power; therefore, it has the power of creating, transforming, and consuming so as to make new torrents of light, of love, and of sanctity flow in the soul.[331]

> While I was thinking about the Holy Divine Will, my sweet Jesus said to me: "My daughter, to enter into My Will... *the creature does nothing other than remove the pebble of her will...* This is because the

pebble of her will impedes My Will from flowing in her... But if the soul removes the pebble of her will, in that same instant she flows in Me, and I in her. She discovers all of My goods at her disposition: light, strength, help and all that she desires... It is enough that she desires it, and everything is done!"[332]

When I came to earth I reunited the Divine Will with the human will. If a soul does not reject this bond, but rather *surrenders itself* to the mercy of my Divine Will and allows my Divine Will to precede it, accompany it, and follow it; if it allows its acts to be encompassed by my Will, then what happened to Me happens to that soul.[333]

Jesus tells Venerable Conchita:

To speak of the Mystical Incarnation is then to consider the soul as entering into a phase of graces of transformation which will bring it, if it *corresponds, to the identification of its will with Mine*... in order that its union with God come to the most perfect likeness possible. Such is the gift of the Mystical Incarnation which the Holy Spirit gives as a gift to certain souls.[334]

In this loving act of supreme *abandonment to the will* of my Father there is perfection, the highest and complete sanctity.[335]

Blessed Dina remarks:

> Quite simply, God in his goodness has to bestow
> this free gift on us. And how can we obtain it? *By*
> *the least act of submission of our will to the will of our*
> *Father in heaven.*[336]

Based on the approved writings of the mystics, to *enter* God's
eternal activity the soul must acknowledge God's presence, invite
his activity and desire to remain faithful to his will in all things. To
continuously remain in this activity—or to "live" in it—is quite
another matter. Most mystics had undergone several years of
testing before they finally "lived" in the eternal state, without ever
leaving. The reason for this is due simply to man's impaired vision
of the good, which is a consequence of original sin. Man's wounded
nature develops within time and space through a progressive
cultivation of the awareness of God's continuous presence through
his exercise of the virtues and reception of the gifts. Although it
may appear unlikely, it is not impossible that a soul should enter
into this eternal state for the first time never to leave. The lives of
Ss. Paul and Mary Magdalene testify to the human ability to make
an immediate and lifelong commitment to God.

2. Daily Challenges

Admittedly, God's most precious gifts never remove the daily
challenges, sufferings and contradictions the soul must sometimes
endure. Immediate access to God's eternal mode of activity does
not cause the crosses in life to disappear. On the contrary, the
crosses become the very means to strengthen man's resolve to live
God's gift, whereby he may apply himself with greater attentiveness

to daily duties and accept whatever crosses God may wish to send him. This truth appears vividly in the Diary of St. Faustina:

> The soul recognizes that God is counting on it, and this knowledge fortifies it. It knows that to be faithful it will have to face various difficulties, but it trusts in God and, thanks to this trust, it reaches that point to which God is calling it. Difficulties do not terrify it; they are its daily bread, as it were. They do not frighten or terrify the soul, just as a warrior who is constantly in battle is not terrified by the roar of the cannon. Far from being frightened, it listens to determine from which side the enemy is launching his attack, in order to defeat him.[337]

Should the soul be so fortunate as to become divinized and live continuously in God's eternal mode, it will find itself at the center of life's challenges, where it maintains the *remote* possibility of losing God's favor. Blessed Dina affirms:

> My eternity has begun... I live in the Heart of God... Is this not the life of the elect in paradise? Undoubtedly, in heaven, the battles are over and we are confirmed in grace. I am still battling, prey to the attacks of the enemy, and I have ample proof of this: I am free; at any moment, I could be unfaithful to grace... but...I let Jesus have his way and concern myself only with him... it is the trust of God himself.[338]

3. Manifold Degrees

It is through life's unexpected challenges that the soul is tested in virtue and, by means of its contrary, disposed for greater holiness. Yet not all souls possess the same degree of virtue or union with their divine Spouse. Jesus reassured Luisa Piccarreta and other mystics that his creatures in varying degrees experience the gift of his continuously eternal activity. After presenting her with a vision of the sea with various objects, Jesus assures Luisa the following:

> The sea symbolizes My Immensity, whereas the objects that varied in greatness, the souls who live in My Will. There are various ways of remaining: some remain on the surface, others penetrate within, while yet others are completely immersed in Me. These are distinguished according to the ways in which they live in My Will: some imperfectly, others more perfectly, and yet others to such profound depths as to lose themselves completely in My Will.[339]

Jesus relates to Venerable Conchita:

> The soul of the priest who embraces and cultivates with his correspondence to grace this gift of God, *is the most disposed to receive and to enlarge* this priceless grace of the mystical incarnation in the soul... This is the final point of the most elevated union.[340]

Once transformation into Jesus is brought

about, the Holy Spirit also becomes the spirit of the creature *raised to a more or less higher degree* according to the intensity and amplitude of transformation, which strictly depends on the growth of the soul in virtue.[341]

Jesus reveals to Vera Grita:

In the beginning, to the soul the journey will consist in being attentive, vigilant in order to rid itself of all obstacles to My permanent indwelling within it. My graces in the souls that are called to this work *are gradual.*[342]

Characteristics of God's Eternal Mode in Man

1. *God's Transtemporal Activity*

Since the eternal works of the Trinity are works that precede and exceed man's abilities, they are works of the Creator, not of man. But by an extraordinary grace, God enables man to participate in his eternal activity. Here the creature is caught up in the Creator's *eternal mode* of operation, which enables the soul to perform acts, motivated and sustained by the Godhead, that exceed all boundaries of time and space. One of the effects of this eternal mode is the ability to go beyond the present and into the past and future, otherwise known as God's *"transtemporal activity."*

There have been several saints of preceding centuries that have experienced God's transtemporal activity. They knowingly influenced the lives of all creatures throughout *time* in a general manner (i.e., Ss. Catherine of Siena; John of the Cross and Ven. Anne Catherine Emmerich) and mystically traversed *space* (Ss. Anthony and Alphonsus were known to bilocate). Saints John of the Cross, Catherine of Siena and Venerable Anne Emmerich are but a few examples of exemplars that intended that their present acts assist in the actualization of the potencies of man in a manner that spanned all of time and creation.

St. Catherine of Siena often prayed and sacrificed herself for "*every* rational creature" and for the salvation "of the *whole* world";[343] Venerable Anne Emmerich was told by our Lord that "her gift of seeing the past, present and future in mystic vision was greater than that possessed by anyone else in history";[344] and St. John of the Cross states that the soul in the high state of transforming union, is given a supernatural sight in which it beholds, "in only one view" the "harmony of every creature" in God's divine life "with such newness."[345]

Moreover, Jesus' aforementioned revelations to Venerable Conchita attest that many saints '*experienced the effects*' of the new mystical reality God had given her, and that he is experientially offering to all the members of his household. While many saints of the past experienced the *effects* of the eternal indwelling in the state of mystical marriage, they did not possess a full experiential or cognitive awareness of God's eternal activity within their souls. Hence, although St. Catherine of Siena's prayers and sacrifices were directed to "every rational creature" and for the salvation "of the whole world," there is no evidence in her writings to suggest that she exerted an "*eternal*," "*continuous*" *and* "*commensurate*" influence on "*every act*" of every creature. These quoted expressions emerge from the approved literature of the late 19ᵗʰ and 20ᵗʰ century mystics in their descriptions of intercessory prayer.

Jesus to Luisa:

> It is only My Will, which is *Eternal* and Immense, that finds everything. *It reduces the past, present and future to a single point,* and in this single point It finds all hearts palpitating, all minds alive and all of My works in act. Moreover, the soul, making this Will of Mine its own, does all, satisfies for all, loves for all, and does good to all and to each one *as if all were one.*[346]

> If a soul does not reject this bond, but rather surrenders itself to the mercy of My Divine Will and *allows My Divine Will to precede it, accompany it, and follow it;* if it allows its acts to be encompassed by My Will, *then what happened to Me happens to that soul.*[347]

Luisa relates:

> I sought to give to my God all the honor, the glory, the submission, etc., of all created minds. I did likewise with all my other senses, *calling into them all the senses of all other creatures.* I did this in his lovable Will where everything is found and nothing escapes, *even those things that presently do not exist.*[348]

> While I was doing this, a voice came forth from the immensity of the light, saying, "As often as

a soul enters into the Divine Will to pray, work, love, or to do anything else, it opens many paths between the Creator and the creature. The Divinity, seeing that the creature is coming to It, opens up paths in order to meet Its creature. In this encounter, the creature imitates the virtues of its Creator, absorbs into itself Divine Life, and *enters more fully into the eternal secrets of the Supreme Will...* That is how, in my Will, the creature approaches likeness to Me, how it realizes my designs, and how it fulfills the purpose of Creation."[349]

My daughter, newborn of My Eternal Will, take a look at where your Jesus calls you and wants you: under the wine press of My Divine Will, so that your will receives a *continuous* death, as did My human will. Otherwise you would not be able to inaugurate *the new Era* and make My Will reign on earth. *What is needed in order for My Will to come and reign on earth is the continuous act,* the pains, the deaths in order to be able to draw down from Heaven the *Fiat Voluntas Tua.*[350]

Though exerting an eternal influence over all creatures, the mystic's transtemporal activity neither alters the history and objective acts of the past, nor the creature's particular judgment. Rather, in God's eternal act time assumes the lineaments of the ongoing present, in which the creature makes reparation to God for all bad actions and glorifies him for all good actions of every creature.

Jesus tells Venerable Conchita:

> All in Me is present, that is to say, it is existing,
> not only was or will be, but it is, always is.[351]

> Know that in God there is no succession of acts. He
> operates eternally in one act of his Will which covers
> all times and eternity, and all creations, all things in
> only one instant, the eternal instant of the Unity in
> which is reflected and exists always past, present and
> future... You must live in this essential Unity.[352]

Jesus tells Sr. Mary of the Holy Trinity:[353]

> Do you understand that if your actions fall into My
> Heart to rejoice it and to bury themselves there,
> I can use them through time and space according to
> the desires of My Heart?[354]

Jesus reveals to Blessed Dina that in the measure that the
soul is faithful to his gifts, the more intimately it can penetrate
and sanctify all other souls:

> In consecrated souls in whom my hands are bound
> by threads, in whom my heart is consequently
> wounded, my rays reach only some souls living in
> the world at the same time. In consecrated souls
> who refuse me only small things, you can see that
> my rays reach many other souls in the world and
> extend further. In consecrated souls that have
> abandoned themselves to me, in whom I can act

freely, see how my rays reach all souls, *even to the end of time.*[355]

It is worthy of mention that the activity of those souls in whom Jesus freely acts to "reach all souls even to the end of time," increases *qualitatively*. For no sooner does the soul enter Jesus' *continuous* and *eternal* activity to influence *every act* of every creature *commensurately*, than it begins a journey of ongoing and exponential penetration into those same acts.

2. God's Eternal Act

The writings of recent mystics also affirm that today God's children can more perfectly approach the original state of holiness for which they were created than in times past. Their internal participation in God's Eternal Act embraces and exceeds the acts of all creatures, makes reparation to God and increases his accidental glory.

Having enabled the soul of the human creature to experience the transtemporal activity, whereby it influences all creatures of all time, God elevates the creature to his one Eternal Act that exceeds all time and space. If in the transtemporal activity the creature is able to mystically trilocate into the past, present and future, in God's one Eternal Act that has neither beginning nor end, it can penetrate eternity, embrace heaven and earth and participate in the eternal life of God himself for as long as God is God. This mystical experience is a participation in the eternal life of God that only eternity can fully fathom.

Jesus reveals to Luisa:

You cannot fully comprehend the entire value of operating in My Divine Will. Operating in My *Fiat* is life that the soul takes within itself, it is divine life. This life in its fullness is the font of all goods, and for every act the soul does in My Will, I enclose within it a life that *has neither beginning nor end*. I enclose within the soul an act that generates all things and whose operation never ceases. And what is it this act generates? It generates continuous sanctity, happiness, beauty and love, while all the divine qualities remain in the continuous act of generating and growing. And if one were able to gather together all the good acts of all the creatures of all centuries, these would never be capable of equaling one act that is done by the soul in My Will, for in the soul that possesses this act done in My Will life reigns, whereas all other acts done outside of My Will are bereft of interior life and operate without life.[356]

My daughter, how does one accomplish an act that is done in My Will? You must know that in order to form this act what is required is the power of My Will, as the creature of itself cannot accomplish this act... The power of My *Fiat* empties the creature of all that which does not belong to It and fills the creature to repletion with the Divine Being, so much so that the creature feels within itself the fullness of the life of its Creator... It feels within itself the fullness and totality of the Supreme Entity insofar as it is possible for the creature.[357]

Whoever enters Our Will truly experiences our Creative Act that is always in act, as well as Our love that is always anew and in the act of giving itself to the creature... And since Our ways are always equal and never change, that which We do through Our always new and never ceasing Act with the Blessed in heaven to increase their beatitude, We likewise do for those that live in Our Divine Will on earth to increase their life with new sanctity, new beauty, new bounty and new love... with this difference: The Blessed acquire nothing new, as they inundate themselves solely in the new joys of their Creator, whereas the fortunate wayfarer (on earth) that lives in Our Will is always in the act of making new conquests.[358]

Let us recall that when Adam failed to properly exercise his office of steward of creation, God did not abandon him, but chose that another should come, namely, his eternal Son, to begin the work of Redemption. The eternal Son exercised his priestly office in redeeming man and the cosmos: to glorify his Father by making *reparation* for sin, by *restoring* God's likeness in man, and by *reestablishing* universal peace. If, on the one hand, Christ's Redemption is complete and definitive, on the other hand, it may be viewed as an ongoing process that actualizes the fruits of Redemption in all men. And it is in this sense that Rev. Walter Ciszek makes the following assertion:

> Christ's redemptive act did not of itself restore all things, it simply made the work of redemption possible, it began our redemption. Just as all men share in the disobedience of Adam, so all men must share in the obedience of Christ to the Father's will. *Redemption will be complete only when all men share his obedience.*[359]

St. Paul further illustrates this idea when he acknowledges his co-redemptive afflictions in the actualization of God's universal plan of restoration:

> Now I rejoice in my sufferings for your sake, and in my flesh I am filling up *what is lacking* in the afflictions of Christ on behalf of his body, which is the church.[360]

When mankind reflects God's original plan in creation, by sharing *"in the obedience of Christ to the Father's will,"* it fully exercises the office of steward of creation. Not only does God invite his chosen and gifted mystics to become sharers in his one Eternal Act, he invites all of his children. He extends this invitation to them to draw them into his one, eternal act, into his eternal mode of operation, whereby they make *reparation* for sin, *restore* God's accidental glory and *reestablish* the rights of all creation lessened by sin. Once the soul has arrived at this simple yet most sublime point of mystical union, everything it does, from the most conscious to the most unconscious acts, is sustained and motivated by God's eternal act that never leaves it so long as it refrains from deliberately offending him.

Jesus tells St. Faustina:

> Involuntary offenses of souls do not hinder My love for them or prevent Me from uniting Myself with them. But voluntary offenses, even the smallest, obstruct My graces, and I cannot lavish My gifts on such souls.[361]

3. God's Omnipresence

Once God inspires his beloved children to glorify him by interceding on behalf of all rational creatures, he then incites them to praise him in the extension of his being through nature. Nature is God's subtle and playful expression of his omnipresence; it offers man a concrete immersion in the God he cannot see; and it is the pathway to God through the body and its senses, where the finite absorbs the reflections of the Infinite. Here the soul is introduced to a new vision of God. It sees God's image in the earth, in the skies, in the seas, in the meadows, in the plains, in the valleys. In all things it beholds the mark of its Creator and a sacred extension of his divine being. Once the soul has arrived at this vision it, in turn, glorifies and praises God in every created being, rational *and* irrational. Jesus tells the Servant of God Luisa:

> I desire, therefore, that My children enter My Humanity and copy what the Soul of My Humanity did in the Divine Will... Rising above every creature, *they will restore the rights of Creation—My*

own as well as those of creatures. *They will bring all things to the prime origin of Creation and to the purpose for which Creation came to be.*[362]

Luisa illustrates her experience:

While fusing myself in the Supreme Will, an immense void becomes present in my mind and the little girl[363] continues her rounds. Elevating herself on high, she desires to compensate her God for all the love He has for all creatures through the work of Creation. She desires to honor Him as Creator of all things, and thus she goes around the stars and in each twinkling of light imprints an "I love You" and "Glory to my Creator." In each atom of the sun's light that descends she imprints an "I love You" and "Glory" throughout the expanses of the Heavens; in the distance of one step to another an "I love You" and "Glory"; in the warbling of the birds, in the movement of their wings, a "Love" and "Glory to my Creator"; in the blades of grass that sprout from the earth, in the flowers that bloom and in the perfumes that rise, a "Love" and "Glory." On the heights of the mountains and in the depths of the valleys, a "Love" and "Glory." She then goes in search of each heart of every creature, as if she wanted to enclose within each one an "I love You" and "Glory to my Creator." *She desires that there be one single Will, one harmony in all things and one single exclamation: "Glory and Love to my Creator."* And

– 158 –

after *having united everything,* such that everything gives God an exchange of love and declaration of glory for all that he has done in Creation, she transports herself before his Throne.[364]

St. Faustina's prayer to God encompasses the whole of creation, intercedes on its behalf, and restores it to its original splendor:

> O my Creator and Lord, I see on all sides the trace of Your hand and the seal of Your mercy, which embraces all created things. O my most compassionate Creator, *I want to give You worship on behalf of all created things and all inanimate creation; I call on the whole universe to glorify Your mercy.* Oh, how great is Your goodness, O God![365]

The opening chapter described how creation is transformed and set free from its slavery to corruption. We now see it unfolding specifically through God's activity in the will of the human creature, who by praying and acting in it, reunites and restores the rightful claims of creation.[366] As man makes his "rounds" in creation by mystically penetrating, transforming and sublimating all creatures in God, there awakens in him a deep respect and awe for the world around him. He acquires a new set of eyes, as it were, with which he beholds all created things as a sacred extension of God's divine being and beauty.

Because man in his desire to better the earth has taken from it without replenishing it, and has managed to disfigure it to the point of extinction, God reawakens within him the first impulse of love for the earth from which he came. Man was created for God through his relation to the earth, to its creatures and the cosmos. Thus the more he learns to respect the world around him, the more its resources and potencies are available to him in his service to God and to all creatures. Once man grasps this fundamental truth, God opens his eyes to a reality that stood before him in the days of Adam, where he beholds the Creator's handiwork in every creature, where he cultivates and shepherds the earth as God intended, and where he gives back to the earth for that which he received. Indeed it is in gaining respect for the earth that man gains respect for all life around him. For God fashioned nature in such a way that it takes very good care of man, it provides for him both physically and spiritually, and by its example, trains him to care for all other creatures.

And so as the soul progresses in its love for God through the world around it, its vision of God extends not only to all created things, but to all *events* and all *circumstances* of life as well. St. Paul affirms, "all things work for good for those who love God, who are called according to his purpose,"[367] and the Servant of God Luisa Piccarreta, Blessed Dina and St. Padre Pio add, "even sin." Here God reveals to the soul his omnipotence to precede, accompany and follow all of its past, present and future acts.[368] He precedes its good acts by performing them before the soul was yet conceived, in order that the soul might repeat his actions with him in time and space through the use of its free will: He accompanies its actions that they might perfectly conform in intention and objectivity to the Divine Will, and he follows every act by applying its beneficent effects to all other creatures.

The fact that God can draw good even from man's evil acts, without condoning the evil, is made evident in the writings of Luisa. Jesus reveals that original sin was permitted to bring about a *greater* good:

> Although when I created men I made them as pure and noble heavens, in the Redemption I adorned them with the brilliant stars of My wounds to cover their ugliness and make them more beautiful... *I clothed them with such magnificence that their appearance surpassed in beauty that of their original state. This is why the Church says: "Happy fault."* With the fault came the Redemption, whereby My Humanity not only nourished you with its Blood, not only clothed you with its very (divine) Person and adorned you with its beauty, but always nourishes My children from its inexhaustible bosom.[369]

> My daughter, do not fear, you have more help than Adam had. You have the help of a humanized God and all his works and pains for your defense, for your sustenance, for your cortege, which he did not have. Why then do you fear?[370]

Jesus tells Blessed Dina:

> *The glory that my Father has received since the Redemption is, in spite of human sinfulness, far greater than if humans had never sinned, because the reparation that I offer my Father is infinite,*

and it makes up infinitely for all the sins of the human race. Each time a soul unites itself to Me to glorify my Father, it gives him infinite glory through Me.[371]

Jesus reveals to his chosen mystic Sr. Mary of the Holy Trinity:

The soul that regrets her sin and makes reparation for it gives Me a greater proof of love than a soul that has avoided sin.[372]

The prophet Ezekiel and the Magisterium reinforce this teaching:

I will be... more generous to you than in the beginning; thus you shall know that I am the Lord.[373]

Father, in restoring human nature you have given us a greater dignity than we had in the beginning.[374]

St. Padre Pio also assures us that God can obtain good even from evil:

And in truth, given that the Lord can obtain good even from evil, for whom will he do this, if not for those who have given themselves to him without reservation? Consider the work of this great mercy: It converts our sins into good... Tell me, therefore, what will he not do with our afflictions, whatever they are, be certain that, if you love God with all your heart, everything will be converted to good. Even if at that moment you cannot understand where this good should come from, be more than ever sure that it will come, without a doubt.[375]

In a word, the soul that sees God in all things has been trained to glorify him vicariously in every person, in every work of nature and in every event. For it is God that governs all things, guides all things and determines all things for the *greatest good* of those who love him. And for many of us this is an encouraging thought indeed.

4. *Knowledge of God's Eternal Mode*

Admittedly, most of the aforementioned *mystics* received private revelations that helped them to recognize, esteem, and embrace God's new activity in the soul. However, many modern *exemplars* who received no private revelations at all experienced this reality as well (here one calls to mind the Servant of God Archbishop Luis Martinez, Blessed Elizabeth of the Trinity, St. Maximilian Kolbe, the Servant of God Rev. Michael Sopo ko, etc.). One may then ask how it was possible for the exemplars to experience the mystical gift of God's continuous and eternal activity of which they had no knowledge? To this question, I submit the only plausible response: They obtained it through the Holy Spirit who prays in the soul to stir and form in it the desire and general knowledge to receive the gift he wishes to grant it.[376]

St. Augustine writes:

There is then within us *a kind of instructed ignorance*, instructed, that is, by the Spirit of God

– 163 –

who helps our weakness… the Apostle said:…
*"the Spirit helps us in our weakness; we do not know
what it is right to pray for, but the Spirit himself pleads
with groans too deep for words. He who searches
hearts knows what the Spirit means, for he pleads for
the saints according to God's will."*

He pleads for the saints because he moves the
saints to plead, just as it says: "The Lord your
God tests you, to know if you love him, in this
sense, that *he does it to enable you to know."* So
*the Spirit moves the saints to plead with groans too
deep for words by inspiring in them a desire* for the
great and as yet *unknown* reality that we look
forward to with patience. How can words express
what we desire when it remains unknown? If we
were entirely ignorant[377] of it we would not desire
it; again, we would not desire it or seek it with
groans, if we were able to see it.[378]

It is not simply man's knowledge of a given private revelation that
contains the power to *actualize* God's new gift in the human creature
or during the era of peace, but the inseparable power of the Father,
Son, and Holy Spirit. Though all divine Persons participate in the
actualization of the Church's gifts, to the Holy Spirit is particularly
attributed the works of "imparting gifts,"[379] "sanctifying,"[380]
"renewing,"[381] and "igniting the Church to cooperate toward the full
realization of God's design".[382] Hence, Jesus' words to Luisa:

If Creation is attributed to the Father – the
Divine Persons always being united in their works

– Redemption is ascribed to the Son, and *the Fiat
Voluntas Tua is attributed to the Holy Spirit.*[383]

Upright works always maintain the fire of Divine
Love kindled in the soul; *the Omnipotent Wind of
God is what ignites it.* On the other hand, if on his
own one wants to ignite this fire in the upright
work, the winds of self-love, human respect, self-
esteem, desire for pleasures, and so many other
things come, and these winds will extinguish
it. *The winds that the upright work maintain are
not what ignite the fire, rather only the continuous
Omnipotent Wind of a God does that.*[384]

It is the breath of the Holy Spirit, that blowing
continually, keeps you burning and consuming
for his love.[385]

On Augustine's teaching, there are two ways by which one may
interpret the *knowledge* of the approved private revelations that
describe God's new mystical gift of Living in the Divine Will. One
may interpret knowledge of this gift in its *particular* sense, in which
case, it had *not* been known by many saints of past centuries, as several
mystics assert. On the other hand, one may interpret knowledge
of this gift in its *general* sense, and, in this case, it has indeed been
known by the saints of past, indeed since the time of Christ.

Let us take for example the Servant of God Luisa Piccarreta.
First, the knowledge of the Divine Will that God revealed to her
is indeed *particular,* but in the manner in which God chose to
revealed it "to her." It is far less particular, or rather it is *general*

in the manner by which he chose to reveal it to many pious souls after Luisa that have not been exposed to her private revelations, or have not experienced private revelations themselves.

Second, God can actualize his gifts in any properly disposed soul through his own power and without its *particular* knowledge of Luisa's revelations. The soul's proper disposition, i.e., the state of grace,[386] is sufficient for God's Spirit to communicate new insights on revealed truths to its intellect and actualize them in its will, at least in part – even without its particular or explicit apprehension of such truths.

Throughout Luisa's revelations, Jesus reminds her that the human creature need not possess complete knowledge, or "realize" what is actually taking place in its soul to *experience* a new mystical reality. God, nevertheless, elevates the soul to what St. John calls a "supernatural" and "infused" knowledge,[387] whereby it may better cooperate with greater spontaneity, agility, and penetration into the graces God holds out before it. Jesus reveals to Luisa:

> As the soul enters into My Will, her volition remains tied with My Eternal Will. Then, although *she doesn't realize it,* since her will has remained tied to Mine, that which My Will does hers also does; and it flows together with Me for the good of all.[388]

> My obligation is that of a more intense love, to reciprocate love with the soul [of the human creature] and allow her to have a foretaste of heavenly happiness. In other words, *I reveal to a*

soul's intellect the knowledge of My divinity, alluring her with the food of eternal truths, refreshing her sight with My beauty and caressing her ears with the gentleness of My voice, covering her mouth with My kisses and embracing her heart with all My affections.[389]

There are numerous examples of mystics and exemplars that have received the gift of "Living in the Divine Will" by *desire*, and with the assistance of revelations other than those of Luisa Piccarreta. Indeed, Luisa is the first human creature conceived in original sin to possess *continuously* this extraordinary gift and introduce it via *particular* knowledge to the Church. But the approved writings of numerous contemporary mystics and exemplars attest to having also experienced and lived this gift *in its fullness* without any knowledge of Luisa's revelations. Their narrations of the characteristics that define their mystical experiences are clear and certain indications that what they experienced was indeed the gift of 'Living in the Divine Will'.

As mentioned earlier, since God entrusts different missions to different souls whom he has chosen, different concepts often accompany the attainment of that mission without implying different realities. Therefore, while nearly all contemporary mystics neither knew nor read anything of the concepts or writings of Luisa Piccarreta, their private revelations and spiritual experiences helped them to recognize, esteem, and fully embrace the same gift Luisa describes.

More needs to be said here. If *desire* and *general knowledge* suffice in the reception of the new gift of Living in the Divine

Will, what positive contribution can the *particular knowledge* of Luisa's writings make to the Church?

First, because the Church allows the faithful to receive its approved spiritual works in the spirit of obedience as an edifying means for growth in holiness, it would seem inappropriate to dismiss Luisa's approved private revelations that best express the gift of Living in the Divine Will as revelations intended for the sanctification of Luisa only. Neither does their informal non-binding character, which is reserved for the *credo*, encourage the faithful to toss them out as rubbish. Their endorsements by Church authorities demand that they be approached with theological assiduousness and discernment.

Second, inasmuch as the Church's private revelations are a means by which the faithful may come to the *particular* knowledge of Living in the Divine Will, they can benefit the faithful in many ways from the knowledge and encouragement they bring. St. Thomas Aquinas reminds us, "the more knowledge one acquires of an object, the more he can love that object." Likewise, the more the soul acquires knowledge of God's new and eternal mode of holiness, the more it is capable of disposing itself to penetrate and persevere in that eternal mode. In this sense, the particular knowledge of Luisa's writings enables the soul tremendously to remain in and to rapidly grow in unending degrees of the Divine Will. The particular knowledge of the Divine Will serves not simply to illuminate the mind (cognitive knowledge), but more importantly to enflame the will (experiential knowledge). And it is above all this *experiential* knowledge of the Divine Will that our Lord emphasizes in the human creature's full reception and the full actualization of the gift of Living in the Divine Will.

Jesus reveals to Luisa:

> To "Live in the Divine Will" and not know it is absurd, for if one does not know it, it is not a reality but a manner of expression, as the first thing that My Will does is to awaken and to *make itself known* to those that *desire* to live together with My Will. [390]

In the writings of the great 20th century mystic Vera Grita, we find that she was able to experience the effects and activity of a gift whose particular knowledge she lacked. It wasn't until Vera became aware of this new indwelling that she could aspire to a greater sharing of its activity and thereby *"assent"* to God's *"eucharistic presence in her soul."*[391] Here Vera reveals her ability to more fully embrace an objective reality through its corresponding particular awareness:

> A Living Tabernacle is... the inhabitation of the Holy Spirit in the soul... who acts, speaks, sees, works... But I am already a living tabernacle in this soul and *she does not realize it. She must realize it because I want her to assent to My eucharistic presence in her soul.*[392]

Here one recalls Jesus' words to Luisa:

> As the soul enters into my Volition, her volition remains tied with my Eternal Volition. Then,

although *she doesn't realize it*, since her volition has remained tied to Mine, that which my Volition does hers also does; and it flows together with Me for the good of all.[393]

Jesus' assurance that Vera would assent to his new presence within her soul only after she had arrived at its realization, reveals the final causality of particular knowledge in the actualization of a new reality. Inasmuch as "one cannot love what he does not know," knowledge fosters love. And since it is God's eternal love that is communicated to the human creature, the more knowledge it obtains of his love, the more it is capable of informing its will to embrace it with a *firm* and *decisive act*.

Jesus tells Luisa that the purpose of her private revelations is to "attract" his children to the knowledge they transmit, so that they may be made more explicitly aware of the truths implicitly contained in the Church's deposit of faith:

> Knowledge of these things will be a powerful magnet *to attract* creatures, to make them receive the inheritance of my Will, and to put in motion this generation of light.[394]

> This is why you have received so many manifestations from Me; why I have revealed to you so many effects of my Will. *These are powerful magnets to attract you, and after you, others to live in my Will.*[395]

Here is the reason for the many manifestations of My Will that I have made to you, because the *knowledge of It will bring the desire of eating It.* When they have tasted what it means to live only to do My Will, if not all, at least part of them will return to the way of My Will, the two wills will give themselves the perennial kiss.[396]

More simply put, in order for the human creature to enter into this new stage of holiness, it must not only know it, it must also *desire it* and *live it.*

5. Jesus' Internal Sorrows

The gift of Christ's continuous and eternal activity in the human soul brings with it a unique personal presence. In the writings of several 20th century mystics this presence is marked by an *increased activity and knowledge of Jesus' internal sorrows.* To the Servant of God Luisa Piccarreta and Blessed Mother Teresa of Calcutta, Venerable Conchita, Ss. Padre Pio and Faustina, Jesus speaks of internal sorrows that have hitherto remained hidden. Jesus illustrates this when describing the mission to the Church that he entrusted to his victim soul Venerable Conchita de Armida:

> The essence of this Work consists in making known the Interior Sufferings of My Heart which are ignored, and which constitute for Me a more painful Passion than that which My Body underwent on Calvary, on account of its duration mystically perpetuated in the Eucharist. I tell

you, up to this day, the worlds had known the love of My Heart manifested to Margaret Mary, but *it was reserved for present times to make known its suffering, the symbols of which I had shown simply and in an external way.* I say again, there must be a penetration into the Interior of this boundless ocean of bitterness and an extension of knowledge of it throughout the world.[397]

The internal sorrows of my Heart are the most fruitful, because they share in the substantial fruitfulness of the Father in the Word made flesh, and those sorrows are divinized and in a certain way are divine... by reason of the hypostatic union... *These mystical sorrows have infinite virtue;* I see on earth the prolongation of Myself in souls so that they may continue in the world by attaining graces in union with Me... *Nothing moves my beloved Father so much as the intimate and hidden sufferings of my Heart...* they are of so much value! Clearly my external Passion saved the world and opened heaven; but what gave life and fruitfulness to my Church were those internal martyrdoms in the very substance of my soul, in which the Father refreshed himself, because he would see the immense glory purchased with them for my priests. *This very great grace, that is only given, and not always, to souls transformed into Me, is a very great grace for the great fruitfulness and virtue of other souls. Transformation into the dolorous Me*

is a very superior step, the highest and most fruitful
of transformation into Me. [398]

Shortly before his death, St. Hannibal di Francia illustrates
his state of interior darkness and sorrow, which resembles the
sorrowful state endured by our Blessed Lord:

> I have also entered a moral, spiritual state in which
> I seem to see and to feel the diabolical operations
> of the infernal enemy. Discouragements and
> oppressions assail me day and night; I feel interior
> abandonments and desolations, profound
> preoccupations within me – in sum, an interior
> state of such anguish and suffering which I have
> never before experienced. All the miseries of
> my life, the responsibilities, my sins, the priestly
> obligations, etc., come before me; and all this
> with an interior depression. I feel my heart and
> my soul as though under the press. [399]

St. Padre Pio of Pietrelcina[400] explains in masterly fashion the
phenomenon of Jesus' interior sorrows, as revealed to his dearest
friends, in stages leading up to purification and divinization. In
his letters St. Pio emphasizes the importance of Jesus' sorrows,
as "the soul can never attain to divine union unless it is first
purified of every actual and habitual imperfection":[401]

> I try in the apex of my spirit to be resigned
> to offer my "fiat," although I experience no
> spiritual solace. But may his will be done, I
> repeat continually and I long for nothing else

but the perfect fulfillment of his will in the precise manner he demands, generously and firmly... In this will and in the declarations of authority I find my only support, the only thing which sustains me in the dark paths into which I have penetrated... my inward gaze is always fixed upon the beloved.

"How many times," said Jesus to me a little while ago, "would you not have abandoned me if I had not crucified you?" Beneath the Cross one learns to love and *I do not grant this to everyone, but only to those souls who are dearest to me.*[402]

God disposes the soul by leading it into his eternal activity through arduous paths of spiritual warfare that require heroic, absolute and immediate trust. St. Faustina was given to understand this vital truth in regard to her spiritual director. Jesus had commissioned Faustina's director Fr. Sopoćko[403] to promote the work of divine mercy while, at the same time, allowing others to thwart and even contradict his efforts. Fr. Sopoćko was persecuted in every conceivable way by laity and priests for years, and without interruption. Despite the severity of the attacks that posed enormous obstacles to God's work of mercy, he did not let up in the face of trials that taxed and even injured his health. Rather, Faustina would later assure him that *all of these trials and setbacks are necessary for the work of mercy,* for through them, the good Lord was mystically drawing many hearts and minds to the very mission he had entrusted him with.

St. Faustina relates:

> One day, I saw interiorly how much my confessor
> would have to suffer; friends will desert you while
> everyone will rise up against you and your physical
> strength will diminish. I saw you as a bunch of
> grapes chosen by the Lord and thrown into the
> press of suffering. Your soul, Father, will at times be
> filled with doubts about this work and about me.

> I saw that God himself seemed to be opposing
> [him], and I asked the Lord why He was acting in
> this way toward him, as though He were placing
> obstacles in the way of his doing what He himself
> had asked him to do. And the Lord said:
> "I am acting thus with him to give testimony that
> this work is Mine. Tell him not to fear anything;
> *My gaze is on him day and night. There will be as*
> *many crowns to form his crown as there will be souls*
> *saved by this work. It is not for the success of a work,*
> *but for the suffering that I give reward."*[404]

> Once as I was talking with my spiritual
> director, I had an interior vision— quicker
> than lightening—of his soul in great suffering,
> in such agony that *God touches very few souls*
> *with such fire.* The suffering arises from this
> work. There will come a time when this work,
> which God is demanding so very much, will be
> as though utterly undone. And then God will
> act with great power, which will give evidence

of its authenticity. It will be a new splendor for
the Church, although it has been dormant in it
from long ago... When his triumph comes, we
shall already have entered the new life in which
there is no suffering. But before this your soul
[Fr. Sopoćko] will be surfeited with bitterness
at the sight of the destruction of your efforts.
However, this will only appear to be so, because
what God has once decided upon, He does not
change. But although the suffering will be such
only in outward appearance, the suffering will
be real. When will this happen, I do not know.
How long it will last? I do not know. But *God
has promised a great grace especially to you and to
all those... who proclaim his great mercy.*[405]

Admittedly, Fr. Sopoćko did not receive revelations from
Jesus, as did his spiritual daughter, St. Faustina. Rather, it
was through her diary, which he commissioned her to write
and which Jesus confirmed, that he came to the particular
knowledge of God's extraordinary activity in him. Jesus
reassured his spiritual daughter that only certain souls allow
him to relive his internal sorrows in them, as he lived them
in Fr. Sopoćko, when he stated, "I enter into *certain* hearts as
into a second Passion."[406]

The Rev. Joseph Neuner, a friend to Mother Teresa[407] and the
senior theologian spoke of the intimate experiences she had and
seldom shared of Jesus' internal sorrows. In the New Delhi Jesuit
circular Rev. Neuner writes: "It came to her at a time when she
embarked upon her new life in the service of the abandoned...

From the beginning, she had to experience not only their material poverty and helplessness, but also their abandonment."

Mother Teresa, in fact, was tempted to return to Europe, writing of "all the beautiful things and comforts, the people they mix with, in a word everything." But she resisted. She wrote in 1949: "Of free choice, my God, and out of love for You, I desire to remain and do whatever be your holy will in my regard."

Some of her most agonizing writings come from 1959 and 1960, when the Rev. T. Picachy, future archbishop of Calcutta, was her spiritual director and had asked her to write out her thoughts. During this period Jesus drew her into the depths of his internal state of the abandonment his soul experienced on the Cross of Calvary:

"Now, Jesus, I go the wrong way," she wrote. "They say people in hell suffer eternal pain because of loss of God. *In my soul, I feel just the terrible pain of loss, of God not wanting me, of God not being God, of God not really existing.* Jesus, please forgive the blasphemy—I have been told to write everything—that darkness that surrounds me on all sides. *I can't lift my soul to God: No light, no inspiration enters my soul.*" Later, in the 1990's she would acknowledge that her sufferings were truly those of Christ: "*I have begun to love my darkness, for I believe now that it is a part, a very small part of Jesus' darkness and pain on earth...* My life is not strewed with roses. Rather, I have more darkness as my fellow friend... I simply offer myself to Jesus."

Her many years of service to the poor would prepare Mother Teresa for the reception of God's greatest gift, that is, the gift of 'Living in the Divine Will.' In her memoirs she affirms that it is not abandonment to suffering that crowns the spiritual life, but living in the Will of God:

> It is not necessary... to consciously experience the sensation that we are talking to God, no matter how nice this would be. *What matters is being with him, living in him, in his will.* To love with a pure heart, to love everybody, especially to love the poor, is a twenty-four-hour prayer.[408]

And Jesus once told Blessed Dina:

> My joy, in which I am allowing you to share, can be found *in aridity, in anguish, and in darkness, because it is the joy of perfect union with my divine will,* it is the joy of my love, the joy of my Heart.[409]

6. *Jesus' Real Presence*

For the soul to arrive at the new stage of holiness it must first allow itself to be divinized by Jesus' internal sorrows and from the graces it receives in the Eucharist. Several mystics emphasize this cardinal point through the power of transforming union produced by the Eucharist, which Vatican Council II defines as "that which contains the entire spiritual good of the Church."[410]

Jesus tells Luisa:

> Now you, my daughter, receive It [Holy Communion] in my Will; unite It to My Humanity.

In this way, you will enclose everything, thereby allowing Me to discover within you the reparations of everyone, the compensation of everyone, and my pleasure—or rather, to discover you once again in Me.[411]

Jesus tells Venerable Conchita:

Nothing helps this transformation so much as the reception of the Eucharist in which one receives me as God-man, in My Humanity and in my Divinity, one with the Father and the Holy Spirit.[412]

St. Faustina relates:

Jesus, there is one more secret in my life, the deepest and dearest to my Heart: it is You yourself when You come to my heart under the appearance of bread. Herein lies the whole secret of my sanctity. Here my heart is so united to Yours as to be one. There are no more secrets because all that is yours is mine, and all that is mine is Yours.[413]

Jesus-Eucharist, life of my soul, You have raised me up to the eternal spheres.[414]

Jesus reveals to Vera Grita:

All souls and every soul that receives Me under the Eucharistic Species can become a Living Tabernacle. Behold, I am such, in the soul that receives Me in humility and in charity with his neighbor. Alas, this soul enables other souls to partake of My gift: of Me, of My grace.[415]

From the [Church's] Tabernacles I effuse My Spirit of Love. Now I have chosen new churches, new Tabernacles to guard Me: Living Tabernacles that bring Me to all parts of the world, that lead Me among the people that do not think of Me, that do not seek Me, and that do not love Me... Those called to this work of Mine will receive a particular fervor toward My Eucharistic of Love that will characterize their predilection...[416]

Never neglect guarding within the intimacy of yourself love for Me in the Eucharist, which I have given to you as a consoling reward: The "consummation" of self in Me to My Father.[417]

Once the soul is transformed by Jesus' internal sorrows, it is then drawn into the 'eternal spheres' by the power of the Eucharist and made into a 'Living Host,' a 'Living Tabernacle,' that is, a perfect reflection of Jesus' internal state. Luisa Piccarreta and other approved mystics explain their union with God's will in terms of his real presence in the Eucharist. Jesus tells Luisa:

My daughter, as the soul progressively encompasses My Will and loves Me, she encompasses Me within My own Will, and in so loving, she forms the accidents to imprison Me within, thus forming for Me a Host. Hence when she suffers, when she

makes reparation, etc., she encompasses My Will.
She forms many Hosts in order to administer Me
and nourish Me in a divine manner that is worthy
of Me. No sooner do I see these Hosts formed in the
soul, than I immediately lay hold of them to nourish
Myself and satisfy My insatiable hunger, in order that
the creature may give Me love for Love. Thus you
can say to Me: "You have administered me, and I
also have administered You."[418]

Jesus tells Venerable Conchita:

I then felt... I had already received Christ in
Communion, but he, as if it were, reading my
mind, continued: "No, no, it is not so. *You have
received Me today quite differently.* I have taken
possession of your heart. I have incarnated Myself
mystically in it *never to leave.*[419]

Jesus tells Blessed Dina:

The grace of My chalice is My real presence which
I am giving to you, as in the sacred Host... you
are really in possession of Me during those few
moments following sacramental communion... *I
am giving you the continual grace of My real presence.*[420]

Jesus relates to Marthe Robin:[421]

The Host for your sacrifice, your Mass, is
yourself... offer yourself to God with Jesus, the

divine victim, ceaselessly immolated for the salvation of all.[422]

Jesus tells Vera Grita:

A Living Tabernacle is... the inhabitation of the Holy Spirit in the soul... who acts, speaks, sees, works... But I am already a living tabernacle in this soul...[423]

In the last days of October 1906, another 19th century mystic from France relates a similar phenomenon using the expression "little host" to define Jesus' eternal activity in her soul. Days before her transit to heaven, Blessed Elizabeth of the Trinity (1880-1906) penned a letter to her prioress, with whom she had forged a deeply spiritual rapport, and in which she detailed the deep gratitude she felt for her spiritual mother:[424]

If you will allow her, *your little host* will spend her heaven in the depths of your soul: she will keep you in communion with Love, believing in Love; it will be the sign of her dwelling in you. Oh in what intimacy we are going to live. Cherished Mother, *let your life also be spent in the heavens... that you too, may live the life of the blessed!*[425]

Jesus and St. Faustina exchange words of the new mystical union:

You are a *living host*, pleasing to the heavenly Father.[426]

I am *a white host* before you, O Divine Priest. Consecrate me yourself, and *may my transubstantiation be known only to you.*[427]

The Mother of God... said to me: ...You are a dwelling place pleasing to God; *in you He dwells continuously* with love and delight... And the living presence of God... will confirm you.[428] Suddenly, when I had consented to the sacrifice with all my heart and all my will, God's presence pervaded me... *A great mystery took place... a mystery between the Lord and myself... At that moment I felt transconsecrated. My earthly body was the same, but my soul was different; God was now living in it with the totality of His delight.*[429]

St. Faustina's "mystery" of Christ's presence in the human soul bears a striking resemblance to a recent statement made by her compatriot Pope John Paul II. After having carefully reviewed and rehabilitated her writings, Pope John Paul II penned an encyclical in which he acknowledged God's limitless capacity for acting in the human soul:

We know in fact that, in the presence of the mystery of grace, *infinitely full of possibilities and implications for human life and history,* the Church herself will never cease putting questions, trusting in the help of the Paraclete... to guide her "into all the truth."[430]

If Faustina speaks of a transubstantial presence of Christ in her soul she is not speaking as a theologian. In its Thomistic sense, transubstantiation implies the replacement of one reality with another, such that at the consecration Christ replaces the reality or substance of bread with the reality of his own divine Person and Nature. Christ's presence in the substance of the bread and of the wine is referred to in theology as his "real presence." Faustina suggests rather God's full and incomprehensible possession of the human soul's intellect, memory and will, such that they no longer operate apart from his one, eternal act. In this eternal act or eternal mode, Christ continuously extends his divine and eternal powers to the soul, that he may act in it *fully* and in such a mysterious way that the human mind cannot completely grasp it. Because the soul's powers are completely captivated by God, the only reality that can be used to shed light on it is the Eucharist.

Theologically, in the Eucharist Christ replaces the substance of the bread with his own divine body, blood, soul and divinity, becoming its subject (*suppositum*). In the soul in which Christ *fully* dwells, on the other hand, Christ does not *replace* the substance of the human creature—who preserves its creaturehood—but so absorbs it in himself that a new state of mystical union is effected. This new union constitutes the creature's "full" participation in God's eternal being and operation in every passing moment of its earthly existence without interruption. It is heaven on earth internalized. This continuous possession of Christ's eternal activity is the key that unlocks the secret of the new gift that God has exponentially revealed at the dawn of the third Christian millennium.

Since the creature, by itself, is not worthy or capable of actualizing this union, it is God's initiative to give himself in the Eucharist. To assuage his burning desire to give himself to us, God goes in search of others souls willing to receive the graces that scores of others have rejected. This he does by progressively extending the duration of his eucharistic presence in the soul of the human creature that is faithful to his graces, until it experiences his eucharistic presence *continuously*. This is made possible only by what the mystics call a 'special grace' that lifts the creature into God's 'eternal mode.' In this state of Living in the Divine Will, the soul participates in the *ad intra operatio* (internal operations) of the three divine Persons. [431] Jesus tells Luisa Piccarreta:

> My daughter, my aforementioned *ad intra* consists precisely in this: that now, I keep you joined together with Me, with My thoughts, whereby you partake in the pains, the works, and the joys of My Humanity. And by drawing you to Me, I cause you to lose yourself in My Divinity... Now, what cause for great wonder is there in saying, that once the soul's will is united to Mine – by her placing her will within Me, thus rendering it indissoluble... – she partakes in the *ad intra* operations?[432]

Does this mean that souls who enjoy the lofty state of Jesus' continuous real presence are exempt from receiving him in his sacrament? On the contrary, the Eucharist is the very cause, sustenance and object of the soul's journey to God. In the life of St. Padre Pio of Pietrelcina, the Eucharist emerges as the chief source of this *continuous* flow of graces poured into the human soul that enable it to live in his eternal will. St. Padre Pio explains:

> Let us adore it [divine providence] and be ready to conform our will *in all things and at all times* with the will of God... The total offering of our will is unfortunately very difficult. We must remember, though, that when our divine Master addressed to His Father on our behalf those words of the Lord's prayer "thy will be done," his divine mind showed Him very clearly how difficult it would be for us to do what He had promised the Father for us...Well, then, His immense love... found an admirable means... What means was this?... He asked Him also: "Give us this day, Father, our daily bread"...But what bread is this?... I recognize primarily the Eucharist...
>
> *How could I fulfill that petition made by Your Son in our name: Thy will be done on earth as it is in heaven, if I did not receive strength from this immaculate flesh?... Yes, give Him to us and we shall be sure to fulfill the request that Jesus Himself addressed to You on our behalf: "Thy will be done on earth as it is in heaven."*[433]

Earlier I referred to Jesus' presence in the human soul as a "pneumatic coming," or a "new Pentecost." It is "pneumatic" because the Spirit of Jesus enters the spirit of the human creature in a new, continuous and eternal way. This notwithstanding, other spiritual writers refer to this coming as the "intermediary coming of Christ,"[434] "the Eucharistic Reign of Jesus" in souls,[435] "the assumption of souls in love,"[436] and, more polyvalently, the *"second coming."*[437] It is noteworthy that the Magisterium refrains from associating the era of peace or an historic triumph of Christian sanctity with the expression, "the second coming," for the simple reason that the latter principally represents the coming of the Holy Spirit in a Second Pentecost to prepare the Church for Christ's final coming in the flesh at the *end* of human history and at the *end* of the world.[438] Insofar as the era of peace constitutes a portion of human history it may indeed be referred to as a "new presence of Christ" in souls, or a "new Pentecost" of the glorified Spirit of Jesus *before* Christ's final coming at the end of the world. Therefore, if several mystics, prophets or locutionists refer to the era of peace as a "second coming of Jesus," it is to be understood as his *pneumatic* coming (of his glorified Spirit) in a way that exceeds all preceding indwellings.[439] One may here recall Jesus' words of Venerable Conchita de Armida and those of Blessed Dina:

> *The time has come to exalt the Holy Spirit in the world...* I desire that this last epoch be consecrated in a very special way to this Holy Spirit... It is his turn, it is his epoch, it is the triumph of love in My Church, *in the whole universe.*[440]

> In this *new divine indwelling,* what strikes me... is the power, the greatness, the immensity of God's attributes. The infinite seems to me to be more and more infinite... My *offering is far more active than in the preceding dwellings.*[441]

a. *Eucharistic Theology*

In approved contemporary spiritual literature, one can translate the new and eternal indwelling to the *full* presence of Christ in his spatial and personal modalities. That Christ may be more *personally* present to one soul than to another is brought out in the historic contributions to the field of eucharistic theology. The scholastics have always held that emphasis should not be placed upon Christ's *"spatial presence"* in the Eucharist (*illocaliter in loco*), even though there had been earlier considerations of it. The scholastic emphasis was given to Christ's ontological and cosmological presence in the Eucharist, which we may translate as Christ's *"personal presence."* The personal presence of Christ is not, for that matter, bereft of all physical relationship to the world, rather Christ transcends the world *and* is in the world, in heaven *and* in the Eucharist. The Council of Trent further teaches that in the Eucharist Christ does not become bread, rather the substance of the bread is replaced and consumed, as it were, by the divine Person of Christ and the Nature of the three Divine Persons.

On a more practical scale, if God can empower himself to become substantially present in an *inanimate* host, may not the same be said of an *animate* subject? And if God were to work such a miracle, how might it affect his modality? We know that if Christ were to transubstantiate himself in the soul of the human person endowed with an intellect, a memory and a will, he cannot replace that substance of the human person that preserves its creaturehood, lest it cease to be a creature altogether.[442] Indeed, God is immutable and cannot add to his divine essence additional *persons.* Yet if Christ were to preserve the creature's personhood by allowing its substance to "continuously participate" in his eternal activity and qualities, he may then effect a union of wills, intellects and memories that is so perfectly united with his own that he can act in them as he acted in the eternal Word. Hence Jesus' words to the Servant of God Luisa Piccarreta:

> All three Divine Persons descended from Heaven; and then, after a few days, We took possession of your heart and took our *perpetual residence* there. We took the reins of your intelligence, your heart, all of you. Everything you did was an outlet of our creative Will in you. It was a confirmation that *your will was animated by an Eternal Will.*[443]

The Servant of God Archbishop Luis Maria Martinez affirms the same teaching:

> The soul gives to the Word that which he does not have: a new human nature, the capacity for pain and immolation. And the Word divinizes the soul, *uniting himself to it in a most intimate way (by union of wills) that imitates the hypostatic union.*[444]

Jesus reveals to Blessed Dina:

> During my thanksgiving after Communion, I was concentrating on remaining closely united with him... I was taken by surprise... He said: "*I want to deify you in the same way as I united My humanity with My divinity*"... The degree of holiness that

I want for you, *is the infinite plentitude of my own holiness, it is the holiness of my Father brought about in you through me.*[445]

The grace of incarnating Me, of Me living and growing in your soul, never to leave it, of possessing you and of being possessed by you *as in one and the same substance...* is the grace of graces.[446]

Similarly, Jesus told Venerable Conchita:

While saying at the last Supper: "This is my Body, this is my Blood," I had in mind the extension of this Body and this Blood in my priests transformed in Me, *fully* formed also, in this sense, *Living Eucharists,* and with the same end of living immolated on behalf of all the world. Then I beheld in my soul that they would disappear, and in a certain sense, like the substance of bread and wine, remain transformed into Me for the salvation of souls.[447]

Since Christ, who existed on earth in time and space, acts in an eternal manner that exceeds both, he is able to be immanent in both while performing eternal acts that transcend both. We find this in the acts of the ordained priest, in whom this eternal activity is present during the eucharistic consecration. We find it also in the aforementioned lay mystics, many of whom experienced the *fullness* of this activity in their lives. Since God's triune activity combines both Christ's divine and human acts,

known in theology as "theandric activity," the three divine
Persons act through the natural union forged by the Person of
the eternal Word, while fully sustaining, motivating and guiding
the soul's powers.[448] Moreover, since it was the eternal Spirit[449]
that empowered Christ to perform divine and eternal acts, the
Spirit becomes the acting principle of the human soul's activity
in a modality of operation that causes it to exit time and space
and remain in the ambience of eternity. As the glorified Christ
possesses an eternal manner of existing that is not bound to the
"accidents" of the spatio-temporal location of the bread, he is free
to subsist in the soul in a manner altogether unrestricted. Thus,
by the power of the glorified Spirit of Christ, the soul vicariously
participates in the eternal processions of the three Divine Persons
(*ad intra operatio*) and becomes a sacramental sign of the Church
in its perfected state (*pignus futurae gloriae*). Urs von Balthasar
describes the unique state of Blessed Elizabeth of Trinity as that
in which God's eternal processions of love are communicated to
the soul:

> "The Holy Ghost raises the soul to such a
> wonderful height as to enable it to witness, in God,
> the same aspiration of love uttered conjointly by
> the Father and the Son..." Man... *is enabled to
> take part in the eternal processions, that is, in the very
> activity of the eternal love.*[450]

Yet in order that the soul may reestablish itself in Christ,
it must advance from the mere satisfaction of his "spatial
presence" to his "personal presence." In their advanced stages
of the spiritual journey, recent mystics acknowledge that both
"spatial" and "personal" presence combine to form within the

soul a participation in God's one, eternal act. The two elements combine as a result of a spatial act of the human person's free will and the personal act of God's eternal will to establish Christ's "*full presence*" in the soul. Jesus tells Venerable Conchita de Armida:

> I want to close the distances that separate Me from souls; I want them to know Me as I am: not Jesus who lived in the past, but a present Jesus, *not only in the tabernacle, but also in the intimacy of each heart.*[451]

Despite Christ's spatial presence in the physical reality of his body, blood, soul and divinity, he is unable to draw us to himself without the "personal presence" that demands a free, self-determined response. Unlike the inanimate bread, the human soul is open to a genuine personal communication. To the extent that we accept another's self-revelation in trust and in faith, or to the extent that we close ourselves off from one another, the other is more or less personally present. Personal presence allows a richly varied range of degrees. God can be present in a number of ways. God is far more present to those who possess the gift of his eternal will than to those who do not, to a mystic than he is to a baptized infant, to a baptized infant than to a blade of grass. As a final illustration of the primacy of personal to spatial presence, I refer you to St. Augustine's presentation of Mary's possession of God's word:

> Mary heard God's word and kept it, and so she is blest. She kept God's truth in her mind, a nobler thing than carrying his body in her womb. The truth and the body were both Christ: he was

kept in Mary's mind insofar as he is truth, he was carried in her womb insofar as he is man; but *what is kept in the mind is of higher order than that which is carried in the womb.*[452]

7. Continuous Immersion in Eternity

Throughout the approved writings of modern-day mystics, we have seen a new infusion of the activity of the Holy Trinity in the human soul wrought by a "special" and "intimate grace." This grace is a gratuitous gift of God who desires to draw all souls into the highest regions of the eternal priesthood of Christ. Inasmuch as Christ's eternal priesthood is "directed to all peoples and all times, and is not confined by any bounds," the soul is empowered to influence the lives of "all creatures past, present and future." At this stage, the soul enters in the eternal mode of God's activity never to leave. If before the soul had intermittently experienced God's eternal act on previous occasions, it has now made a "firm and decisive act" never to leave that eternal act and remains faithful in its resolve. Recent mystics affirm that very few souls arrived at this most sublime point of mystical union that is there for the asking.[453] Yet once the soul has entered this ambience of God's eternity, it mystically exits time and space and participates continuously in the life of God for as long as God is God.

The new reality of God's continuously eternal activity, or eternal mode, admits the soul into the same interior state of glory as the blessed in heaven. In this new state, the soul experiences infusions of God's sublime knowledge and consolations, as well as the temporal desolations that enable the eternal Word to relive his entire human existence in the soul, mystically incarnated. Since the soul is purified, illuminated, unified and divinized, it is perfectly disposed to accept and embrace God's Will in all things and give him the glory he would have received if his beloved creatures had never sinned. Whence the soul expiates its sins of the past and embraces the penalty of sin incurred by others; it endures on earth the pains of purgatory and participates in Jesus' internal sorrows. Jesus underscores this characteristic note of *continuity* in the following passages:

Jesus tells Luisa:

> I Myself knew how many graces were necessary, having to work the greatest miracle that exists in the world, which is that of *living continuously in My Will*: the soul must assimilate everything of God in its act, so as to give it back again intact, just as the soul assimilated it, and then to assimilate it again.[454]

> Whoever lives in my Will finds himself already in this single Act. As the heart always palpitates in human nature and constitutes its life, so my Will palpitates *continually* in the depth of the soul, but with a single palpitation. As It palpitates, It gives it beauty, sanctity, strength, love, goodness, wisdom... This palpitation encloses Heaven and earth... This single Act, this palpitation of the soul, reigns completely, it has full vigor and is *a continuous prodigy that only a God can perform.* Therefore, new Heavens are unveiled in it, new

abysses of graces, and surprising truths.[455]

All three Divine Persons descended from Heaven; and then, after a few days, we took possession of your heart and took our *perpetual residence* there. We took the reins of your intelligence, your heart, all of you. Everything you did was an outlet of our creative Will in you. It was a confirmation that your will was animated by an Eternal Will.[456] Living in my Will is the apex of sanctity, and it bestows continuous growth in Grace.[457]

Blessed Dina writes:

I need a perpetual and very powerful grace to *maintain me in this blessed state*: I am enjoying perfect beatitude... *It is truly eternity!*[458]

As the soul advances in its continuous immersion in God, it acquires a keener understanding of the eternal realities of the blessed in heaven. Jesus tells Luisa:

My Will has the power to make everything that enters into My Will infinite, and to elevate and transform the acts of creatures into Eternal Acts. This is because *what enters into My Will acquires the Eternal, the Infinite, and the Immense*, losing what has beginning, what is finite, and what is small... In My Will I will hear the note of My Eternal Love, I will feel created love hidden in Uncreated Love, and I will feel Myself loved by the creature with Eternal,

Infinite, and Immense Love; hence a love worthy of
Me, that substitutes for Me and can requite Me with
the love of all.[459]

Although the soul's ultimate reward remains the *beatific
mode*[460] outside of time, more meritorious still is its internalization
within time. Jesus tells Luisa:

> The soul who is still wandering unifies herself with
> my Will in such a way as to *never separate herself from
> It*. Her life is of Heaven, and I receive from her the
> same glory that I receive from the Blessed. Further,
> I take more pleasure and satisfaction in her. This
> is because what the Blessed do in Heaven they do
> without sacrifice, and with delight.[461]

> I must tell you the great difference which passes
> between the newborn creature of my Supreme Will
> *in time* and the creatures that are reborn *at the doors
> of eternity*. An example is My Holy Queen Mother
> who was the newborn of the Divine Will *in time*.
> Precisely because She was the newborn, She had
> the power to make her Creator descend to earth…
> Because She was the newborn, She formed seas of
> graces, light, sanctity and knowledge as to be able
> to contain Him who had created Her. With the
> power of the Life of the Supreme Will that She
> possessed, She was able to do all and to intercede
> for all. And God Himself could not refuse what
> this Celestial Creature asked, for what She asked
> she asked with My own Will.

Therefore, the creature that is newborn in My Will *in time* is formed with seas of grace while it is on this exilic earth. Parting from the earth, this creature takes with itself all the seas of the blessings My Divine Will possesses and, therefore, takes God Himself... On the other hand, to the creature that is born into My Will *when leaving this earth*, the Divine Will reveals Its immense seas so that its soul may be reborn in the Divine Will. This creature does not carry God with itself, but God lets Himself be found by this creature. And what a difference there is between the two.[462]

We find the continuous state of union with the Divine Will in the writings of God's chosen instrument Sr. Mary of the Holy Trinity. Jesus tells Sister Mary:

To let Me live within you is to fill your heart with the utter surrender of little children... to apply all your intelligence to understanding My ways of working and to imitate them... It is to keep in the truth with all the strength of your will, cost what it may, *at every instant and on every occasion.*" To this Sister Mary replied: "Fix them on yourself *as in their eternity.*[463]

A few days later, Jesus defined the supernatural character of Sr. Mary's obedience that enabled his will to truly "live" and "reign" in her:

Silence, respect for all creatures... Stripping oneself in the joy of giving. Patience. Love which obeys the Voice of God, not in appearance, *but*

*from the depths of one's being, in complete adhesion to
the divine will...* I need all of that to live in a soul,
to grow there and to reign there...[464] Obedience is
a state of the soul, *a permanent state* which makes
the soul *cling perseveringly to the will of God...*[465]
You must be firmly united to Me, and to the will of
God alone, and detached from all else... in order
to help Me to penetrate everywhere...[466] I live in
you with a *continuous* and progressive life.[467]

Overjoyed with Jesus' words of confirmation on the new
state of union she presently enjoyed, Sr. Mary cried out:

My Lord, yes, to all you desire, with your help,
with all my will... it is Your will that I desire...
my immense desires for union among souls of
goodwill for Your glory! I will intercede until the
end of the world.[468]

8. *A New State of Mystical Union*

That God's mystics were aware that they possessed a new
"state" of mystical union is affirmed in their writings that bear
the Church's seals of approval. For purposes of brevity I here
recall two mystics, the Servant of God Luisa and Blessed Dina:

But now the time has come for the creature to
enter into this plane (of God's eternal mode) and
do his acts in mine... This means that the time
had not arrived in which my Goodness should
call the creature to live in this sublime *state*.[469]

> This morning, I received a special grace that I
> find difficult to describe. I felt taken up into God,
> as if in the *eternal mode*, that is in *a permanent,
> unchanging state*... I feel I am continually in the
> presence of the adorable Trinity.[470]

It is often only after the soul is trained in the knowledge and
desire of God's eternal will that it enters his will in a new way,
that is, in the eternal mode and never to leave. And it is here, at
this point of entry that the new "state" of mystical union begins.

Although the new union the mystics knowingly describe may
seem to be reserved to a select few far removed from society,
nothing could be farther from the truth. Venerable Conchita
was a mother of nine children. "Being a wife and a mother was
never an obstacle to my spiritual life," she asserted. Speaking
as a woman to one of her daughters-in-law, she added: "I have
been very happy with my husband." And the Lord himself told
her one day: "You married in view of My great designs for your
personal holiness, and to be an example for many souls who
think that marriage is incompatible with holiness." The most
sublime mystical graces described by spiritual masters are not
privileges reserved to souls who have fled the world, to priests
and religious; they are offered to all Christians of every state in
life. Vatican II forcefully testifies to this:

> Thus it is evident to everyone that all the faithful
> in Christ of whatever rank or status are called
> to the *fullness* of the Christian life and to the
> perfection of charity.[471]

Jesus reveals to his chosen mystic Vera Grita that the time has arrived for him to call a new militia of victim souls to service *in the world*, that are willing to set out for deep waters in search of lost souls. It is precisely because the world misleads many souls in these times of great grace that Jesus requests their presence in the world:

> In a living tabernacle I want to be crucified in order to draw sinners close to me. Therefore, in the most mystical silence My [living] tabernacle *must live in society*, for I, Jesus desire My divine presence among men... A living tabernacle must not lose contact with the world or with society; although living in the world, it must act, speak and love with a spirit that is interiorly animated by My Spirit and that reflects My Spirit.[472]

Since the victim souls in society are more prone to the unexpected attacks and temptations of the evil one, God provides for them by means of the graces they receive from the Eucharist and from a life of prayerful solitude. Hence Jesus' words to Sr. Mary of the Holy Trinity:

> I desire a great army of victim souls who will join Me in the apostolate of My Eucharistic Life... I desire an army of victim souls who will confine their efforts to imitating My Apostolate... so that my Spirit may spread... I desire these victim souls to be everywhere: *in the world and in the cloisters*...[473]

As far back as the early centuries, one can find many exemplary figures who, through a contemplative-active apostolate, revealed the conditions for the attainment of union leading up to this new stage of holiness. St. Augustine, Maximus the Confessor, Ss. Catherine of Siena, Ignatius of Loyola, Teresa of Avila, John of the Cross and other mystics that lived an active life, provided a skeletal framework of the steps leading up to divinization and the recovery of man's full participation in God's Divine Will. Approved Modern mystics, on the other hand, show how in recent years the Holy Spirit has actualized the gift of Living in the Divine Will, by empowering and divinizing the human creature to fully participate in God's Will. This gift, they affirm, is available to all of us so long as we desire it with a sincere heart.

Chapter 5

THE FINAL COMING OF JESUS

The Parousia

As mentioned earlier, the new stage of holiness is a period of preparation for Christ's final return in glory. St. Paul's description of the future Church that is presented to Christ in a *"holy and immaculate"* state before his final return intimates this period of preparation. Admittedly, the Church's holiness and immaculacy proceed from the Holy Spirit's action in the sacraments and in the gifts that build up the body of Christ, *"until we all attain to the unity of faith and knowledge of the Son of God… to the full stature of Christ."*[474] If the "unity of faith" and "knowledge in the Son of God" are wrought by the Holy Spirit's power at work in the sacraments and through his gifts – especially through the gift of Living in the Divine Will – it advances the teaching that they are the means by which the Church approaches her state of immaculacy. Therefore, when Christ returns in glory, he will indeed encounter his beloved Church beautifully adorned as a bride awaiting her Spouse's return. This nuptial encounter between Christ and the Church is often referred to in Greek as the *"Parousia."*

The Magisterium teaches that Christ's *final coming* in the flesh coincides with the *Parousia*, that is, after the historic era of peace and at the end of human history:[475]

> The kingdom will be fulfilled, then, *not by a historic triumph* of the Church through the progressive ascendancy, but only by God's victory over *the final unleashing of evil, which will cause his Bride to come down from heaven.*[476]

> Indeed, the [final] resurrection is closely associated with Christ's Parousia.[477]

> The resurrection of all the dead, "of both the just and unjust," will precede the Last Judgment... *Then Christ will come 'in his glory,* and all the angels with him... Before him will be gathered all the nations, and he will separate them one from another...[478]

> *The Last Judgment will come when Christ returns in glory,* Only the Father... determines the moment of its coming. Then through his son Jesus Christ he will pronounce the final word on all history.[479]

> The Antichrist's deception already begins to take shape in the world every time the claim is made to realize within history that messianic hope which *can only be realized beyond history* through the eschatological judgment.[480]

…Baptism is only the beginning from which the figure of the glorious Church will emerge… as a *definitive* fruit of the redemptive and spousal love, only with *the final coming of Christ (parousia)*.[481]

The Scripture scholars Russel Adwinkle and A. Winklhofer acknowledge the immediate relationship between the Parousia and the end of human history:

The parousia will be a real event… in that the parousia brings to an end the long process of historic development. It will not be an historical event… It is literal in the sense that the union of Christ with his people at the end of history will be a meeting between a real Christ and a real community of persons.[482]

It is this coming [the parousia] and nothing else that brings history to its fulfillment. It gives all history its meaning, and its course is understandable only in view of it… which consists in a mysterious transformation of the entire creation and particularly man… it is an event visible to all men in every part of the earth.[483]

One can gain from the Church's teachings on the Parousia and its association with Christ's Final Coming in the flesh, the final resurrection and the Last Judgment, a deeper appreciation for the Church's antecedent era of peace. As mentioned earlier, St. Paul affirms that the Church must clothe herself with holiness and immaculacy in order to present herself worthily before her divine Spouse's return in glory, which fittingly suggests that the Parousia occurs *after* the Church's era of holiness.

The Rapture

> Two men will be out in the field; one will be taken,
> and one will be left. Two women will be grinding
> at the mill; one will be taken and one will be left.
> Therefore, stay awake! For you do not know on
> which day your Lord will come.[484]

> For the Lord himself, with a word of command,
> with the voice of an archangel and with the
> trumpet of God, will come down from heaven,
> and the dead in Christ will rise first. Then we who
> are alive, who are left, will be caught up together
> with them in the clouds to meet the Lord in the
> air. Thus we shall always be with the Lord.[485]

While most *Premillenarians* hold that the quoted passages
from Matthew and Paul signify a pre-tribulation "rapture," a
more careful study reveals elements of Scripture foreign to their
belief. The *Premillenarians* believe the rapture will occur *before*
Satan and his adherents are released for the final battle, such
that all believers in Christ are conveniently spared the ravages
of war. However, not only does this eliminate all possibility of
believers obtaining the glorious crown of martyrdom, it deprives
the world of its efficacious fruits extolled throughout the Book
of Revelation (cf. 6:9; 7:13-14; 13:7.10.15; 17:6; 18:24; 20:4).
Moreover, a pre-tribulation rapture contradicts Jesus' words on
the final tribulation:

> When you see the desolating abomination spoken
> of through Daniel the prophet standing in the

holy place (let the reader understand), *then those in Judea must flee to the mountains, a person on the housetop must not go down to get things out of his house, a person in the field must not return to get his cloak.* Woe to the pregnant women and nursing mothers in those days. *Pray that your flight not be in winter or on the Sabbath, for at that time there will be great tribulation,* such as has not been since the beginning of the world until now, nor ever will be. And if those days had not been shortened, no one would be saved; but for the sake for the elect they will be shortened.[486]

If understood as a general resurrection of all the living and the dead at the *end* of history, the rapture then finds its relevancy in Tradition. It was part of the early patristic thought to maintain a rapture *outside* of history, when the New Jerusalem comes down from heaven as a bride adorned to meet her spouse. In that moment, all the just that have lived from the beginning of the world will be rapt up into Christ's eternal embrace to remain with him for all eternity (For more information on the personages accompanying the final battle, please refer to my book entitled *Antichrist and the End Times*).

Based on the quoted texts, it appears that the rapture will occur after the era of peace and the final tribulation. Shortly thereafter follows the resurrection of the dead, the General Judgment, the consummation of the heavens and earth, and the establishment of the New Jerusalem, the New Heavens and New Earth. Below I present the last events associated with Christ's Final coming in tabloid form:

Characteristics of Christ's Final Coming

- *Resurrection of the Living and The Dead*

> But your dead shall live, their corpses shall rise;
> awake and sing, you who lie in the dust.[487]

> I saw the dead, the great and the lowly, standing
> before the throne, and scrolls were opened. Then
> another scroll was opened, the book of life.[488]

> But when the thousand years shall be
> completed, the world shall be renewed by
> God, and the heavens shall be folded together,
> and the earth shall be changed, and God shall
> transform men into the similitude of angels,
> and they shall be white as snow; and they
> shall always be employed in the sight of the
> Almighty, and shall make offerings to their
> Lord, and serve Him forever. At the same
> time shall take place that second and public
> resurrection of all, in which the unrighteous
> shall be raised to everlasting punishments.[489]

- *The Last Judgment*

> The resurrection of all the dead... will precede
> the Last Judgment... Then Christ will come
> 'in his glory, and the angels with him... Before
> him will be gathered all the nations, and he will
> separate them one from another'...[490]

The Last Judgment will come when Christ returns in glory. Only the Father knows the day and hour; only he determines the moment of its coming. Then through his Son Jesus Christ he will pronounce the final word on all history.[491]

Thrones were set up and the Ancient One took his throne. His clothing was snow white, and the hair on his head as white as wool; His throne was flames of fire, with wheels of burning fire. A surging stream of fire flowed out from where he sat... The court was convened, and the books were opened.[492]

The heavens will pass away with a mighty roar and the elements will be destroyed by fire, and the earth and everything done on it will be found out.[493]

But fire came down from heaven and consumed them [the Devil, Gog and Magog]... I saw a large white throne and the one who was seated on it. The earth and sky fled from his presence... I saw the dead, the great and the lowly, standing before the throne, and the scrolls were opened. Then another scroll was opened, the book of life. The dead were judged according to their deeds, by what was written in the scrolls. The sea gave up its dead; then Death and Hades gave up their dead. All the dead were judged according to their deeds. Then Death and Hades were thrown into the pool of fire...[494]

- *Consummation of the Heavens and Earth*

> Lightning illumines the world; the earth sees and trembles. The mountains melt like wax before the Lord, before the Lord of all the earth... because of your judgments, O Lord... Light dawns for the just.[495]

> The heavens shall be rolled up like a scroll...[496]

> The Day of the Lord will come like a thief, and then the heavens will pass away with a mighty roar and the elements will be dissolved by fire, and the earth and everything done on it will be found out... But according to his promise we await new heavens and a new earth.[497]

- *New Heavens and New Earth*

> Lo, I am about to create new heavens and a new earth, the things of the past shall not be remembered or come to mind. Instead there shall always be rejoicing and happiness in what I create; For I create Jerusalem to be a joy and its people to be a delight.[498]

> Then I saw a new heaven and a new earth. The former heaven and the former earth had passed away, and the sea was no more. I also saw the holy city, the new Jerusalem, coming out of heaven from God, prepared as a bride adorned for her husband.[499]

For man, this consummation will be the final
realization of the unity of the human race...
Those who are united with Christ will form the
community of the redeemed, 'the holy city' of
God, 'the Bride, the wife of the Lamb.' She will
not be wounded any longer by sin... The visible
universe, then, is... restored to its original state.[500]

But when the thousand years shall be completed,
the world shall be renewed by God, and the
heavens shall be folded together.[501]

In 1459 Pope Pius II condemned the view that the world
would be *naturally destroyed* by the heat of the sun consuming
the humidity of the land and air in such a way that the elements
are set on fire.[502] More recently, Vatican II instead favored the
"transformation" view. In *Lumen Gentium* the Church is described
in its imperfect and changing pilgrim state, which "*will attain its
perfection only in the glory of heaven... then the human race as well
as the entire world will be perfectly re-established in Christ.*"[503] Thus
all that God has created will not end in "destruction" or natural
disaster, but will be *transformed* and *divinized*.

New Heavens and New Earth

The depictions of Revelation 21 and 22 present the New
Jerusalem as a luminous and unblemished city whose gates never
close. Like Mary and the Apostles who behold God face-to-face,
those who enter this heavenly city partake of the beatific vision.
It is in this eternal and perfected kingdom which Christ hands

over to his Father after destroying every ruler and authority that the Lord's elect reign with him. Unlike the New Jerusalem, the "New Heavens and New Earth" is not just the planet earth, but the entire cosmos with all its galactic systems transformed by God for mankind's new modality of existence.

Scripture scholar A. Winklhofer affirms that in man's eternal mode of psychosomatic existence, the universe will become "*directly accessible to man's new sense in its entire being, in all its relationships, in all its intelligible content.*"[504] The renewed universe will reflect the countenance of the Trinity in its omnipresence and omniscience. St. Thomas Aquinas, in his work entitled *Quaestiones Disputatae*, comments on the earth's final transformation and on the duration of its composite substances:

> The sense of the passages quoted (2 Pt 3:10: "The heavens shall pass away"; Lk 21:33: "Heaven and earth will pass away") is not that the substance of the world will perish, but that its outward appearance will vanish according to the Apostle (1 Cor 7:31).[505]

The breathtaking reflections of God in nature will become sublimated, perfected and deified in God to conform to his deified children. Some theologians, such as E.J. Fortman, believe that mountains, valleys, plains, fields, meadows, rivers and seas will assume new forms for the glorified sons and daughters of God, such that their enigmatic "passing away" is correctly understood not as an annihilation but as a transformation. As the dwelling place for the Incarnate Son of God, of the Redeemer not only of man but of the entire universe, the earth will remain in substance and will be received by him in all its beauty. Since God sent his only Son to the world not to condemn but to save it, it follows that he will indeed save it.

The Beatific Mode

As for the sons and daughters of God who possess the earth, they will be the same persons they were in their pilgrim state and yet different—with the same bodies and souls they had in history, yet different. Like Jesus, they will possess material bodies that have been "glorified" to conform to their new modality of existence. Since they retain their humanity, their senses will remain. They will be able to see, hear, taste, smell and feel without being confined to time or space, but in a *"beatific mode"* of existence, "for the kingdom of God is not a matter of food and drink, but of righteousness, peace and joy in the Holy Spirit."[506] Their "spiritual bodies," comprised of glorified bodies and glorified souls, will continue to increase in power. These powers of soul and body may be called paranormal, telepathic, clairvoyant, cognitive, retrocognitive, psycho-kinetic, projective and communicative. They will be impassible and immortal, resplendent, beautiful and radiant with the glorious light of their souls illuminating their bodies. They will compenetrate other bodies of matter at will; and they will be agile, so as to move easily from one place to another, perhaps from one planet to another with the speed of thought.

In contrast to former notions of heaven as a static place of eternal rest and immobility, contemporary theology admits growth and progress in perfection, happiness and beauty throughout eternity. In heaven mobility is admitted on the more human level, for the ongoing human perfections of glorified man. Surely a God who carefully molded the human traits in his only begotten Son, to be assumed and sanctified for man's Redemption, would adopt this standard for the mankind he redeemed. For this reason all bodies rejoined to their souls will continue to admit growth in perfection, even in their perfected state.

The New Jerusalem

At the center of the New Heavens and New Earth is the New Jerusalem, a place one may imagine filled with God's eternal light, singing, rejoicing, in perfect communion with the saints in heaven, who may visit or dwell therein. One of the most fascinating passages in Scripture is St. John's description of the New Jerusalem:

> The earth and the sky fled from his presence and there was no place for them… Then I saw a new heaven and a new earth. The former heaven and the former earth had passed away, and the sea was no more. I also saw the holy city, a new Jerusalem, coming down out of heaven as a bride adorned for her husband. I heard a loud voice from the throne saying, "Behold, God's dwelling is with the human race…" I saw no temple in the city, for its temple is the Lord God almighty and the Lamb… the river of life-giving water sparkling like crystal, flowing from the throne of God and of the Lamb down the middle of its street… Nothing accursed will be found there anymore. The throne of God and of the Lamb will be in it, and his servants shall worship him. Night will be no more, nor will they need light from lamp or the sun.[507]

Interpreters have been impressed by this imagery of the New Jerusalem. W.M. Smith stated that since it is seen coming down from heaven, the New Jerusalem *"is not to be identified with heaven... rather it is part of the new heaven and new earth."*[508] Interestingly, the Old Jerusalem was the religious center of Israel, the city over which the redeemer wept and centered on the temple area where he prayed and taught. If the New Jerusalem merits the name it bears, it must then signify to some degree the religious center where God will be with his people in a very special and eternal way; where there will be no man-made temple but a temple which *"is the Lord God almighty and the Lamb."*[509]

Unlike a static chamber where the dead rest in immobility, heaven emerges in light of recent scholarship as a dynamic dimension with two extensions: the New Jerusalem that stands at the center of the entire cosmos, and the New Heavens and New Earth. These two extensions of God's abode—where his supreme glory and presence are manifest—are created by God for the glory and splendor of creation. The separations of earth and sky, matter and spirit coalesce to form the New Heavens and New Earth, with Christ Jesus as its center. The sublime fusion of the spiritual and material orders welcome the sons of God into its endless regions of uninterrupted and eternal communion with the angels and their Creator.

Characteristics of the New Jerusalem

- *Christ's Eternal Dwelling with Men*

> I heard a loud voice from the throne saying, "Behold, God's dwelling is with the human race. He will dwell with them and they will be

his people and God himself will always be with them"... They will look upon his face... and they shall reign forever and ever.[510]

Jesus answered and said to him... "Amen, amen, I say to you, you will see the sky opened and the angels of God ascending and descending on the Son of Man."[511]

The throne of God and of the Lamb will be in it, and his servants will worship him.[512]

- *Eternal Rest, the Eighth Day*

The followers of Christ would dwell in Jerusalem for a thousand years, and that afterwards the universal and, in short, everlasting resurrection and judgment would take place. To this our Lord himself testified when He said: "They shall neither marry, nor be given in marriage, but shall be equal to the angels, being sons of God, (that is) of the resurrection."[513]

After its thousand years are over, within which period is completed the resurrection of the saints... there will ensue the destruction of the world and the conflagration of all things at the judgment: we shall then be changed in a moment into the substance of angels, even by the investiture of an incorruptible nature, and so be removed to that kingdom in heaven.[514]

But when the thousand years shall be completed, the world shall be renewed by God, and the heavens shall be folded together, and the earth shall be changed, and God shall transform men into the similitude of angels, and they shall be white as snow; and they shall always be employed in the sight of the Almighty, and shall make offerings to their Lord, and serve Him forever.[515]

- *The Garden of Eden Repossessed*

  But these things seduce the wary, who fail to realize that the tree of life which once grew in Paradise has now been made to bloom again... He (Christ) is the first principle, the "tree of life."[516]

  To the victor I will give the right to eat from the tree of life that is in the garden of God.[517]

  On either side of the river grew the tree of life... Blessed are they who have washed their robes so as to have the right to the tree of life...[518]

- *Creation's Freedom*

  Then the wolf shall be a guest of the lamb, and the leopard shall lie down with the kid; the calf and the young lion shall browse together, with a little child to guide them. The cow and the bear shall be neighbors, together their young shall rest; the lion shall eat hay like the ox. The baby shall play by the cobra's den, and the child lay his hand on the adder's lair. There shall be no harm or ruin on my holy mountain...[519]

'The wolves and lambs feed together, and the lion shall eat like the ox, and the serpent shall eat earth like bread. They shall not hurt nor destroy on my holy mountain, saith the Lord...'[520]

All the animals who use the products of the soil will be at peace and in harmony with one another, completely at man's beck and call.[521]

Throughout this time beasts shall not be nourished by blood, nor birds by prey; but all things shall be peaceful and tranquil.[522]

- *Perpetual Light*

No longer shall the sun be your light by day, nor the brightness of the moon shine upon you at night; the Lord will be your light forever... No longer shall your sun go down, or your moon withdraw, for the Lord will be your light forever.[523]

The city had no need of sun or moon to shine on it, for the glory of God gave it light, and its lamp was the Lamb.[524]

Night will be no more, nor will they need light

from lamp or sun, for the Lord God shall give them light, and they shall reign forever and ever.[525]

The city had no need of sun or moon to shine on it, for the glory of God gave it light...nor will they need light from lamp or sun, for the Lord God shall give them light and they shall reign forever and ever.[526]

He will change the sun and the moon and the stars.[527]

- *Infused Knowledge*

All your sons shall be taught by the Lord...[528]

I will place my law within them, and write it upon their hearts... No longer will they need to teach their friends and kinsmen how to know the Lord. All, from the least to the greatest, shall know me, says the Lord...[529]

It is written in the prophets: "They shall all be taught by God."[530]

And they shall not teach their fellow citizens or brothers, saying, "Know the Lord," for all shall know me, from the least to the greatest.[531]

- *Terminating Point of the Sacramental Economy*

Until there is realized new heavens and new

earth...the pilgrim Church, in her Sacraments and institutions, which belong to this present age, carry the mark of this world which will pass...[532]

I am with you always, until the end of the age.[533]

For as often as you eat this bread and drink the cup, you proclaim the death of the Lord until he comes.[534]

- *Sin's Defeat*

See that we shall then indeed sanctify it when we enjoy true repose... because we have been made just ourselves and shall have received the promise, when there is no more sin, but all things have been made new by the Lord.[535]

God is preparing a new dwelling place and a new earth, where justice will reign (cf. 2 Cor. 5:1; 2 Pt 3:13)... Then, with death defeated... what had been sown in weakness and corruption will be clothed with incorruptibility (cf. 1 Cor. 15:42.53)... and this whole creation made by God for our sake will be freed from the bondage of vanity (cf. Rom. 8:9-21)...cleansed of all sin, illuminated and transfigured, when Christ will hand over to the Father an eternal and universal Kingdom.[536]

When we have come to know the true God,

both our bodies and souls will be immortal and incorruptible. Friends of God and coheirs with Christ, we shall be subject to no evil desires or inclinations, or to have any affliction of the body or soul, for we shall have become divine.[537]

• *Death's Defeat*

And again another prophet says: "...And there was a river flowing on the right hand, and beautiful trees grew of it, and whoever shall eat of them shall live forever"... This means: Whoever hears these things spoken and believes shall live forever.[538]

We shall then be changed in a moment into the substance of angels, even by the investiture of an incorruptible nature, and so be removed to that kingdom in heaven.[539]

The Lord shall come in his majesty, and all his angels with him, (Mt 25:31) and, death having been destroyed, all things shall be subject to him (1 Cor. 15:26-27).[540]

...and there shall be no more death.[541]

As humankind enters the third Christian millennium, it will witness an explosion of mystical gifts, particularly that of "Living in the Divine Will." By means of this most powerful gift that elevates man's internal powers to God's continuously eternal activity, all creation will be set free from its former slavery to corruption and enjoy the glorious freedom of the sons of God. This liberating process of man and the cosmos introduces God's sons and daughters to the splendor of creation, where a 'new Pentecost' will assist his creatures to live in harmony and in holiness. If God chose to actualize this gift in recent years for the sake of presenting to himself a 'holy and immaculate' Church, many of the early Church Fathers and Doctors have foretold it, and several approved modern mystics have internalized it. It is a gift for the asking for those of you who are seeking holiness. To receive this incredible gift all you have to do is follow four simple steps: 1) *desire it*; 2) *know it*; 3) *grow in its virtue*; 4) *live it*.

Chapter 6

THE FOUR EASY STEPS
TO LIVING IN THE DIVINE WILL

To prepare oneself for the approaching, breathtaking era of peace and the New Heavens and New Earth, it is fitting that we should explore the steps leading up to possession of the gift that admits us to these celestial realities. The gift of Living in the Divine Will not only prepares us for the bright future that awaits us, it enables us to partake of the future in the eternal now. Earlier I gave evidence to support the reception of this gift through the *eternal mode* that brings the past, present and future to a single point. Now, for all practical purposes, I show that it is quite simple to receive this gift through four easy steps: These steps are as follows: 1) *desire*; 2) *knowledge*; 3) *growth in virtue*; 4) *life*.

Step 1: Desire

In the approved writings of the Church's mystics Jesus makes it abundantly clear that *desire* is the most important ingredient to *enter into* and to *live in* God's Divine Will. Since it is ultimately the Holy Spirit that enables the human creature to desire and to correspond to God's will, *knowledge* of his will occupies an ancillary role. Let us take for example the particular knowledge of Luisa

Piccarreta's writings on the Divine Will. While the knowledge of Luisa's writings is valuable, it does not per se *actualize* the Divine Will in the soul of the human creature. One can glean from the magisterial documents that the Spirit of God actualizes his gifts in the soul of human creature. Certainly knowledge of the inspired writings of Luisa and other recent mystics occupies an important role in the penetration and development of God's gifts, but without *desire*, such knowledge is of little or no value. It is only when the soul, literate or illiterate, learned or unlearned *desires* to live in God's will that the entrance to the new mystical way has taken place. And as the soul more earnestly desires to live in God's will, the more his will unfolds, where time and eternity unify in the sanctification of mankind and the entire cosmos. Living in the Divine Will is a mystical phenomenon that sometimes surpasses human sensory experience and eternally unifies the creature with the Creator. Jesus tells Luisa all that is required to obtain the gift of Living in the Divine Will is that the human creature offer its will entirely to God with a firm *desire*:

> While I was thinking about the Holy Divine Will, my sweet Jesus said to me: "My daughter, to enter into My Will there are neither paths, nor doors, nor keys, because My Will is found everywhere. It runs beneath the feet, to the right and to the left, over the head, everywhere. The creature does nothing other than remove the pebble of her will... This is because the pebble of her will impedes My Will from flowing in her... If the soul removes the pebble of her will, *in that same instant* she flows in Me, and I in her. She finds all of My goods at her disposition: light, strength, help, and

– 224 –

all that she wants. That is why there are neither paths, nor doors, nor keys. *It is enough that she desires it, and everything is done!*[542]

Step 2: Knowledge

The particular knowledge we encounter in the writings of recent mystics on Living in the Divine Will attracts and disposes the human creature to a continuous, transforming union with God. Yet what directly motivates, actualizes, and perpetuates the human will in God's will is the *Holy Spirit*, the sanctifier, who, attracted by our *desire*, "helps us in our weakness" by pleading in us "with sighs too deep for words." I here recall St. Augustine's teaching:

> There is then within us a kind of *instructed ignorance*, instructed, that is, by the Spirit of God who helps our weakness… the Apostle said:… "the Spirit helps us in our weakness; *we do not know what it is right to pray for, but the Spirit himself pleads with sighs too deep for words. He who searches hearts knows what the Spirit means, for he pleads for the saints according to God's will… he does it to enable you to know.*[543]

Undoubtedly particular knowledge is an effective *means* to attract and dispose us to Live in the Divine Will, but the absence of such knowledge does not keep us from experiencing this magnificent gift. And this is good news! By the power of the Holy Spirit who prays, sighs and pleads in the souls of the faithful, we can immediately receive the *desire* to obtain whatever gifts God wishes to grant us, in particular, the gift of the Divine Will. Now, the more we grow in the *knowledge* of God's gifts, the more we can appreciate them, correspond to them and live them. In this sense, knowledge is an integral means and ingredient to Living in the Divine Will.

Step 3: Virtue

In order for the creature to "Live" in God's Divine Will, that is to remain in it without ever leaving, the creature must perfect its *desire continuously*. To do this, it sets out to inform its mind with sound spiritual teaching that will foster a greater awareness of God's will, which will, in turn, set its will ablaze with love for him and for all creation. As the creature draws continuous enlightenment from God's revealed word, it seeks to prove its love in exchange for all that God has bestowed on it by continuous confirmations of desire. The creature confirms its desire through the development of the Christian virtues. Here we encounter the words of St. Hannibal di Francia, who captures the essential human ingredient for remaining in the Divine Will:

> In order to form, with this new science, saints who may surpass those of the past, the new Saints *must also have all the virtues, and in heroic degree, of ancient Saints* – of the Confessors, of the Penitents, of the Martyrs, of the Anachorists, of the Virgins, etc.[544]

Jesus confirms this teaching to Venerable Conchita:

> Once transformation into Jesus is brought about, the Holy Spirit also becomes the spirit of the creature raised to a more or less higher degree

according to the intensity and amplitude of transformation, *which strictly depends on the growth of the soul in virtue.*[545]

Hence the more one develops the Christian virtues the more the Divine Will expands in that individual. Needless to say, this stability in virtue is grounded in a lifestyle of prayer and work, like that of the saints of old. A life of prayer may include a varied form of pious practices such as meditation, spiritual reading, discursive and contemplative prayer, fasting, abstinence, which, in turn, compliment a life of work.

As the creature exchanges love with its Creator, no sooner does it realize its awfully *finite* character of love, than it turns to its Creator to take from him his *infinite* love that embraces heaven and earth and every act of every creature in time and in eternity, in order to fuse itself within his divine and eternal being. In this way the creature and the Creator form *one* synergetic action in two distinct but inseparable wills. And if the human creature's will remains free to break from God's eternal will to commit sin, its stability in God's divine virtue disposes it to refrain from doing so. The creature's virtues, under the influence of the Holy Spirit, have faithfully reared and trained it to *Live* in the Divine Will with a continuous respect and with a holy fear.

Step 4: Life

The more the union of wills increases between Creator and creature, the more graces and wonders the creature discovers while advancing in unending degrees of holiness. The advancement in one single degree of holiness is a new life of grace that only eternity can fathom – so incredible is its achievement. It is the life of the blessed internalized on earth ordered to exponential growth. To *Live* in the Divine Will is to live eternity on earth, it is to mystically traverse the present laws of time and space, it is the human soul's ability to simultaneously trilocate into the past, the present and the future, while influencing every act of every creature and fusing them in God's eternal embrace! Initially most souls will often enter and exit the Divine Will until they arrive at *stability in virtue*. Yet it is this stability in divine virtue that will help them to participate *continuously* in the Divine Will, which defines *Living* in the Divine Will.

As for the date of our permanent entry in the Divine Will, though God seldom reveals this date to his creatures, he reassures us that at the moment when we possess a continuously 'upright intention' and 'firm desire' to live in his will, that is by all standards the most fitting day when we Live in the Divine Will.

May we strive to live the greatest gift God has given humankind in these days preceding the universal era of peace. May we immerse ourselves in God's eternal life in order to become Living Tabernacles of the Eucharistic Jesus. It is a gift that is ours for the asking, and all we have to do is *desire it, know it, grow in its virtue, and live it.*

Chapter 7

MAGISTERIUM AND MILLENARIANISM

U ntil recently, most patristic teachings on the era of peace were dismissed as heresy and associated with *millenarianism*. But thanks to recent scholarship, what had once appeared fragmentary and incomplete has re-emerged as a coherent doctrine in the synthesis of Church teaching. In this final chapter we will discover the underpinnings of the Church's official position on *millenarianism* to distinguish it from the orthodox writings of several early Church Fathers, Doctors and mystics.

Apropos of the Church's official position, it is imperative to distinguish the *extraordinary* from the *ordinary Magisterium*. The Vicar of Christ on earth—the Roman pontiff alone—exercises the *extraordinary Magisterium*. The exercise of this gift, freely bestowed by Christ is exercised *ex Cathedra* (from the Bishop of Rome's St. John Lateran Cathedral) on revelations and issues of morals and faith. [197] The *ordinary Magisterium* is the episcopal sharing of this gift. Though the college of bishops may *"participate"* in the exercise of the pontiff's supreme gift of infallibility through a sharing in his singular authority, their authority depreciates when divorced from it. The laity, for their part, are required to lend loyal respect to both the pope and the bishops in union with him.[546] Whence the Magisterium emerges as the teaching office of the Catholic Church expressed through the pope and college of bishops to enlighten its members on God's revealed truths.

The Magisterium condemned the teachings of *millenarianism* on several counts for its unrefined interpretation of Scripture:

> Pope Zephyrinus in 217 declared the millenarian doctrines of Montanus to be heretical.

> On St. Augustine's authority, the Council of Ephesus (431) condemned belief in millenarianism as a superstitious aberration.[547]

> Augustine had stated the following: "But as they [carnal millenarians] assert that those who then rise again shall enjoy the leisure of immoderate carnal banquets, furnished with an amount of meat and drink such as not only to shock the feeling of the temperate, but even to surpass the measure of credulity itself, such assertions can be believed only by the carnal. They who believe them are called by the spiritual Chiliasts, which we may reproduce by the name of Millenarians..."[548]

> The Magisterium and Pope Pius XI declared that "the Church has rejected even modified forms of the falsification of the Kingdom to come under the name of millenarianism, especially the

'intrinsically perverse' political form of a secular messianism."[549]

Pope Pius XII and the Holy See stated that millenarianism may not be sustained even in its mild form: "The system of mitigated Millenarianism, which teaches that Christ the Lord will come visibly to this earth to rule..." cannot be safely taught.[550]

"Spiritual millenarianism" was formally declared as being in opposition to the teachings of the symbols of the faith, for in the prospect of Matthew 16:27: "Filius hominis venturus est in gloria Patris sui cum Angelis, tunc reddet unicuique secundum opera sua" (For the Son of man will come with his Angels in his Father's glory, and then he will repay everyone according to his conduct). Christ cannot come in the Father's glory unless with the scope of requiting each individual according to his deeds.[551]

Question: What must one think regarding the system of mitigated Millenarianism, which teaches that Christ the Lord, before the final judgment — whether or not it precedes the resurrection of the majority of the righteous — will come visibly to reign on this earth? [Qu.: Quid sentiendum de systemate Millenarismi mitigati, docentis scilicet Christum Dominum ante finale iudicium, sive praevia sive non praevia plurium *iustorum resurrectione, visibiliter in hanc terram regnandi causa esse venturum?]*

Response (confirmed by the Holy Father, 20 July 1944): The system of mitigated Millenarianism cannot be safely taught. [*Resp. (confirmata a Summo Pontifice, 20 Iul.): Systema Millenarismi mitigati tuto doceri non posse.*][552]

Pope Paul VI briefly touched upon the misleading notion of a sensual or carnal millenarianism.[553]

Contained in these magisterial anathemas are several nuances, all of which depict an earthly kingdom imbibed with pleasures ranging from the flesh to the spirit. One might wonder what constitutes the *millenarian doctrines of Montanus?* What is its *mild form?* What is *spiritual millenarianism?* What is *modified millenarianism?*

To begin, millenarianism at its birth was swiftly nipped in the bud. In its early stages it was a relatively simplistic and conspicuous doctrine: Christ will *reign on earth*, in the *flesh*, for *a thousand years*, and will revel with his saints in *immoderate carnal banquets* replete with foods and drinks of all imaginable species. The immediate images this generates are understandably mind-boggling. Since we are still in the nascent stage of Christian doctrine, this utopian hedonism was denounced by St. Augustine and the early corpus of faithful Christians, and later formally condemned at the Council of Ephesus. As we have seen, it was a heresy that was attributed to the early Jewish converts to the Christian faith who, perhaps being accustomed to dependency on an oral tradition, misinterpreted the allegories of Sacred Scripture:

> The text of the Apocalypse conveys with utmost discretion the happiness of the elect during the thousand year reign. Whereas the Hebrew exegesis and literal millenarianism describe such paradisal happiness with bizarre imagery.[554]

The ecclesiastically revered Catholic theologian Jean Daniélou, provides additional information on the Judaic misinterpretation of Scripture while acknowledging the elements in Tradition that favor the Fathers' teachings on the era of peace:

> *Millenarianism, the belief that there will be an earthly reign of the Messiah before the end of the time, is the Jewish-Christian doctrine which has aroused and continues to arouse more argument than any other.* The reason for this, however, is probably a failure to distinguish between the various elements of doctrine. On the one hand, it seems hard to deny that *it contains a truth which is a part of the stock of the Christian teaching,* and which occurs in the New Testament, in I-II Thessalonians, in I Corinthians, and in the Revelation of John... *It implies a period of time, the duration of which is unknown to men...* I-II Thessalonians show that it was the belief of Christians in Greece, since Paul is content merely to add some precision in detail, and assumes that his correspondents were expecting this earthly reign of Christ. Moreover,

the doctrine underlies the various developments to be found in the Revelation of John. The essential affirmation is of *an intermediate stage in which the risen saints are still on earth and have not yet entered their final stage, for this is one of the aspects of the mystery of the last days which has yet to be revealed.*[555]

The newborn heresy known by the early Christian community as *Chiliasm*, and later *millenarianism*, would continue to assume doctrinal nuances and the following titles: *carnal millenarianism, gross* or *crass millenarianism, radical millenarianism, mundane millenarianism, secular millenarianism, false millenarianism, mitigated millenarianism, modified millenarianism* and *spiritual millenarianism.*

Let us begin with the first heresy of *Chiliasm*. Chiliasm, from the Greek *kiliàs* (1,000), was the name given to the belief that the 1,000 years mentioned in St. John's Book of Revelation is to be read in the literal sense only. When Latin began to exercise its influence over the Christian-speaking world, Chiliasm became known as *millenarianism*, from Latin *mille* (1,000). It professed the belief that Christ would soon *return to earth* to reign *visibly*, in the *flesh* and with his saints for *literally* 1,000 years. Those who held these beliefs were called *Millenarians* and are divided into two camps. While both camps believe in an historic tribulation and rapture, one group places the rapture before the tribulation (*Premillenarians*), and the other group immediately after (*Postmillenarians*).

The succeeding centuries brought with it an infiltration of their beliefs into many religions, predominating much of the 19th century thinking in the Church of the Mormons, Adventists and Jehovah Witnesses, but were countered by an extreme reaction in the opposite direction. The *Amillenarians* espoused the errors of Amillenarianism that stemmed from the Missouri Synod Lutheran Church, the Christian Reformed Church, the Orthodox Presbyterian Church and the Reformed Presbyterian Church.[556] Not only did the *Amillenarians* disavow belief in the Pre- and Postmillenarians' literal views of biblical eschatology, they denied and opposed the possibility of the magisterial "historic period of triumphant Christianity." Needless to say, the Magisterium condemned their beliefs due to faulty interpretations of the 20th chapter of the Book of Revelation. As Millenarianism continued to gain notoriety under various forms, it became enmeshed in the thought of many new Christian movements.

Millenarianism was soon presented in its most gross display. By placing *matter* over *spirit* it became identified as a 1,000-year reign of surfeited materialism. A Gnostic adherent by the name of Cerinthus was the chief proponent of this jaded spirituality that flourished toward the end of the first century. According to the school of Cerinthus, Christ would *return to earth* to reign *visibly* and in the *flesh* with his resurrected saints amid *immoderate banquets* for *literally* 1,000 years. Not long thereafter Cerinthus' teachings were condemned as a form of *carnal, gross* and *radical millenarianism*. Worthy of mention is St. Augustine's condemnation of *carnal* millenarianism, which stems from its hedonistic interpretation of the same chapter of Revelation.

Saint Jerome condemned the next form of millenarianism in his commentary on Isaiah 66, where he explains the proper way of interpreting the millennium the *Ebionites* misunderstood.

The Ebionites were a heretical sect known chiefly in Palestine from the 1ˢᵗ to the 4ᵗʰ centuries that sprouted from early Jewish communities. Having conserved much of the Judaic practice and its literal biblical method, it interpreted the 1,000-year prophecy in the Book of Revelation in a *strictly secular sense*. It initially held that Jesus would return in the *flesh* vested in royal garb befitting a King to bring prosperity to the human race. Eventually, their Judaic beliefs devolved into a form of Gnosticism, which the early Fathers "spotted immediately and endeavored to eliminate."[557]

The next group to make a public debut was the *Montanists*. About 170 A.D., Montanus founded a heretical sect, which based its belief on the conviction that the millenary kingdom had already begun, and that the heavenly Jerusalem had descended upon the Phrygian borough of Pepuza (Asia Minor). Unlike their predecessors who sought their reward in carnal banquets, the Montanists awaited purely "spiritual pleasures." Hence their view of the flesh as a mere warring instrument against the spirit, subject to *bizarre rigorism* and *extreme asceticism*, as the spirit anxiously awaited the Great Day of the Lord. And when the Lord descended in the *flesh*, he was expected to inaugurate the millenary kingdom, the "kingdom of the Spirit." Though formally condemned by Pope Zephyrinus, the Montanist heresy prepared the groundwork for Jansenism 15 centuries later.[558]

It is worthy of mention that the "spiritual blessings" of which the Church Fathers speak do not resemble the "spiritual pleasures" of the Montanists. For one thing, the Fathers never encourage extreme violence to the body in expectation of a physical descent of Christ to a determinate locale for literally 1,000 years. Secondly, the Fathers' biblical allegories refer to the spiritual blessings as effects of the dispensation of the baptismal grace procured by the shedding of the Blood of Christ, which sanctifies and strengthens both body and soul. St. Thomas Aquinas provides a timely commentary on these spiritual blessings: *"The quoted text [Jer 31:38] refers not to the carnal but to the spiritual Israel."*[559]

Apollinaris of Alexandria introduced millenarianism to the 4th century. Church writers of the 4th century tell us that in addition to teaching that Christ had no human intellect, and that his flesh was of one substance with his divinity, Apollinaris caused millenarianism to spread throughout Alexandria and its neighboring countries.

In the 16th century, Protestantism ushered in a new epoch of millenarian doctrines. It promoted the belief in a new golden age under Christ, wherein the Papacy would be overthrown along with its secular empires. In 1534, the Protestant movement, known as the Anabaptists, set up the "new kingdom of Zion" as a prelude to the new kingdom to come. Increasingly aware of the inherent dangers to their cause, the Lutherans refused to come to their aid, despite their call for assistance.

With the dawn of the 17th and 18th centuries, new apocalyptic trends emerged. In certain countries, such as Germany, France and England, *Pietism* became increasingly fashionable in Protestant circles. Jacob Spener who sought to awaken dormant Protestantism through an increased and intensified prayer life began pietism in the late 17th century. Eventually it degenerated into strange forms of apocalyptic beliefs. Eva Buttlar preached a *spiritual* millenarian doctrine that regressed into the old, hedonistic heresy of *carnal* millenarianism, which the Labadists, in turn, adopted.

In the 19th century, United States millenarian groups proliferated, usually based on the Books of Daniel and Revelation and sometimes reinforced by private revelations. Spearheading these groups were William Miller and Ellen G. White (Seventh-Day Adventists), Joseph Smith (Mormons), Charles T. Russell (Jehovah Witnesses) and their disciples. In some evangelical groups sharp divisions arose between *Premillenarians* and *Postmillenarians*: the former held that Christ's second coming in the flesh would end all evils and inaugurate the golden age of the Church; the latter that the golden age would come, not from Christ's second coming, but from a gradual transformation by natural progress and religious reform.

Pietistic doctrines were soon introduced within Catholic circles. The rebirth of the old heresy of *Chiliasm* would now go by the new titles of *mitigated, modified* and *spiritual millenarianism*. This heresy is easily distinguishable from its predecessors by the exclusion of inordinate carnal indulgences (Cerinthians and Ebionites) and total carnal abstinence (Montanists). Hence the titles *mitigated, modified* and *spiritual*. Much like the Chiliasts, the Pietists believed that before the General Judgment Christ would descend to a geographical location on earth where he would remain in the *flesh* and reign *visibly* for 1,000 years. He would not, however, participate in immoderate carnal banquets, nor were his followers required to abuse their bodies.

In opposition to the teachings of the Millenarians, the early Fathers preached a prolonged period of triumphant Christianity symbolized by 1,000 years. Jean Daniélou defines this future, historic event that "contains a truth which is a part of the stock of the Christian teaching," as an *"intermediate stage in which the risen saints are still on earth and have not yet entered their final stage, for this is one of the aspects of the mystery of the last days which has yet to be revealed."*[560] If indeed a future, intermediate stage forms part of the stock of the Christian teaching, it cannot be identified with the millenarian teachings that foretell an historic, definitive and corporeal reign of Christ on this earth. The Church's teachings in this regard are clear:

> Pope Pius XII and the Holy See stated that millenarianism may not be sustained even in its mild form: *"The system of mitigated Millenarianism, which teaches that Christ the Lord will come visibly to this earth to rule..."* cannot be safely taught.[561]

> "Spiritual millenarianism" was formally declared as being in opposition to the teachings of the symbols of the faith, for in the prospect of Matthew 16:27: "For the Son of man will come with his Angels in his Father's glory, and then he will repay everyone according to his conduct." *Christ cannot come in the Father's glory unless with the scope of requiting each individual according to his deeds.*[562]

Since the era of peace is principally characterized by a spiritual reign of Jesus in souls, one cannot postulate theories of him definitively reigning on earth in his Person or in the flesh. The Septuagint text of the Bible (Greek translation), as well as other sources of Tradition affirm Christ's personal reign from above:[563]

> Show yourself *over* the heavens, God; may your glory appear *above all the earth.* [564]

> Some Catholic Scholars believe that the 'thousand years' is a figure of speech for a long period of time before the end of the world, when the Church will enjoy a great peace and *Christ will reign over the souls of men.* All the just who live during this time have a first resurrection. [565]

> The Divine Mercy will triumph *over the whole world* and will be worshipped by *all souls...* Today, I saw the Sacred Host of Jesus, in the midst of a great brilliance. The rays were issuing forth from the wound [in his side] and *spreading out over the entire world.* [566]

Although the Church had never condemned the eschatological teachings of the early Fathers, she expressly forbad the teachings of *mitigated, modified or spiritual millenarianism.* In a formal declaration issued by the Holy See, the Church had stifled once and for any potential heretical revivals of the past: *"The system of mitigated Millenarianism cannot be safely taught."* [567] This second condemnation of 1944 formally rejected all ideas that advocate a carnal, historic and definitive reign of Christ on earth before the Final Judgment. [568]

The reason Christ cannot return to earth in the flesh and in human history stems from the Church's teaching, which associates the *end* of human history with Christ's return to earth in the flesh. [569] History's terminating point signals the end of three principal themes:

a) God's providential action and the various phases of the divine plan in relation to the human race as contained in revelation; b) man's free response to the divine action; and c) the struggle between the forces of good and evil, grace and sin, God and Satan. St. Augustine has much to offer in this regard. The Church esteems his exposition on human history as an authoritative and theological pedagogy. His vast yet simple concept describes "Two Loves" building two cities or two commonwealths, which exist side by side as invisible protagonists from the beginning to the end of history, *"both locked in conflict and competition throughout the ages and providing the dynamic historical development until the issue shall be decided between them, in the grand denouement of the Parousia, the Last Judgment, and the triumph of Christ and the Church."*[570] Although man's pilgrim state will come to an end and history will cease, man himself will not cease to be. Man will continue to glorify God in his body long after history is ended in the eternal, New Jerusalem and the New Heavens and New Earth.

In conclusion, after the heresy of millenarianism spun off of the orthodox teachings of the Apostles and early Church Fathers, Eusebius the historian and scores of academics misinterpreted these teachings and attributed the errors of millenarianism to the Fathers themselves. The medieval epoch, in turn, stripped the Augustinian treatment of the era of its three-fold presentation, and poor hermeneutical scholarship removed this treatment from Catholic literature. A brief review of the threefold objective of hermeneutics reveals the extent of this injustice.

Catholic Hermeneutic Principles

The first objective governing proper interpretation of Scripture is called *noematics* (from Greek *nòema*): to determine the nature of the different kinds of the biblical methods (i.e., historical, literal, allegorical, moral, which God, the principal author of the text, intends to express through the words written by the sacred writer, the secondary author); the second is called *heuristics* (from Greek *eurìsko*): to establish the interpretation of the text; and finally the third is *prophoristics* (from Greek *propsèro*): to find the most convenient way of proposing, according to the various aptitudes of the readers, the true sense of the text.[571] Given this framework, it is easy to acknowledge the errors of those who failed to disclose the true meaning of the Fathers' texts. Since the Fathers' allegories were interpreted literally, the intended sense of their texts was neither determined (noematics) nor established (heuristics) for the readers' understanding (prophoristics).

In short, the Church's condemnations were never directed toward the Fathers' eschatology, but toward all forms of literal and faulty interpretations of the millennium of the Book of Revelation. The Catholic Encyclopedia states, *"millenarianism is that thought which stems from a too literal, incorrect, and faulty interpretation of Chapter 20 of the Book of Revelation... This can only be understood in a spiritual sense..."*[572]

May the information I have provided in this book, particularly in this chapter, restore to those early Church Fathers that foretold an era of peace their rightful place among orthodox Christian literature. May it forever remove the stigma of millenarianism from their teachings and rehabilitate their names. Many early Church Fathers, Doctors and mystics have consistently foretold an era of peace and great Christian holiness, thereby giving evidence to support the position that this teaching is part and parcel of the Church's Tradition. It began with Christ, was faithfully transmitted by his apostles and carefully handed down to us. Let us therefore join creation with eager longing for that day when we will all be set free from our slavery to corruption, and exclaim, "*Thy kingdom come, Thy Will be done on earth as it is heaven.*"

PROPHECIES OF ROMAN PONTIFFS ON THE ERA OF PEACE

*I*t will at length be possible that our many wounds be healed and all justice spring forth again with the hope of restored authority; that the splendors of peace be renewed, and the swords and arms drop from the hand and when all men shall acknowledge the empire of Christ and willingly obey His word, and every tongue shall confess that the Lord Jesus is in the Glory of the Father.[585]

—*Pope Leo XIII*

Should anyone ask us for a sign… We will give this one and no other: "To re-establish all things in Christ." This great perversity may be the foretaste and perhaps the beginning of those great evils reserved for the last days…. In very truth, we cannot think otherwise…In the very moment when man, under the delusion of his triumph shall break the heads of his enemies, then all may know that God is King of all the earth. When human respect is banished and prejudices and doubts dispelled, great numbers will be won over to Christ. These (converts) in turn will become promoters of His knowledge and love, the road to true and lasting happiness.

When in every city and village God's law is faithfully observed, reverence shown for sacred things, the sacraments frequented and the ordinances of a Christian life carried out, then... we need labor no further in re-establishing all things in Christ... When we arrive at this state of affairs, the wealthy classes will be more just and charitable to the lowly, and the latter will be capable of bearing with more tranquility and patience the trials of a very hard lot. Then citizens will not follow lust... but law... Then reverence and love... a sacred duty towards those who govern... What more can be expected?... The Church must enjoy full liberty.[586]

—*Pope Pius X*

"And they shall hear my voice, and there shall be one fold and one shepherd." May God... shortly bring to fulfillment His prophecy for transforming this consoling vision of the future into a present reality... It is God's task to bring about this happy hour and to make it known to all... When it does arrive, it will turn out to be a solemn hour, one big with consequences not only for the restoration of the Kingdom of Christ, but for the pacification of... the world. We pray most fervently, and ask others likewise to pray for this much-desired pacification of society...[587]

—*Pope Pius XI*

Prophecy order, tranquility and peace, peace, peace for this world of ours, which although seemingly seized by a murderous and suicidal armament folly still yearns for peace, in any event and together with us, confidently asks the God of Peace for it.[588]

—*Pope Pius XI*

Man's cause is not only not lost, it is secure. The great ideas which are the guiding lights of the modern world shall be achieved. The dignity of the human person shall be recognized not only formally but effectively... Unworthy social inequalities shall be overcome. Relationships between peoples shall be peaceful, reasonable and fraternal. Neither egoism... shall impede the establishment of a true human order, a common good and a new civilization. Neither misery nor the loss of goals attained, nor sorrow nor sacrifice nor temporal death shall be able to be abolished. But every human misery shall be able to have assistance and comfort. It shall even know that higher value which our secret can confer on every human weakness. Hope will not be extinguished because of the inner power of this secret which in fact is not a secret for anyone which is listening to us today. You understand it. It is the secret which we speak, it is the Easter message.[589]

—*Pope Paul VI*

ABOUT THE AUTHOR

D̲r̲. Joseph L. Iannuzzi is a doctoral alumnus of the Gregorian Pontifical University. He has obtained 5 post-graduate degrees with studies that include medicine, music, anthropology, sociology, philosophy, and theology.

An accomplished violinist and wrestler, Joseph travelled to an international Marian sanctuary where he was inspired to enter the seminary. Subsequently, he obtained a BA in Philosophy and was awarded the Kilburn Award. After having obtaining a B.A. in theology with honors from the Pontifical University for the Catholic Missions (Pontifical Urbaniana University), he was ordained and asked to assist in parishes in Italy and the USA.

Fr. Joseph pursued his licentiate *summa cum laude* and doctorate *magum cum laude* in Sacred Theology at the Gregorian Pontifical University with theses respectively entitled, *"The Eschatology of the Early Church Fathers"* and *"The Gift of Living in the Divine Will in the Writings of the Servant of God Luisa Piccarreta – An Inquiry into the Early Ecumenical Councils, and into Patristic and Scholastic and Contemporary Theology"*. In the academic year of his licentiate, he was one of four selected students to receive a grant from the Pontifical Biblicum University of Rome to study theology in Israel.

Fr. Joseph has appeared on EWTN and was host of several television and national radio programs. He has translated numerous theological works into English, is the author of twenty publications on mysticism, revelation and prophecy, and is the theological consultant in the causes of the Beatification of several mystics.

BIBLIOGRAPHY

Altaner, Berthold. *Patrology*, Herder and Herder, NY, 1961.

Aquinas, Thomas. *La Somma Teologica*, edizione Studio Domenicano, Bologna, 1985.

Aquinas, Thomas. *Quaestiones Disputatae*, Vol. II De Potentia, Marietti, Roma, Italy, 1965.

Aquinas, Thomas. *Summa Theologica*, Benzinger Bros., NY, 1947.

Aquinas, Thomas. *Summa Theologica*, editio quarta, Lethielleux, Paris, 1939.

Augustine of Hippo. *De Civitate Dei* [*The City of God*], Catholic University of America Press, Washington, 3rd Printing, 1977.

Bélanger, Blessed Dina. *The Autobiography of Blessed Dina Bélanger*, translated by Mary St. Stephen, R.J.M., 1997.

Bellarmine, Robert. *De Romano Pontefice*, Neapoli, apud Josephum Giuliano, 1856.

Bernard of Clairvaux. "Adventu Domini," *Opera Omnia*, Edit. Cisterc. 4, 1966.

Bianchi, Enzo. "Chaghiga," *La Festa Escatologica*, Edizioni Qiqajon, Monastero di, Bose, Italy, 1996.

Cabrera de Armida, Venerable Concepciòn. *To My Priests [A Mis Sacerdotes]*, Archangel Crusade of Love, Cleveland, OH, 1996.

Ciszek, Father Walter. *He Leadeth Me*, Ignatius Press, San Francisco, 1995.

Congar, Yves. *The Meaning of Tradition*, Hawthorn Books, NY, 1964.

Congar, Yves. *Tradition and Traditions*, translated by M. Naseby and T. Rainborough, Macmillan, NY, 1967.

Coyle, Kevin J. *Augustine's "Millenarianism" Reconsidered*, Augustinus 38, 1993.

Delumeau, J. *Mille ans de bonheur. Une histoire du paradis*, Paris, 1995.

De Montfort, St. Louis Grignion, *True Devotion to Mary*, Rockford, IL Tan Books, 1985.

Denzinger, Heinrich. *Enchiridion Symbolorum*, cura di Johannes B. Umberg SJ, 1951.

Denzinger, Heinrich. *Enchiridion Symbolorum*, definitionum et declarationum de rebus fidei et morum, cura di Peter Hünermann, Barcinone, Herder Pub., 1965 [ed. Dehoniane Bologna 1995].

Dubay, Thomas. *Fire Within*, Ignatius Press, Colorado, 1989.

Dulaey, M. "L'Apocalypse, Augustin et Tyconius," *St. Augustine et la Bible*, a cura di A.M. la Bonnardière, Paris, 1986.

Emmerich, Anne Catherine. *The Life of Christ*, Tan Books, Rockfort, IL, 1968.

Fitzmeyer, J.A. *Jerome Biblical Commentary*, Prentice-Hall, Engelwood Cliffs, NJ, 1968.

Fortman, E.J., S.J. *Everlasting Life after Death*, Alba House, NY, 1976.

Grita, Vera. *Opera di TabernacoliViventi (Living Tabernacles)*, translated by Rev. Joseph L. Iannuzzi, a cura di Giuseppina e Liliana Grita, Edizioni Segno, Udine, Italy, 1989.

Herbert, Albert J. S.M. *Signs, Wonders and Response*, LA, 1988.

Hippolytus, *The Fragments from Commentaries on Various Books of Scripture*, in "The Anti-Nicene Fathers," Vol. V authorized edition, WM. B. Eerdmans Publishing Company, Grand Rapids, MI, 1978.

Hulsbisch, A., O.S.A. *God in Creation and Evolution*, translated by Martin Versfeld, Sheed and Ward, NY, 1965.

Irenaeus of Lyons. "Adversus Haereses," *The Fathers of the Church*, CIMA Publishing Co., NY, 1947.

Jerome. *De Viris Illustribus*, Sansoni, Firenze, 1964.

John of the Cross. *The Collected Works of St. John of the Cross*, translated by Kieran Kavanuagh, O.C.D. and Otilio Rodriguez, O.C.D., ICS Publications Institute of Carmelite Studies, Washington, D.C., 1991.

John Paul II, "Letter on the Centenary of the Rogationist Fathers," in

L'Osservatore Romano, Vatican City, English ed., July 9, 1997.

John Paul II. "Novo Millennio Inuente," http://www.ewtn.com/library/PAPALDOC/JP2MIL3.HTM.

John Paul II. *Prayers and Devotions*, translated by Firman O'Sullivan. (Pope John Paul II, *Prayers and Devotions*, translated by Firman O'Sullivan, December 20 Advent Mediation by Pope John Paul II, Penguin Audiobooks (December 1994).

John Paul II. "Redemptoris Mater" http://www.vatican.va/holy_father/john_paul_ii/encyclicals/documents/hf_jp-ii_enc_25031987_redemptoris-mater_en.html.

John Paul II. *Theology of the Body*, Pauline Books and Media, Boston, 1997.

Jurgens, W.A. *The Faith of the Early Fathers*, Liturgical Press, Collegeville, MN, 1970.

Kowalska, St. Maria Faustina. *Diary, Divine Mercy in My Soul*, Marians of the Immaculate Conception, MA, Stockbridge 2000.

Kramer, H.B. *The Book of Destiny*, Tan Books and Publishers, Inc., Rockford, IL, 1975.

Lactantius. "The Divine Institutes," *The Ante-Nicene Fathers*, Henrickson Pub., Peabody, MA, 1995.

Leo XIII. "Consecration to the Sacred Heart of Jesus," http://www.ewtn.com/library/ENCYC/L13ANNUM.HTM.

Leo XIII. "Providentissimus Deus," Boston: Pauline Books & Media, Slough, England 1999.

Manteau-Bonamy, H.M., O.P. *Immaculate Conception and the Holy Spirit*, Translated by Brother Richard Arnandez, F.S.C. Franciscan Marytown Press, Kenosha, 1977.

Martyr, Justin. "Dialogue with Trypho," *The Fathers of the Church*, Christian Heritage, 1948.

McGratty, Rev. Arthur. S.J. *The Sacred Heart: Yesterday and Today*, Benzinger, NY, 1951.

Meagher, Father James L., D.D. "De Religione Hebraeorum," *How Christians Said the First Mass*, Tan Books and Pub., Inc. IL, 1984.

Methodius. *The Banquet of the Ten Virgins*, Discourse IX, in "The Anti-Nicene Fathers," Vol. VI authorized edition, WM. B. Eerdmans Publishing Company, Grand Rapids, MI, 1978.

Methodius. "The Symposium", Logos 9, *Ancient Christian Writers*, The Newman Press, Westminster, MD, Ed. Quasten & Plumpe, 1958.

Migne, Jacques Paul. *Patrologiae Graeca*, Paris, 1857.

Molnar, Thomas Steven. *Utopia: the Perennial Heresy*, Sheed & Ward, NY, 1967.

Newman, John Henry. *Discussions and Arguments on Various Subjects*, Basil Montagu Pickering, London, 1872.

Ortíz de Orbina, Ignacio. "Das Glaubenssymbol von Chalkedon: sein Text, sein Werden, seine dogmatische Bedeutung," Das Konzil von Chalkedon, Würzburg, Echter, 1959.

Papias of Hierapolis. "The Fragments of Papias," *The Fathers of the Church*, CIMA Publishing Co., NY, 1947.

Penasa, Padre Martino. *È imminente una nuova era di vita cristiana?*, Il Segno del Soprannaturale, Udine, Italia, 1990.

Penasa, Padre Martino. *IL Libro Della Speranza*, Padova, 1989.

Philipon, Marie Michel, O.P. *Conchita: A Mother's Spiritual Diary*, Alba House, NY, 1978.

Piccarreta, Luisa. *Pro-manuscripts*, Assocazione del Divin Volere, Milano, Italy, 1977.

Pius X. "E Supremi Apostolatus," http://www.ewtn.com/library/ENCYC/P10SUPRE.HTM.

Pius XI. "On the Peace of Christ in His Kingdom," http://www.catholictradition.org/arcano.htm.

Poupard, Paul. "Articolo sul Millenarianismo," *Il Grande Dizionario delle Religioni*, Cittadella Editrice, Assisi, Italy, 1990.

Ratzinger, Cardinal Joseph. *On the Threshold of a New Era*, Ignatius Press, San Francisco, CA, 1996.

Serra, Aristide. *Parola, Spirito e Vita*, Centro editoriale dehoniano, Bologna, Italy.

Sheen, Archbishop Fulton J. "Sermon On the Story of Fatima", produced by St. Bernard's Institute, 1942 cassette number 13, side A, distributed under the exclusive license by The Fulton J. Sheen Co., Inc. and JAE-DSC Ventures.

Smith, W.M. *The Biblical Doctrine of Heaven*, Moody Press, Chicago,1968.

Soulen, Richard N. *Handbook of Biblical Criticism*, John Knox Press, second edtion, Atlanta, GA, 1981.

Teresa of Avila. *The Interior Castle*, translated by the Benedictines of Stanbrook, Tan Books, IL, 1997.

Tertullian. "Adversus Marcion," *The Ante-Nicene Fathers*, Henrickson Pub., Peabody, MA, 1995.

Tertullian. "Apologia del Cristianesimo," *The Ante-Nicene Fathers*, Henrickson Pub., Peabody, MA, 1995.

Trese, Leo John. *The Faith Explained*, Fides Pub. Assn., Chicago, IL, 1959.

Von Balthasar, Hans Urs. *Elizabeth of Dijon: An Interpretation of Her Spiritual Mission*, Pantheon, NY, 1956.

Vincent of Lérins. "Commonitory of 434," Johannes Quasten, *Patrology*, Spectrum Pub., Utrecht, Brussels, 1850.

Winklhofer, A. *The Coming of His Kingdom*, Herder and Herder, New York, 1963.

BIBLIOGRAPHY OF REFERENCE SOURCES

Acta Apostolicae Sedis, 36, Rome, 1944.

Adversus Haereses, Irenaeus of Lyons, *The Fathers of the Church*, CIMA Publishing Co., NY, 1947.

Adversus Marcion, Tertullian, *The Ante-Nicene Fathers*, Henrickson Pub., Peabody, MA, 1995.

A History of Early Christian Doctrine, Before the Council of Nicea, Jean Danielou, London, Darton, Longman & Todd, Westminster Press, Philadelphia, PA, 1964.

Ananstasii Abbatis, Sanctae Romanae Ecclesiae Presbiteri et Bibliothecarii, in Opera Omnia, Anastasius of Sinai, accurante J.P. Migne, Lutetiae Parisiorum,

Migne, 1852.

A New Catechism — Catholic Faith for Adults, Herder and Herder, NY, 1969.

Apologia del Cristianesimo, Tertullian, in *The Ante-Nicene Fathers*, Henrickson Pub., Peabody, MA, 1995.

Catechism of the Catholic Church, Libreria Editrice Vaticana, St. Paul Books & Media, 1994.

Catechism of the Council of Trent, Christian Press Co., NY, 1905.

Catholic Dictionary, edited by Donald Attwater, The Macmillan Company, NY, 1941.

Catholic Dictionary of Dogmatic Theology, Bruce Publishing Co., Milwaukee, WI, 1952.

Catholic Encyclopedia, Sunday Visitor Pub., Huntington, IN, 1991.

Catholic Encyclopedia Revised, Nashville, TN, Thomas Nelson, 1987.

Chronikon, syntomon ex diaphoron chronographon te kai exegeton synlegen kai syntheom upo Georgiou Monachou tou epikale Hamartolou, Lipsiae, Parisiorum, 1863.

Codex Vaticanus Alexandrinus, Nr. 14 Bibl. Lat., Romae, 1747.

Cursus Patrologiae, Omnium SS. Patrum Ecclesiasticorum, Archiepiscopi Caesarae Cappadociae, Commentarius in Joannis Theologi Apocalypsin, Tomus Unicus, J.P. Migne Editorem, Paris, 1863.

Dei Verbum, Vatican Council II, Costello Pub. Co., Northport, NY, Rev. Ed., 1988.

Dictionary of the Bible, Bruce Pub. Co., Milwaukee, WI, 1965.

Enciclopedia Cattolica, Città del Vaticano, Ente per l'Enciclopedia Cattolica e per il libro Cattolico, 1948.

Encyclopedia of the Early Church, Vol. II, Edited by Angelo DiBerardino, James Clarke & Co., Cambridge, England, 1992.

Epitome Historiarum, 471/5, Lipsiac, Teubner, 1868.

Gaudium et Spes, Vatican Council II, Costello Pub. Co., Northport, NY, Revised Ed., 1988.

Georgii Monachi Chronicon, in aedibus B.G. Teubneri, Lipsiae, Parisiorum, 1904.

Jesus Living in Mary: Handbook of the Spirituality of St. Louis de Montfort, Montfort Publications, Bayshore, NY, 1994.

"Letter of Barnabas," *The Fathers of the Church*, CIMA Co., NY, 1947.

Lumen Gentium, Vatican Council II, Costello Pub. Co., Northport, NY, Revised Ed., 1988.

Nestle-Aland Greek-English New Testament, Deutsche Bibelgesellschaft, Stuttgart, Germany, 1992. translated by Fr. Joseph Iannuzzi from the original Greek text.

New Catholic Encyclopedia, McGraw-Hill Pub., NY, 1967.

Septuaginta, 1d est Vetus Testamentum graece iuxta LXX interpretes; edidit Alfred Rahls; Duo volumina in uno; Deutsche Bibelgesellschaft, Stuttgart, Germany, 1979.

Tertio Millennio Adveniente, Inside the Vatican, Martin de Porres Printshop, New Hope, KY, 1994.

Theological Dictionary, Karl Rahner and Herbert Vorgrimler, Herder and Herder, Third Printing, London, 1968.

The Ante-Nicene Fathers, Henrickson Pub., Peabody, MA, 1995.

The Apostolic Fathers: First and Second Clement, R.M. Grant and H.H. Graham, Thomas Nelson & Sons, NY.

The Christian Faithful, Society of St. Paul, 6th Ed., 1995.

The Christian Faith in the Documents of the Catholic Church, J. Neuner & J. Dupuis, Harper Collins, London, 1995.

The Liturgy of the Hours, Catholic Book Publishing Co., NY, Vol. I-IV, 1975.

The Spiritual Legacy of Sister Mary of the Holy Trinity, Tan Books, IL, 1981.

The Teaching of the Catholic Church: A Summary of Catholic Doctrine, Burns Oates & Washbourne, London, 1952.

ENDNOTES

[1] Archbishop Fulton J. Sheen, *On the Story of Fatima*, St. Bernard's Institute Distributed under the exclusive License by The Fulton J. Sheen Co., Inc. and JAE-DSC Ventures, cassette number 13, side A.

[2] *Our Sunday Visitor's Catholic Almanac* (Huntington, IN: Our Sunday Visitor, 1998) p.309. Archbishop Daniel M. Buechlein, O.S.B. of Indianapolis is head of the bishops' Ad Hoc Committee to Oversee the Use of the Catechism. He made this timely statement in June, 1997 at a meeting of the United States bishops.

[3] *Patristic eschatology* is the doctrine of the Last Things as found in the writings of the early Church Fathers. The Fathers were early century followers of Christ entrusted with the task of faithfully transmitting the apostolic teachings to the Church in its beginnings. *Millenarianism*, on the other hand, was a heresy that infiltrated the early Church and that was condemned for its faulty interpretation of the Church's doctrine on the Last Things.

[4] *Dei Verbum* (Dogmatic Constitution on Divine Revelation), Vatican Council II, edited by Austin Flannery, O.P. (Northport, NY: Costello Pub. Co., 1988), 8.

[5] *The Ascent of Mount Carmel*, Saint John of the Cross, *The Collected Works of St. John of the Cross* (Washington, DC: ICS Publications Institute of Carmelite Studies, 1991), translated by Kieran Kavanuagh, O.C.D. and Otilio Rodriguez, O.C.D. p.217; Bk. II, Ch. 19, 10.

[6] *Chaghiga'*, II,1; in *La Festa Escatologica*, Enzo Bianchi (Monastero di Bose, Italy: Edizioni Qiqajon, 1996), p.8.

[7] The Talmudic commentary was the written record of Jewish canon and civil law not contained in the Pentateuch, consisting of the *Mishna* and *Gemara*.

[8] Discorso del Santo Padre Giovanni Paolo II durante l'incontro con i giovani di Roma, 21 marzo 2002, article nn. 4,5. Cf. also http://web.tiscali.it/avvocaturainmissione/giovani%20roma.htm.

[9] Pope John Paul II, *Novo Millennio Inuente* (Libreria Editrice Vaticana, Citta' del Vaticano, 1994) 1, 16, 23, 30.

[10] Ibid., 18.

[11] Rom. 8:19-21: *Nestle-Aland Greek New Testament* (Stuttgart, Germany: Deutsche Bibelgesellschaft, 1992), translated by Fr. Joseph Iannuzzi from the original Greek text.

[12] Joseph Cardinal Ratzinger, *Salt of the Earth* (San Francisco: Ignatius Press, 1997), translated by Adrian Walker.

[13] Luisa Piccarreta was born on April 23, 1865 in the small town of Corato, Italy of poor and hardworking parents. Luisa's spiritual journey began while on a farm where she spent many years of her childhood. When she was nine, Luisa received first Holy

Communion and Confirmation, and from that moment learned to remain for hours in prayer before the Blessed Sacrament. She only received a first grade education, and at the age of eleven she enrolled in the Association of the Daughters of Mary. At the age of eighteen she became a third-order Dominican, taking the name of Sr. Magdalene after St. Mary Magdalene. At the age of thirteen, she was asked by the Lord to become a "victim soul." This occurred when, from the balcony of her house in Corato, she experienced a vision of Jesus suffering under the weight of the Cross, who, raising his eyes to her, said: "*Soul, help me!*" From that moment she accepted the state of victim to suffer for Jesus and for the salvation of souls. Gradually she came to experience a most peculiar condition: Every morning she found herself rigid and immobile in bed, with no one able to either raise her arms or move her head or legs. Only the blessing of a priest enabled her to return to her usual tasks of lace making and needlepoint.

On February 2, 1899, Luisa was asked in obedience to her spiritual director Fr. Gennaro di Gennaro to write down the revelations she received from Jesus. These revelations, which she would continue to write until 1938, are popularly referred to as her "diary." Her revelations comprise 36-volumes and contain her intimate and mystical experiences, with dictations from Jesus and Mary on how to "Live in the Divine Will" and hasten its universal reign on earth.

Luisa possessed numerous mystical gifts such as ecstasy, apparitions, visions, the stigmata and bilocation. She was confined to bed with hardly any food or drink except the Eucharist for about 60 years. She occasionally ate and retained other food in very small amounts. Although she was confined to bed, she never suffered any physical illness except for the pneumonia that took her life in 1947.

In 1926 she wrote her autobiography in obedience to her extraordinary spiritual director and confessor St. Hannibal di Francia. St. Hannibal edited her writings, of which the first 19 volumes were properly examined and approved by the local ecclesiastical authorities. He published various writings of Luisa, including the book *L'Orologio della Passione (The Hours of the Passion)*, which was reprinted four times in Italian.

The Cause of Beatification of the Servant of God Luisa Piccarreta was opened by Rome in 1994 and is still under way. At present, the first 19 of Luisa's 36 volumes bear the local Church authority's *imprimatur* and *nihil obstat*. Luisa's Bishop Joseph Leo and her spiritual director and *censor librorum* St. Hannibal di Francia, found nothing in her works contrary to the Catholic Faith. However, this does not ensure immunity from error on the part of those who may present or interpret her works in ways that contradict Catholic teaching. For this reason, the Church requests that until the completion and approval of the critical edition of Luisa's collected works, Catholics should exercise caution when reading the translations of her writings (*Pro-manuscripts*) that have been made available to the public in recent years.

[14] Luisa Piccarreta, *Pro-manuscripts* (Milano, Italy: Assocazione del Divin Volere, 1977); February 24, 1917.

[15] Ibid., Oct 6, 1922.

[16] Ibid., Sept 11, 1922.

[17] Msgr. Anthony D. Muntone, S.T.L., the postulator, went to Rome to present to Rev. Paul Molinari a list of Fr. Walter Ciszek's materials that consisted of 400 letters, 45 testimonies, numerous homilies and videos. Fr. Molinare highly praised the exemplary life of Rev. Walter Ciszek.

[18] Fr. Walter Ciszek, *He Leadeth Me* (San Francisco: Ignatius Press, 1995), pp.116-117.

[19] *Gaudium et Spes*, Vatican Council II, edited by Austin Flannery, O.P. (Northport, NY: Costello Pub. Co., 1988), 34.

[20] For a more comprehensive understanding of the concept of divinization, I refer you to the chapter *Divinization and the Divine Will*.

[21] John Paul II, *Novo Millennio Inuente*, op. cit.

[22] Of the numerous expressions used to describe the Fathers' historic period of universal Christianity, we limit ourselves to the nomenclature "era of peace," coined by our Lady of Fatima on July 13, 1917: *"In the end my Immaculate Heart will triumph. The Holy Father will consecrate Russia to me and she will be converted, and the world will enjoy an era of peace."*

[23] Is. 25:6.

[24] St. Justin Martyr, *Dialogue with Trypho, The Fathers of the Church* (Christian Heritage, 1948). Concerning the meaning of the "resurrection of the flesh," I refer you to the chapter on *The First Resurrection*.

[25] The expression "rising from the dead," is addressed in the chapter on the First Resurrection.

[26] St. Irenaeus of Lyons, *Adversus Haereses*, Book V, 33.3.4, in *The Fathers of the Church* (NY: CIMA Publishing Co., 1947), pp. 384-385.

[27] See footnote to Luke 11:2 in the *New American Bible, St. Joseph Edition* (NY: Catholic Book Pub. Co, 1991), p. 119.

[28] *Gaudium et Spes*, Vatican Council II, op. cit., 26.

[29] Rom. 8:15-16.

[30] Pope Leo XIII affirmed that Sacred Scripture is the principal source of our faith (*Providentissimus Deus*, Pope Leo XIII, 10, 16 (Boston: Pauline Books & Media, Boston: Pauline Books & Media, Slough, England 1999) and other pontiffs have emphasized the role of Sacred Scripture in the development of theology, among whom Popes Benedict XV (*Spiritus Paraclitus*) and Pius XII (*Humani Generis*) are worthy of mention.

[31] Karl Rahner and Herbert Vorgrimler, *Theological Dictionary* (London: Herder and Herder, Third Printing 1968), p. 171; *New Catholic Encyclopedia* (NY: McGraw-Hill Book Co., 1967), vol. V, p.853-854.

[32] Ignacio Ortíz de Orbina, "Das Glaubenssymbol von Chalkedon: sein Text, sein Werden, seine dogmatische Bedeutung," *Das Konzil von Chalkedon* (Würzburg: Echter, 1959) v.1, p.398.

[33] R.M. Grant and H.H. Graham, *The Apostolic Fathers: First and Second Clement* (NY:

Thomas Nelson & Sons), 1 Clement 42,2.

[34] *Dei Verbum*, Vatican Council II, edited by Austin Flannery, O.P., op. cit., 7-8.

[35] "I have much to tell you, but you cannot bear it now. *But when he comes, the Spirit of truth, he will guide you to all truth... And he will declare to you the things that are coming*" (Jn. 16:13).

[36] *Dei Verbum*, op. cit., 8.

[37] St. Thomas Aquinas, *Summa Theologica* (NY: Benzinger Bros., 1947), Treatise on the Theological Virtues, Question 1: Of Faith; Art. 7: Whether the articles of faith have increased in the course of time?

[38] Vincent of Lérins, *Commonitory of 434*, Johannes Quasten, *Patrology* (Utrecht—Brussels: Spectrum Pub., 1850), vol. I, Ch. 41, pp. 9-10.

[39] Pope Leo XIII, *Providentissimus Deus*, Libreria Editrice Vaticana, Rome 1893, p.18.

[40] John Henry Newman, *Discussions and Arguments on Various Subjects* (London: Basil Montagu Pickering, 1872), II, 1.

[41] *Catholic Dictionary of Dogmatic Theology* (Milwaukee, WI: Bruce Publishing Co., 1952), pp. 80-81.

[42] *Novo Millennion Inuente*, op. cit., 42.

[43] Yves Congar, *The Meaning of Tradition* (NY: Hawthorn Books, 1964), pp. 99-100.

[44] Yves Congar, *Tradition and Traditions* (NY: Macmillan, 1967), translated by M. Naseby and T. Rainborough, p.24.

[45] Augustine of Hippo, *De Civitate Dei* (Washington: Catholic University of America Press, 3rd Printing, 1977), Bk. XX, Ch. 7.

[46] There is but one remedy for our secularized world, steeped in the spirit of comfort and pleasure: the Spirit of God. He alone can revive the Church by a new Pentecost. Pope John XXIII proclaimed this truth vigorously in his introductory remark at the Second Vatican Council: "*The Church needs a new Pentecost.*" In all Catholic churches throughout the world, these words were prayed in preparation for the Second Vatican Council: "*Renew your wonders in our midst as in a New Pentecost!*" Fifty years before Pope John XXIII's Second Vatican Council, Jesus had told his mystical secretary, the Venerable Conchita de Armida:

"On sending to the world *a new Pentecost*, I want it inflamed, purified, illuminated, inflamed and purified by the light and fire of the Holy Spirit. The last stage of the world must be marked very specially by the effusion of the Holy Spirit. He must reign in hearts and in the entire world, not so much for the glory of His Person as for making the Father loved and bearing testimony of Me, although His glory is that of the whole Trinity" (Marie Michel Philipon, O.P., *Conchita: A Mother's Spiritual Diary* [New York: Alba House, 1978] message of Jan. 26, 1916).

"May the whole world have recourse to this Holy Spirit since the day of His reign has arrived. *This last stage of the world belongs very specially to Him* that He be honored and exalted... May all at once this Holy Spirit begin to be called on with prayers, penances and tears, with the ardent desire of His coming. *He will come, I will send Him again clearly manifest in His effects, which will astonish the world and impel the Church to holiness"* (Ibid., Sept. 27, 1918).

Pope John Paul II proclaimed to Latin Americans in 1992, "Welcome the Spirit, so that a *new Pentecost* may take place in every community!"

[47] Blessed Dina Bélanger, *The Autobiography of Blessed Dina* Bélanger, (third edition, 1997), translated by Mary St. Stephen, R.J.M., pp. 323-324, 333.

[48] Padre Martino Penasa, *È imminente una nuova era di vita cristiana?*, Il Segno del Soprannaturale (Udine, Italia, 1990). The statement came in response to the question put before him by the biblical scholar Fr. Martino Penasa. Fr. Penasa visited the Msgr. S. Garofalo, presently a Consultant to the Congregation for the Cause of Saints, and spoke to him on the scriptural foundation of an historic and universal era of peace, as opposed to millenarianism. Msgr. Girofalo, convinced by the force of Fr. Penasa's presentation, encouraged him to discuss the matter directly with the Prefect of the Sacred Congregation for the Doctrine of Faith, Cardinal Joseph Ratzinger. The cardinal responded to Fr. Penasa's question stating, "the question is still open to free discussion, as the Holy See has not made any definitive pronouncement in this regard" {in the original Italian: *"La questione è ancora aperta alla libera discussione, giacchè la Santa Sede non si è ancora pronunciata in modo definitivo"*}.

[49] The Venerable Anne Catherine Emmerich was told by our Lord, "her gift of seeing the past, present and future in mystic *vision* was greater than that possessed by anyone else in history" (cf. *The Life of Anne Catherine Emmerich*); St. Catherine of Siena prayed for the salvation "of the whole world" and for "every rational creature" (cf. *The Dialogue of St. Catherine of Siena*); and St. John of the Cross states that the soul in the high state of transforming union, is given a supernatural sight in which it beholds, "in only one view" the "harmony of every creature" in God's divine life "with such newness" ("The Living Flame of Love," John of the Cross, *The Collected Works*). This notwithstanding, unless the Holy Spirit confers upon the soul the gift of Living in the Divine Will, the soul's aforesaid "mystical vision" or "desire" of all creatures remains bereft of the "eternal activity" or "eternal operation" of the three divine Persons that alone enables the soul to impact all creatures of all time.

[50] Luisa Piccarreta, Ibid., April 8, 1918.

[51] Ibid., Nov 26, 1921

[52] Born in 1905 in the village of Glogowiec near Lodz, Helena Faustina was the third of ten children. From a very early age, Faustina was devoted to prayer, work, and the poor. She attended less than three years of elementary school and at the age of eleven Helen heard for the first time a voice in her soul, calling her to a more perfect way of life. At the age of 14, Helen began working as a domestic servant to help her parents. At the age of 20, she entered the Congregation of the Sisters of Our Lady of Mercy in which, as Sister Maria Faustina, she spent 13 years. Despite a seemingly simple and monotonous life, Sister Faustina had an exceptionally profound union with God. Even from her earliest childhood, she desired to become a saint, and she consistently worked with Jesus for the salvation of lost souls, even to the extent of offering her life as a sacrifice for poor sinners. As such, she was given the grace of much suffering, as well as numerous mystical graces. To Sister Faustina, Jesus said, *"In the Old Covenant I*

sent prophets wielding thunderbolts to my people. Today I am sending you with My mercy to the people of the whole world. I do not want to punish aching mankind, but I desire to heal it, pressing it to My Merciful Heart." This simple, though trusting religious, was to be trusted with one of God's most amazing declarations, to spread devotion to his Divine Mercy.

Racked and broken by tuberculosis, and from the many sufferings that she bore in the sacrifice for sinners, Sister Faustina died October 5, 1938 at the young age of 33, the same age as our Lord when He died. In 1993, on the first Sunday after Easter, in St. Peter's Square in Rome, Pope John Paul II declared her Blessed. In his statement to his General Audience, the Holy Father said, "God has spoken to us through the spiritual wealth of Sister Faustina Kowalska. She left to the world the great message of Divine Mercy and an incentive to complete self-surrender to the Creator. *God endowed her with a singular grace* that enabled her to experience his mercy through mystical encounter and by *a special gift* of contemplative prayer." Blessed Faustina was canonized in Rome on the first Sunday after Easter during the Great Jubilee Year 2000. I had the privilege of personally attending both her beatification and canonization ceremonies in St. Peter's Square. During the canonization ceremony, the pope stated: "The Second Sunday of Easter throughout the Church from now on will be called "Divine Mercy Sunday." She was the first saint of the new millennium.

[53] Faustina Kowalska, *Diary, Divine Mercy in My Soul* (Stockbridge, MA: Marians of the Immaculate Conception, 2000), entry 137.

[54] Ibid., entries 1789, 1796.

[55] Rev. Arthur McGratty, S.J., *The Sacred Heart: Yesterday and Today* (NY: Benzinger, 1951), p.229.

[56] Vera Grita was a Salesian cooperator who was born in Rome, Italy on January 28, 1923. After having obtained her degree in law in Savona, at the tender age of 21, Vera fell victim to the 1944 World War II military air incursion on the city of Savona. The crowd of fleeing citizens trampled over Vera, who remained lying on the ground motionless for hours beside several other wounded and dead bodies. The injuries she underwent would accompany her for the rest of her life. She suffered grave lesions to her internal organs, to her head, lungs and liver that caused her frequent fevers, severe headaches, which, in turn, gave rise to other related illnesses. Despite Vera's allergies that often kept her from taking medications or pain relievers, she accepted her pains out of love for Jesus and for the salvation of souls. Despite her fragile health Vera continued to teach in schools for many years. She became a third-order Salesian in 1967, and on September 19, 1967, began receiving messages from Jesus and Mary, which she recorded in her Diary of "Living Tabernacles."

Jesus asked Vera to submit all of her works to her spiritual director Fr. Gabriel Zucconi (cf. message of December 26, 1967), who was the priest chosen by Jesus to initiate and diffuse the message of 'Living Tabernacles.' Vera bound herself to this work through the vow of victim for the Eucharistic reign of Jesus in souls, and through the vow of obedience to her spiritual director. In exchange, Jesus gave Vera his own name: *"I have given My Holy Name, and from now on I will call you and you will be 'Vera of Jesus.'"*

Vera would confess to Fr. John Bocchi, while Fr. Joseph Borra, the director of the

Salesian Institute of Rome examined her writings. Amazingly, not one of Vera's relatives was aware of her mystical experiences, which she safely confided to her spiritual director. It was only after Vera's death at Savona, Italy on December 22, 1969 that her friends and neighbors came to know of the great mission she received for the entire Church. To Vera, Jesus left an important message concerning the institution of Living Tabernacles. Due to the scarcity of adorers of the Eucharist, as well as the profanations, transgressions and irreverences toward the Sacred Host, many graces are lost that would otherwise have been granted through Jesus' Sacrament of love. In response to man's abuses, God calls the human creature to return to the original state, purpose and order for which it was created, to become a "Living Tabernacle" for the sanctification of others and of the world. This, in essence, is the mission God entrusted to 'Vera of Jesus.'

Jesus reveals to Vera that among his creatures the Pope is *the first missionary* whom God has called to become a Living Tabernacle (cf. massage June 11, 1968), and whom he invites to acknowledge this gift publicly, before the world (cf. message July 15, 1969). In Vera's messages, a Living Tabernacle is not only the soul that adores the Eucharist, it is a willing victim of his Divine Will that "lives in the world and in society" and welcomes in its "fullness" the eternal activity of the three Divine Persons in the Sacred Host. Jesus called Vera to the state of victim, to a "New and Holy Martyrdom" that consists in accepting all obstacles and trials that Satan places in the path of those who promote this work (cf. message June 30, 1968). Lastly, Jesus revealed that all Living Tabernacles must have a strong devotion to Mary: Since Mary is the first creature to carry Jesus, the Living Tabernacle Himself, she fills the office of forming all other Living Tabernacles for the imminent triumph of her Immaculate Heart in the world and in the era of peace.

[57] Vera Grita, *Opera di Tabernacoli Viventi (Living Tabernacles)*, a cura di Giuseppina e Liliana Grita, Edizioni Segno, Udine, Italy 1989 (translation from the original Italian text by Rev. Joseph L. Iannuzzi) pp. 45, 47.

[58] Ibid., pp. 38, 118.

[59] Ibid., p. 116.

[60] Ibid., pp. 33, 160, 162.

[61] Ibid., p.17.

[62] H.M. Manteau-Bonamy, O.P., *Immaculate Conception and the Holy Spirit* (Kenosha: Franciscan Marytown Press, 1977), translated by Brother Richard Arnandez, F.S.C., p.117.

[63] Millenarianism is the belief in a hedonistic utopia inaugurated by Christ, whose physical reign on earth with his saints will last literally for 1,000 years (cf. the chapter "Magisterium and Millenarianism").

[64] *Epitome Historiarum*, 471/5 (Lipsiae: Teubner 1868); cf. *Historiae* 7,18 (Lipsiae: Teubner 1887).

[65] Berthold Altaner, *Patrology* (NY: Herder and Herder, 1961), p. 263.

[66] *Chiliasm*, from the Greek *kiliàs* (1,000), was the name given to the belief that the

1,000 years mentioned in St. John's Book of Revelation were to be understood literally. When Latin began to exercise its influence over the Christian-speaking world, Chiliasm became known as *millenarianism*, from Latin *mille* (1,000). The Fathers, who were privy to the symbolism and allegory of Sacred Scripture, avoided such literalisms.

67 *The Ante-Nicene Fathers* (Peabody, MA: Henrickson Pub., 1995), vol. V, fragment VI, 25. Unlike the millenarian heresy that ascribes gluttony and carnal pleasures to the golden age of the spirit, the Church Father Papias uses nature's imagery in the allegorical genre of his day to paint a portrait—simple enough for the average folk of his day to understand—of the future universal era of reconciliation between God and creation:

"The days will come in which vines shall grow, having each ten thousand branches, and in each branch ten thousand twigs, and in each true twig ten thousand shoots, and in every one of the shoots ten thousand clusters, and on every one of the clusters ten thousand grapes, and every grape when pressed will give five-and-twenty metres of wine. And when any one of the saints shall lay hold of a cluster, another shall cry out, `I am a better cluster, take me; bless the Lord through me.' In like manner, [He said] that a grain of wheat would produce ten thousand ears, and that every ear would have ten thousand grains, and every grain would yield ten pounds of clear, pure, fine flour; and that apples, and seeds, and grass would produce in similar proportions; and that all animals, feeding then only on the productions of the earth, would become peaceable and harmonious, and be in perfect subjection to man" (Ibid., fragment, IV).

[68] *New Catholic Encyclopedia*, op. cit., vol. X, p. 979.

[69] W.A. Jurgens, *The Faith of the Early Fathers* (Collegeville, MN: Liturgical Press, 1970), p. 294.

[70] St. Jerome, *De Viris Illustribus*, 18 (Firenze: Sansoni, 1964), Ed. Vallarsi II, p. 845. *"So the say"* refers to Eusebius' adherents.

[71] Papias of Hierapolis, *The Fragments of Papias*, nn. 3-4, in *The Fathers of the Church*, op. cit., p. 374

[72] St. Irenaeus of Lyons, *Adversus Haereses*, *The Fathers of the Church*, op. cit., pp. 384-385. St. Irenaeus refers to the Apostles as presbyters, *"quemadmodum presbyteri meminerunt"* (*Adversus Haereses*).

73 Scripture scholars point out that in the Acts of the Apostles, where seniors are mentioned for the first time, is not only a distinction made between their role [*presbyteros*] and that of the Apostles [*apostolos*] (Acts 15:2.6.23), but their function is explained as one of safeguarding the apostolic Tradition and governing the Christian community (Acts 20:17-35). The author of Acts [presumably St. Luke] refers to presbyters as *episkopoi* (Acts 20:28), and St. Peter the Apostle modestly refers to himself as a presbyter [*syspresbyteros*] (1 Pt 5:1).

While Acts 20:17 and 1 Pt. 5:1 both share the original Greek title "presbyter," they do not imply a sharing in the same office. The presbyters were reputedly a group of holy and wise elders of the early Christian community who, although appearing to lack the faculties to absolve others of their sins (Jas 5:16), safeguarded the apostolic Tradition and governed the flock entrusted to them. This is especially evidenced in Saint Paul's epistles, where he, unlike Ss. Peter and Luke, never refers to the elders as *presbyteros* but as *diakonos*, thereby emphasizing perhaps the most important function of their office: service toward neighbor, especially within the household of God. Further illustrating the presbyteral office is the author of the "pastoral letters" (it is uncertain whether he is the same Paul of the epistles), who describes its purpose as that of forming, guiding and organizing the Christian community: as leaders, they are to preach and teach (1 Tm 5:17). Of its multi-faceted characterizations, the title *presbyteri*, in Tradition, refers especially to the Apostles and the Fathers.

In the face of the apparent confusion on the usage of the title *presbyteros*, recent biblical scholarship aids us in understanding its traditional two-fold distinction. While it is true that *presbyteros* was a personal title given to the Apostles, it also developed into an honorific title for a "college" that had the explicit obligation of safeguarding the faith and governing God's flock. Whenever we hear of the early Church Fathers referring to *presbyteros* it is, therefore, understood as both the Apostles and the college instituted for the welfare and maintenance of the members and faith of the early Christian community.

Tradition, moreover, indicates that *"seniors"* were not mere acquaintances, but well-known faithful and wise Christians, who accurately conveyed the apostolic Tradition. These *seniors* also lived in the company of the Apostles and carefully understood their teachings. It is to these apostolic teachings that Papias declares his fidelity.

[74] *Codex Vaticanus Alexandrinus*, (Romae, 1747), Nr. 14 Bibl. Lat. Opp. I. p. 344.

"The last of these Evangelists, John, surnamed son of thunder, at a very advanced age... dictated his Gospel... to his own disciple, the virtuous Papias of Hierapolis" (Jaques Paul Migne, *Patrologiae Graeca* (Paris 1857)).

"Drawing their inspiration from the great Papias of Hierapolis, who lived in the company of the Apostle who leaned on Christ's breast" (Anastasii Abbatis, *Sanctae Romanae Ecclesiae Presbyteri et Bibliothecarii, Opera Omnia*, Anastasius of Sinai, accurante J.P. Migne, Lutetiae Parisiorum, Migne 1852; [Commentary on the Hexameron, 1. Migne, Patrologiae Graeca LXXXIX, p. 860]).

"Papias, Bishop of Hierapolis, an ocular witness of John" (*Georgii Monachi Chronicon*, in aedibus B.G. Teubneri, Lipsiae, Parisiorum, 1904; cf. *Chronikon, syntomon ex diaphoron chronographon te kai exegeton synlegen kai syntheon upo Georgiou Monachou tou epikale Hamartolou*, Lipsiae, Parisiorum, 1863).

[75] Martyr, *Dialogue with Trypho*, in *The Fathers of the Church*, op. cit., pp. 277-278.

[76] Sir 39:1-3.

[77] Richard N. Soulen, *Handbook of Biblical Criticism* (Atlanta, GA: John Knox Press, second edtion, 1981), p.15.

[78] Rev. 17:3.9.

[79] *"Adam died in the year 930 when Mathuselah was ninety-four years old. The latter lived till Sem, called also Melchisedech, was in his fiftieth year. Sem, or Melchisedech, died on Sion when Isaac was thirty-three years of age, and the latter lived till he was 180 – 2288 years after the creation of Adam, but a short time before the birth of Amram, Moses' father. Thus history came down from Adam and the patriarchs to Moses the great lawgiver, Founder of the Hebrew nationality and writer*

of the five books of the Bible" ("*De Religione Hebraeorum*", n. 68, Father James L. Meagher, D.D., *How Christians Said the First Mass*, IL: Tan Books and Pub., Inc. 1984).

[80] Martyr, *Dialogue with Trypho*, op.cit., pp. 277-278. From the Apocalypse and Isaiah, by perhaps a mistaken interpretation, Justin inferred a somewhat utopian existence of man in his relation to beasts. He affirms that *before* the Final Coming of Christ in the flesh, man will not eat the flesh of animals. It is noteworthy that this teaching was not unanimously taught by the Church Fathers. Let us recall that the teaching authority of the Church Fathers derives from their "unanimity". I here recall the words of Pope Leo XIII: "It is permitted to no one to interpret Holy Scripture against such sense or also against *the unanimous agreement of the Fathers... The Holy Fathers, we say, are of supreme authority, whenever they all interpret in one and the same manner* any text of the Bible, as pertaining to the doctrine of faith or morals; for *their unanimity* clearly evinces that such interpretation has come down from the Apostles as a matter of Catholic faith" (Pope Leo XIII, *Providentissimus Deus*, art. 14, Vatican City, 1893). Cf. also Pope Pius IV's Bulls *Injunctum Nobis*, November 13, 1564 and *In Sacrosancta*, December 9, 1564 and the 1st Vatican Council, *Dogmatic Constitution on the Catholic Faith*, Session III, April 24, 1870.

[81] Irenaeus, *Adversus Haereses*, IV, op. cit., 20,7.

[82] Ibid., IV, 38,1; 20,5.

[83] Ibid., Bk. 28, Ch. 3; Bk. 30,4; Bk. 33,2.

[84] Ibid.

[85] Ps. 91:7.

[86] Ps. 144:13.

[87] Ps. 68:18.

[88] 1 Sm. 18:7; 21:11.

[89] *Preface of the Apocalypse*, in "The Apostolic Fathers", Christian Heritage Inc., NY 1948, pp. 381-382.

[90] The Letter of Barnabas, in "The Apostolic Fathers", op. cit., pp. 215-216.

[91] Ibid., pp. 191-222.

[92] Much like St. Augustine, Tertullian, was a convert since 197 and the first great ecclesiastical writer in Latin. He lived during the age of Christian dogmatic discovery, when the Persons and Natures of Christ were not yet dogmatically defined. In his pioneering efforts to assist the Church in her discovery of the truths rooted in Scripture and Tradition, his rigorous moral beliefs became unbalanced. While the Church respects his contributions to the field of eschatology as having stemmed from the teaching of the apostles, his moral beliefs, on the other hand, are believed to have stemmed from the doctrines of the Montanists. Among their false beliefs, the Montanists forbade second marriages to the widowed; flight from persecution (the Christian soldier should willingly die for his faith); and imposed rigorous fasts. While noting his shortcomings, the *Catholic Encyclopedia* acknowledges Tertullian's patristic contributions (cf. *New Catholic Encyclopedia*, vol. V, p. 854).

[93] "*Millenarianism, the belief that there will be an earthly reign of the Messiah before the*

end of time, is the Jewish-Christian doctrine which has aroused and continues to arouse more argument than any other. The reason for this, however, is probably a failure to distinguish between the various elements of the doctrine. On the one hand, it seems hard to deny that it contains a truth which is a part of the stock of the Christian teaching, and which occurs in the New Testament in I-II Thessalonians, in I Corinthians, and in the Revelation of John" (Jean Danielou, London, Darton, Longman & Todd, A *History of Early Christian Doctrine Before the Council of Nicea* [Philadelphia: Westminster Press, 1964), p. 377]. *New Catholic Encyclopedia,* vol. XIII, p. 1021.

[94] *New Catholic Encyclopedia,* op. cit., vol. XIII, p. 1021.

[95] Tertullian here refers to the *spiritual* resurrection of saints to the life of grace as earlier presented in the writings of St. Justin Martyr.

[96] The *spiritual blessings* to which Tertullian refers, are described at greater length in the writings of Ss. Justin and Irenaeus.

[97] Tertullian, *Adversus Marcion, The Ante-Nicene Fathers* (Peabody, MA: Henrickson Pub., 1995), vol. 3, pp. 342-343.

[98] Tertullian, *Apologia del Cristianesimo,* in *The Ante-Nicene Fathers,* op. cit, vol. 3, pp. 53-54.

[99] St. Hippolytus, *The Fragments from Commentaries on Various Books of Scripture,* in "The Anti-Nicene Fathers," vol. V authorized edition, WM. B. Eerdmans Publishing Company, Grand Rapids, MI, (1978) Ch.4, p.163.

[100] *The Catholic Encyclopedia* acknowledges his pastristic contributions (cf. *New Catholic Encyclopedia,* op. cit., vol. V, p. 854).

[101] *New Catholic Encyclopedia,* op. cit., vol. IX, p. 742.

[102] St. Methodius, *The Banquet of the Ten Virgins,* Discourse IX, *The Banquet of the Ten Virgins,* Discourse IX, in "The Anti-Nicene Fathers," Ibid., vol. VI, Ch. 1, p.309. The expression "cease to form this creation" does not spell out the end of God's grace in history, but rather the end of an era of the formation of God's elect destined for the era of peace. Likewise, the expression "great resurrection day" alludes to Rev. 20:4-7, which, further into this book, St. Augustine interprets spiritually: *a spiritual resurrection of the saints at the end of the six thousand years of man's existence.*

St. Methodius places the "resurrection day" in lower case alluding not to the Final Resurrection of all the dead, but to the "first resurrection" of Rev. 20:6: "Blessed and holy is the one who shares in the first resurrection. The second death has no power over these...". This concept is reaffirmed in his treatise on Virginity where he calls it *"the first resurrection"* (ch.3) and *"the first day of the resurrection"* (ch.5), and it is bolstered by the teachings of the Church Father Ss. Justin Martyr, Tertullian and Lactanitus (cf. also the section entitled, The First Resurrection).

[103] Lactantius, "The Divine Institutes", *The Ante-Nicene Fathers* (Peabody, MA: Henrickson Pub., 1995), vol. 7, p. 211.

[104] "They who shall be alive shall not die" is an allegorical rendering of the "second death" of Rev. 20:6. Insofar as death accompanies all stages of mankind's progression in human history, it affects the lives of all those affected by original sin. However, not

all those that die experience the "second death," that is eternal condemnation.

[105] Lactantius, *The Divine Institutes*, op. cit., vol. 7, p. 211.

[106] Leo John Trese, *The Faith Explained* (Chicago, IL: Fides Pub. Assn., 1959), pp. 183-184.

[107] *A New Catechism —Catholic Faith for Adults* (NY: Herder and Herder, 1969), p. 480.

[108] *Catechism of the Council of Trent* (NY: Joseph F. Wagner Inc., 11th printing, 1949), translated by John A. McHugh, O.P. and Charles J. Callan, O.P., p. 84.

[109] *The Teaching of the Catholic Church: A Summary of Catholic Doctrine* (London: Burns Oates & Washbourne, 1952), p. 1140.

[110] Ibid.

[111] Mk. 13:9-10: The conversion of all nations.

[112] Not only did Ss. Cyril and Bernard write on the hidden coming in the present tense, but Bernard's "three comings," taken from his Advent Meditation, were interpreted by Pope John Paul II as an "interior Advent" that is continuously unfolding in the man who makes a choice to live according to God's law "within the depths of the personal conscience":

"This Interior Advent is brought to life through constant meditation on and assimilation of the Word of God. It is rendered fruitful and animated by prayer of adoration and praise of God. It is reinforced by constant reception of the Sacraments, those of reconciliation and Eucharist in particular, for they cleanse and enrich us with the grace of Christ and make us 'new' in accordance with Jesus' pressing call: 'Be converted'" [cf. Mt. 3:2; 4:17; Mk. 1:15] (Pope John Paul II, *Prayers and Devotions*, translated by Firman O'Sullivan, December 20 Advent Mediation by Pope John Paul II, Penguin Audiobooks (December 1994).

[113] J.A. Fitzmeyer, *Jerome Biblical Commentary* (Engelwood Cliffs, NJ: Prentice-Hall, 1968), pp. 316-317.

[114] *Gaudium et Spes*, Vatican Council II, op. cit., 26.

[115] *Encyclopedia of the Early Church*, (Cambridge, England: James Clarke & Co., 1992), vol. II, Edited by Angelo DiBerardino, p. 707.

[116] Cf. footnote to Luke 11:2 in the *New American Bible, St. Joseph Edition*, op. cit., p. 119.

[117] Pope John Paul II, *Tertio Millennio Adveniente* (Libreria Editrice Vaticana, Città del Vaticano, 2000), 16, 34.

[118] Anastasius of Sinai, "Anagogical Considerations on the Hexameron", Jacques Paul Migne, *Patrologiae Graeca*, Francis Gallicis 1865, LXXXIX, p. 860.

[119] *Letter of Barnabas*, op. cit., p. 208.

[120] *The Catechetical Instruction by St. Cyril of Jerusalem, Bishop*, Cat. 15, 1-3: PG 33, 870-874, in "The Liturgy of the Hours", vol. I, Catholic Book Pub. Co., NY, pp. 142-244.

[121] *New Catholic Encyclopedia,* op. cit., vol. III, p. 337.

[122] Ibid.

[123] Bernard of Clairvaux, *Sermo 5, Adventu Domini, 1-3,* in Opera Omnia (Edit. Cisterc. 4, 1966) pp. 188-190 *The Liturgy of the Hours,* (NY: Catholic Book Pub. Co., 1975), vol. I, p. 169.

[124] Cf. footnote 112.

[125] Cf. *L'Apocalypse, Augustin et Tyconius,* in: M. Dulaey, *St. Augustine et la Bible,* (Paris: a cura di A.M. la Bonnardière, 1986), pp. 369-386.); J. Kevin Coyle, *Augustine's "Millenarianism" Reconsidered,* Augustinus 38, 1993, pp. 155-164; J. Delumeau, *Mille ans de bonheur. Une histoire du paradis,* (Paris, 1995), in "Il Millenarismo Cristiano, e i suoi fondamenti scritturistici",* Annali di storia dell'esegesi 15/1 (Bologna: Edizioni Dehoniane 1998).

[126] G. Folliet, *La Typologie du sabbat chez saint Augustin.* Son interprétation millenariste entre 389 et 400 (Revue études Augustiniennes II, 1956), pp. 371-390.

[127] St. Augustine of Hippo, *De Civitate Dei* (Washington: Catholic University of America Press, 1977), Bk. XX, Ch. 7.

[128] Ibid., Ch. 7.

[129] Ibid., Ch. 8.

[130] CCC, op. cit., 676.

[131] At the Council of Ephesus in 431, Apollinaris, the former bishop of Alexandria, was criticized for having taught that our Lord had neither a human intellect nor a human body; his intellect and flesh came directly from heaven. He also propagated the erroneous doctrine of Christ's divine flesh returning to earth before the Final Judgment for 1,000 years.

[132] Thomas Aquinas, *Summa Theologica,* op. cit., Qu. 77, art. 1, rep. 4.

[133] Titus 1:10-14.

[134] Mt. 10:34-36.

[135] Jn. 17:11.

[136] Rev. 20:1-3.4.

[137] Heb. 4:4-11.

[138] In his book entitled *Il Libro Della Speranza* (Padova, 1989), the biblical scholar Fr. Martino Penasa affirms that the hermeneutical key to interpreting the many symbolisms in Scripture is biblical parallels. These parallels, found in both the Old and New Testaments, have gained the approval of scores of professors and theologians from the universities of Rome whose ecclesiastical endorsements are prefaced in his book.

[139] Isaiah appears to place Christ's eschatological apparitions within human history, while man sows seed and harvests wheat: "The Lord will give you the bread you need and the water for which you thirst. *No longer will your Teacher hide himself, but with your own eyes you shall see your Teacher,* while from behind, a voice shall sound in your ears: 'This is the way; walk in it,' when you would turn to the right or to the left. And you

shall consider unclean your silver-plated idols and your gold-covered images; you shall throw them away like filthy rags to which you say, 'Begone.' He will give you rain for the seed that you sow and the wheat that the soil produces will be rich and abundant. On that day your cattle will graze in spacious meadows; the oxen and the asses that till the ground will eat silage tossed to them with the shovel and pitchfork" (Is 30:20-24).

[140] Acts 1:3. We know from Scripture that after his Resurrection, Christ appeared on the road to Emmaus, at the Sea of Tiberias, and that many had risen from their graves to testify on his behalf. Some scholars present the scriptural foundation for an intermediary coming of Christ according to the pattern of his Resurrection.

[141] Mt. 27:51-53.

[142] Thomas Aquinas, *Summa Theologica*, op. cit., Qu. 77, art. 1, rep. 4.

[143] Irenaeus, *Adversus Haereses*, *The Fathers of the Church*, op. cit., pp. 384-385.

[144] Tertullian, *Adversus Marcion*, *The Ante-Nicene Fathers*, Henrickson Pub., Peabody, MA, 1995.

[145] Lactantius, *The Divine Institutes*, op. cit., vol. 7, p. 211.

[146] Danielou, *A History of Early Christian Doctrine*, op. cit., pp. 377, 379.

[147] Since sin remains in the spiritual DNA of historic man's wounded nature, it will always accompany him throughout human history, though not of the same intensity that strained and scarred his past. Though unable to rise above sin by its own efforts, mankind will receive a new impulse of love through the Holy Spirit's "new Pentecost." The Spirit's outpouring of grace will strengthen and perfect the graces of Baptism and Confirmation that began and accompany mankind's spiritual journey for the sake of presenting the Church holy and immaculate, without spot or wrinkle before Christ's return in glory. It is only after the era of peace, upon Christ's final return in glory, that the very roots of sin will be definitively eradicated.

Because death is the consequence of original sin (Rom.5:12), whose "concupiscence or the inclination to sin remains in the baptized," though not sin itself, death cannot be vanquished prior to sin's defeat (*The Christian Faith*, Ibid., p.187, Council of Trent, nn.3,5). Thus sin's defeat occurs at the end of the era of peace. If the fifth session of the General Council of Trent condemned the idea of an historic, sinless society in which the inclination to sin no longer remains in the baptized, it has refrained from condemning the modification of its *active* psychosomatic influence. While the law of sin remains in us till death, the lives of the saints remind us of the mitigation of its active influence. Ss. Catherine of Siena, John of the Cross and Teresa of Avila speak of the state of spiritual union where voluntary sins cease altogether. Some Fathers generally ascribe this spiritual state to the elect who make it into the era of peace. Because original sin remains, so must the sacraments that are ordered to the soul's purification and perfection. If, as several fathers suggest, the devil will be released toward the end of the era (Rev 20:7ff), sin, it follows, will once again intensify. Sin subsequently is the reason for the final defection from the faith.

[148] Job 5:15-23.

[149] Irenaeus, *Adversus Haereses*, op. cit., Bk. 32, Ch. 1; 33, 4.

150 Lactantius, *The Divine Institutes*, op. cit., vol. 7, p. 211.

151 Is. 29:20.

152 Justin Martyr, *Dialogue with Trypho*, op. cit.

153 Irenaeus, *Adversus Haereses*, op. cit., Bk. 34, Ch. 4.

154 Is. 54:1.

155 Is. 65:22-23.

156 Ez. 36:9-11.

157 Zep. 2:7.

158 Ps. 72:3. The trees, plants, fruits are portrayed in the poetic allegories often associated with the Old Testament writers. Just as God foretold of the Promised Land "flowing with milk and honey" that would refresh, enliven and cheer men's hearts, likewise the Fathers (cf. Ex 3:8: "God called out to him from the bush, 'Moses! Moses!'... I have come down to rescue them from the hands of the Egyptians and lead them out of that land into a good and spacious land, a land flowing with milk and honey..." [Ex 13:5; 33:3; Dt 6:3; 11:9; Jos 5:6; Jer 11:5; Bar 1:20; Ez 20:6]).

159 Is. 51:3.

160 Ez. 36:8.

161 Ez. 36:35.

162 Irenaeus, *Adversus Haereses*, op. cit., pp. 384-385.

163 Lactantius, *The Divine Institutes*, op. cit., vol. 7, p. 211.

164 Ps. 67:7.

165 Is. 65:9.

166 *Letter of Barnabas*, op. cit.

167 Is. 65:19.

168 Jer. 31:13, 14.

169 Zec. 8:4-5; 10:8.

170 Is. 58:11.

171 Zec. 12:8.

172 Is. 35:3.5-6.

173 Is. 42:16.

174 Ps. 102:22-23.

175 Is. 66:18.

176 Zec. 8:23.

177 Is. 66:23.

178 During the era, light assumes the lineaments of God's eternal activity in the soul of the human creature and its luminous effect on his vision of creation. Through the outpouring of a new Pentecost of grace, man is drawn into the uncreated and eternal activity of the three divine Persons by virtue of the Redemption of the eternal Word

and the Sanctification of the eternal Spirit. The *eternal* Word ("the light of the world") and the *eternal* Spirit ("the living fire") restore God's *likeness* to man, which illuminates and sublimates his vision of all created things, so much so that he beholds in all things the mark of his Creator in a new, eternal light.

An increase in Divine Light is not intended in the literal sense. In my previous book *The Triumph of God's Kingdom* bearing the Church's *imprimi potest*, I affirm that some sort of radical transformation in the arrangement of time will occur, and that "*time, in the sense of its being regulated by the sun and moon, will cease altogether only in the very end, that is, at the end of human history and the General Judgment of all the dead... Only after the temporal kingdom of light (era of peace) will there take place what St. Thomas calls 'the cessation of the movements of the heavenly bodies'*" (*The Triumph of God's Kingdom*, St. Andrew's Productions, McKees, PA, 1999, p.83). Thus any allegorical allusion to the cessation of the regulation of days and nights during the era "*does not preclude the continuance of the movement of the heavenly bodies: 'From one new moon to another, and from one Sabbath to another, all mankind shall come to worship before me, says the Lord' [Is. 66:23]*" (Ibid., p. 82).

It is noteworthy that the aforesaid transformation in time (Ibid., pp.80-81) represents principally a change in mankind's vision of the world around him, who, through the gift of living in the Divine Will, will exercise a positive, transforming influence over the natural laws without changing them. Men, women and children of the era of peace will be the same persons they were during the preceding era of the human will and yet different – they will have the freedom of will wounded by original sin, yet different. Like the apostles, they will receive an outpouring of grace, a new Pentecost to conform to the new, transformed world around them. Since they retain their wounded humanity, they will be born in original sin but not slaves of sin, they will continue to work but not toil, and they will live in the Divine Will in varying degrees and enjoy worldwide righteousness, peace and joy in the Holy Spirit.

[179] Lactantius, *The Divine Institutes*, op. cit.

[180] Is. 30:26.

[181] Is. 42:16.

[182] Justin Martyr, *Dialogue with Trypho*, op. cit.

[183] Is. 30:23-25.

[184] Is. 65:21-23.

[185] Jer. 31:1-6.

[186] Am. 9:14.

[187] Is. 61:6.

[188] 1 Pt. 2:5.

[189] 1 Pt. 2:9.

[190] Rev. 5:10.

[191] Rev. 20:6.

[192] *Catholic Dictionary of Dogmatic Theology*, op. cit., p.208.

193 Piccarreta, *Manuscripts*, op.cit., Feb 8, 1921.

194 Ibid., May 2, 1923.

195 Ibid., May 17, 1925.

196 Venerable Concepción Cabrera de Armida, affectionately known as Conchita, was a fiancée, wife, mother of nine children, grandmother, mystic and spiritual writer. She was born December 8, 1862, in San Luis Potosí, México. She died March 3, 1937, in Mexico City. Conchita was chosen by God to spread in the Church the works of the Cross. These Works include the Reign of the Holy Spirit, the Mystical Incarnation, the internal sorrows of Jesus and the internal martydom of Mary's solitude. For more than forty years, on the advice of her spiritual directors, she faithfully kept a spiritual diary that numbered 66 handwritten manuscripts which equals in amplitude the Summa of St. Thomas Aquinas. Her works are addressed to people from all walks of life: to single and married people, to priests and to bishops, to religious and to all consecrated souls.

As a mystical writer she heard God telling her: *"Ask me for a long suffering life and to write a lot... That's your mission on earth"*. She faithfully followed the obedience of all of her spiritual directors: Father Alberto Mir, S.J. (Dec. 13, 1852 - Dec. 22, 1916), Father Félix Rougier, S.M. (Dec. 17, 1859 - Jan. 10, 1938), Canon Emeterio Valverde y Tellez (March 1, 1864 - Dec. 26, 1948), Msgr. Dr. Ramon Ibarra y Gonzalez (Oct. 22, 1853 - Feb. 1, 1917), and Msgr. Luis Maria Martinez (1881-1956), auxiliary bishop of Morelia, then archbishop-primate of Mexico.

At the time her canonization process began in 1959, about 200 volumes of her writings were presented to the Congregation for the Causes of Saints. On December 20, 1999, she was declared Venerable by Pope John Paul II.

197 Philipon, *Conchita*, op. cit., pp. 195-196.

198 Ibid., pp. 23, 62.

199 John Paul II, *Theology of the Body* (Boston: Pauline Books and Media, 1997), pp. 116. Cf. also pp. 253, 256.

200 Pope John Paul II, *Redemptoris Mater*, Libreria Editrice Vaticana, 1987, n. 13.

201 Ibid., nn. 14, 18, 25.

202 Pope John Paul II, *L'Osservatore Romano*, Weekly Edition in English, Baltimore, 21 August 1996, p. 7.

203 Monteau-Bonamy, Immaculate Conception and the Holy Spirit, op. cit., p. 70. Fr. Manteau-Bonamy was a French theologian at the 2nd Vatican Council. In the 1970's he became captivated by St. Maxamillian Kolbe's understanding of the mystery of Mary and her intimate union with the Holy Spirit.

204 Lk.1:28.

205 Zech. 9:9. Cf. also Ez. 36:27-28; 37:26-28; Zeph. 3:16-17.

206 CCC, op. cit., 972; *Lumen Gentium*, Vatican Council II, op. cit., 68.

207 *Lumen Gentium*, 63. The Latin word for "type"– *typus* – signifies a figure, image or model. In the case of Mary, she is the image of the Church's future state of "perfect union with Christ."

[208] Aristide Serra, *Parola, Spirito e Vita,* semestrale - n.2, luglio – dicembre 1998/2, collana 38 Lo Spirito Santo (Centro editoriale dehoniano, Bologna, Italy); article *Lo Spirito Santo e Maria* in Lc 1,35. *Antico e Nuovo Testamento a confronto,*, pp.119-140. The staff of editors include Enzo Bianchi, Giancarlo Biguzzi, Clara Burini, Alceste Catella, Francesca Cocchini, Rinaldo Fabris, Eleuterio Fortino, Daniele Garrone, Luciano Manicardi, Luca mazzinghi, Alberto Mello, Luciano Monari, Salvatore Natoli, Gianfranco Ravasi, Gerard Rosse, Aristide Serra, Patrizio Rota Scalabrini, Horacio Simian-Yofre, Paolo Vian, Alexandre Winogradsky and Giorgio Zevini.

[209] Ibid.

[210] De Montfort, St. Louis Grignion, *True Devotion to Mary,* Rockford, IL Tan Books, 1985, Article n.35, p.299.

[211] Ibid., Article n. 47, p. 302.

[212] Ibid., n.49, p.303. St. Louis' polyvalent expression "the second coming" reflects his eschatology on an historic era of Christian holiness in which Christ reigns in the souls of human creatures. St. Louis interprets Christ's second coming through his Incarnation and his reign in Mary, through whom he extends his reign in other creatures. He describes Mary's catalytic role in the rise of "the great saints" who hasten the era of Christ's reign in souls. Montfort's 'second coming' is understood as an "interior" reign of Christ at a time of universal outpouring of grace and its preparation by the action of the Spirit and Mary.

When speaking of Christ's second coming, Montfort describes it in distinctly interior and spiritual terms: Christ will reign in the souls of human creatures within history. Although Monfort affirms that Christ's reign will be spiritual and within human history, he also relates it to Christ's definitive and physical return on earth outside of human history, whereby Christ's second coming begins with his interior reign in souls and culminates with his "exterior, physical and final" return in glory to conclude human history.

Montfort's thought may be summarized as follows: As Christ's "first coming" embraces the Incarnation, his public life and the Cross, so his "second coming" embraces his interior reign in souls (era of peace), which discovers its final and definitive moment in his return in the flesh and the final judgment (Parousia). The interior coming prepares the Church for the exterior and final return of Jesus. Jesus came the first time "in self-abasement and privation," whereas he will come the second time interiorly to "reign over all the earth" and externally "to judge the living and the dead," Monfort affirms.

One cannot overemphasize the point that Montfort's interior reign of Christ occurs within human history, whereas his judgment of "the living and the dead," occurs outside of history. These are two distinct and critical points that define Montfort's thought, without which, indiscriminately lend to the heresy of millenarianism. (*Nota bene*: This very error has recurred in recent years in the USA through a privately owned lay printing press that misinterprets the writings of the early Fathers by combining as one event Christ's "interior" reign in souls with his "exterior" and "physical" return at the end of human history. For more information on Montfort's thought, I refer you to the work entitled, Jesus Living in Mary: Handbook of the Spirituality of St. Louis de

Montfort, (BayShore, NY: Montfort Publications, 1994).

213 Yves Dupont, *Catholic Prophecy*, Tan Books, Rockford, 1973, p.33.

214 St. Maximilian was born Raymond Kolbe in Poland, January 8, 1894. In 1910, he entered the Conventual Franciscan Order. After having been sent to Rome to study, he was ordained a priest in 1918. He returned to Poland in 1919 and began spreading devotion to Mary through his Militia of the Immaculata movement of Marian consecration, which he founded on October 16, 1917. In 1927, his missionary spirit inspired him to establish a center of evangelization near Warsaw called *Niepokalanow*, the "City of the Immaculata."

His contributions to the field of theology anticipated the Mariology of the Second Vatican Council and further developed the Church's understanding of Mary as "Mediatrix" of all the graces of the Trinity.

Father Maximilian was captured by the Nazi's in 1941 and imprisoned in Auschwitz. There he offered his life for another prisoner and was condemned to slow death in a starvation bunker. In that same year his impatient captors ended his life with a fatal injection. Pope John Paul II canonized Maximilian as a "martyr of charity" in 1982. St. Maximilian Kolbe is considered a patron of journalists, families, prisoners, the pro-life movement and the chemically addicted.

215 Yves Dupont, *Catholic Prophecy*, Tan Books, Rockford, 1973, p.33.

216 St. Maximilian Kolbe, quoted in Albert J. Herbert, S.M., *Signs, Wonders and Response*, (LA: 1988), p.126.

217 Hugh Owen, *"New and Divine": The Holiness of the Third Christian Millennium* (John Paul II Institute of Christian Spirituality, 2001), *passim*.

218 "Mary alone can instruct each one of us at every instant, can guide us and draw us to herself, so that it may no longer be we but she who lives in us, even as Jesus lives in her, and as the Father lives in the Son... to understand better the Lord Jesus and the mysteries of God... Such souls will come to love the Sacred Heart of Jesus much better than they would have ever done up to now... Through her divine love will set the world on fire and will consume it; then will 'the assumption of souls in love' take place" (St. Maximilian Kolbe, quoted in Monteau-Bonamy, *Immaculate Conception and the Holy Spirit*, pp. 110, 117).

219 Eph. 3:1; 4:1; 6:20.

220 Eph. 3:9-10.

221 Acts 19:10.

222 Eph. 1:3-15; 2:22.

223 The word "immaculate" is the best translation of Paul's original Greek word "amomos" (ἄμωμος), which St. Jerome translated into the Vulgate as "immaculatus" or immaculate and attributed to our loving Mother Mary. This word is used seven times in the New Testament: four times by St. Paul and once by Ss. Peter, Jude and John. In English it is usually translated in a negative sense only, namely "without blemish", even though the Greek word has also a positive quality to it. In addition to the mere absence of blemish, the Greek word expresses the quality of pure, active and

perfect obedience to God's will. It is for this reason that St. Jerome attributed this word to Mary, who best exemplified the state of immaculacy.

[224] John Paul II, *The Theology of the Body*, op.cit., p.317.

[225] CCC, op.cit., 152; 243, 685, 686.

[226] *The Teaching of the Catholic Church*, op. cit., p. 1140.

[227] Eph. 4:11-13.

[228] 1 Pt. 1:4-5.

[229] In Scripture the "white garment" not only refers to a totally new creature reborn in Baptism, but to one that is made immaculate and holy (Rev 7:14; 19:8).

[230] Heb. 8:3.

[231] Heb. 9:13.

[232] Jn. 5:30.

[233] Heb. 5:8.

[234] Heb. 7:27

[235] Heb. 9:15.

[236] Heb. 8:13.

[237] Heb. 7:27.

[238] CCC, op. cit., 1076.

[239] Heb. 9:14.

[240] Vatican II, op. cit., *Presbyterorum Ordinis*, 10, 12, 13, 16.

[241] Rom. 8:29.

[242] 1 Cor. 15:49

[243] Vatican II, op.cit., *Lumen Gentium*, 10.

[244] St. Iranaeus states: "He (God) could have offered perfection to man from the very beginning, but man would have been incapable of supporting it... God prepares man for the vision of Himself by a constant increase in the activity and presence of his Word among men" (Irenaeus, op. cit., *Adversus Haereses*, IV, 38,1; 20,5).

[245] "*The Church with all her sacraments and institutions lives from the air of eternity of heaven; she cannot avoid mediating something of this*" (Hans Urs Von Balthasar, *Die himmlische Kirche und ihre Erscheinung*, in idem, Homo creatus est [Einsiedeln, 1986, 148-64] Skizzen zur Theologie, vol. V); cf. also Christoph Schönborn, *From Death to Life, The Christian Journey*, (CA: Ignatius Press, 1995), p. 74.

[246] Luisa Piccarreta, *Manuscripts*, op. cit., June 15, 1926.

[247] Venerable Concepciòn Cabrera de Armida, *To My Priests [A Mis Sacerdotes]*, (Cleveland, OH: Archangel Crusade of Love, 1996) p.107. Cf. also Ibid., p. 217.

[248] Dina Bélanger was born in 1897 in St. Roch Parish, Quebec City. Her parents taught her to pray while she was still very young. She was intelligent, studious and gifted, yet remained simple and unassuming. Very gifted musically, she spent two

years completing her studies at the New York Conservatory. On returning to Quebec, in June 1918, she gave concerts for the benefit of various works of charity for the poor. On August 11, 1921, Dina entered the novitiate of the Religious of Jesus and Mary, at Sillery. After her religious profession, she gave piano lessons. Her pupils were impressed by her kindness, her work ethic and her remarkable musical talent. Dina lived a life of extraordinary love for God. However she kept the depth of her intimacy with Jesus well hidden. Only her autobiography reveals the secret depths of the eternal life of God in which she was continuously immersed. One day, she heard Jesus say: "My Heart overflows with graces for souls. Lead them to my Eucharistic Heart." She died peacefully on September 4, 1929, in the 33rd year of her life.

[249] Piccarreta, Manuscripts, op. cit., April 8, 1918

[250] Leger, Irene, R.J.M, The Courage to Love, Ipswich, England: East Anglian Magazine, 1986, p. 135.

[251] St. Padre Pio assured his spiritual children that poor style and form should not be of hindrance to them:

"As regards to your reading there is very little to be admired and hardly anything by which to be edified. It is absolutely necessary for you to add to such reading that of the Holy books (Sacred Scripture) so highly recommended by all the Holy Fathers of the Church. I cannot dispense you from such spiritual reading, for I have your perfection too much at heart. If you want to gain the quite hoped-for fruit from such reading, it will be well to rid yourself of the prejudice you have with regard to the style and form in which these holy books are set forth. Get to work then. Make an effort in this respect and don't neglect to ask the Divine assistance with all humility " (Have a Good Day, edited by Fr. Alessio Parente, OFM, National Center for Padre Pio, Barto).

[252] Vatican II, op. cit., Dei Verbum, 4, 8.

[253] CCC, op. cit., 84.

[254] Mk. 16:6; Vatican II, op. cit., Dei Verbum, 8.

[255] Mt. 13:52.

[256] Hans Urs von Balthasar, Présence et Espirit, essai sur la Philosphie religieuse de Grégoire de Nysee, Book Pub Co. Paris, 1942, p.10. in Hawthorn, v.3, in pp.110-111.

[257] Rom. 12:6

[258] St. Thomas Aquinas, Summa Theologica, Benzinger Bros. New York 1947; Treatise on the Theological Virtues, Question 1: Of Faith; Art. 7: Whether the articles of faith have increased in the course of time?

[259] Eph. 3:18.

[260] Vatican II, op. cit., Lumen Gentium, 12.

[261] CCC, op. cit., 2014. The Catholic Catechism distinguishes the gift of the Holy Spirit given to all at Baptism from the mystical gifts granted only to some.

[262] John of the Cross, The Collected Works, op. cit., "The Dark Night", p.380.

[263] Faustina Kowalska, Diary, op.cit., entry 1558.

[264] Luisa Piccarreta, Manuscripts, op. cit., May 17, 1925.

[265] Philipon, *Conchita*, op. cit., p. 129.

[266] "Thus it is evident to everyone that *all the faithful in Christ of whatever rank or status are called to the fullness of the Christian life and to the perfection of charity*" (*Lumen Gentium*, Vatican Council II, op. cit., 5, 40). And Pope John Paul II recalls: "The Church opens to *all* people the prospect of being *divinized* and thus of becoming more human" (Pope John Paul II, from the papal Bull *Incarnationis Mysterium*, Libreria Editrice Vaticana, 1998, n.2).

[267] John of the Cross, "The Living Flame of Love", *The Collected Works*, op. cit., stanza 37, pp.615-616.

[268] *L'Eglise du Verbe Incarné*, vol. II (Burges, 1951) pp.997, n.1; cf. 60-91 and *Nova et Vetera* 38 (1963) pp.307-310.

[269] *Osservatore Romano, Realizzare il Concilio*, Vatican City, Europe, October 2, 1982, p.2. Confer also the Dogmatic Constitution *Lumen Gentium*: "In order to accomplish the Father's will, Christ founded the kingdom of heaven on earth, revealed his mystery to us, and brought about our redemption through his obedience. *The Church, i.e., the kingdom of Christ, which is already present in mystery, grows visibly in the world through the power of God*" (*Lumen Gentium*, Ibid., n.3). The same document reveals how the Church is the kingdom of Christ although only in its "seed form" (*Ibid.*, n.5), which "buds and grows until the harvest time"(Mk. 4:26-29; LG 5).

[270] Every priestly ministry *shares* in the fullness of the mission entrusted by Christ... For the priesthood of Christ, of which priests have been really made sharers, is necessarily directed to all peoples and all times, and is not confined by any bounds (*Presbyterorum Ordinis*, 10, 12, 13, 16).

[271] *Gaudium et Spes*, Vatican II, op. cit., 34.

[272] Maximus was born at the end of the sixth century in Consantinople. He renounced his noble estate to join the monks in the Chrysopolis Monastery, where he was later elected superior. His extraordinary philosophical and theological education prepared him for the many hardships he would face in defense of the faith. He successfully demonstrated the incorrectness of the Monothelite heresy, for which he was subjected to persecutions many times. After being sent into exile on numerous occasions he would each time be called back to Constantinople. For his refusal to recognize the Monothelite Patriarch of Constantinople as legitimate, his opponents cut off his right hand and tongue, so that he could not proclaim or defend the truth either by word or by pen. They then dispatched him to confinement in Lazov in the Caucasus, where he remained until his death in 662. His efforts did eventually lead the Monothelite Patriarch of Constantinople to renounce his heresy in 645. Among his many theological works in defense of the faith, the most outstanding is the *Philokalia* (a collection of patristic instructions on prayer and the ascetic life). In his works Maximus speaks of the divinization of man through the synergetic operations of the human and the divine will.

[273] I refer you to the footnote on the Characteristics of the Era of Peace, Modification of Sin. If the fifth session of the General Council of Trent condemned the idea of an historical sinless society, inasmuch as the "concupiscence or the inclination to

sin *remains* in the baptized," and not sin itself, it refrained from condemning the modification of its active psychosomatic influence in the same (*The Christian Faith*, p.187, *Council of Trent*, nn.3,5). While the law of sin "remains" in us till death, the lives of the saints remind us of the mitigation of its active psychosomatic influence. Ss. Catherine of Siena, John of the Cross and Teresa of Avila speak of the state of spiritual union where voluntary sins cease altogether. Some Fathers ascribe this spiritual state to the elect who partake of the universal era of peace. Because original sin remains, so must the sacraments that are ordered to the soul's purification and perfection.

[274] What Maximus calls the "full natural will" St. Augustine calls the "free will". Augustine refers to the human will in the original state of Adam as the "libera voluntas" (free will), and the state of sinful man after original sin as the "improba voluntas" (perverse will). Like Maximus, Augustine acknowledges that it is possible for man to recover the original and uninhibited activity of the will that Adam possessed before original sin, but only by a special grace of God.

[275] Luisa Piccarreta, *Manuscripts*, op. cit., Jan. 12, 1900.

[276] Ibid., March 19, 1926.

[277] Venerable Conchita's last spiritual director was Msgr. Luis Maria Martinez (1881-1956), auxiliary bishop of Morelia, then archbishop-primate of Mexico and in charge of the Affairs of the Holy See at an extremely difficult time in the history of his country. A famous and saintly author of spiritual theology, he directed Conchita from July 7, 1925 to the more mature period of her spiritual life, until the day of her death March 3, 1937.

[278] Archbishop Luis Maria Martinez, The Unification with the Divine Will, op. cit., p.15.

[279] Dina Bélanger, *The Autobiography*, op. cit., p. 346.

[280] Luisa Piccarreta, *Manuscripts*, op. cit., Oct. 24, 1925.

[281] Dina Bélanger, *The Autobiography*, op. cit., pp. 219, 227, 235-236.

[282] Pico is revered by the Church as a pioneer in his sketches on the images of man's original beauty. Henry de Lubac quotes him on the importance of the human will in relation to the reflection of God's likeness:

"*O Adam... the rest of the creatures are determined according to the laws of their nature... you are not limited by any boundary; rather, you are to establish your own nature through your own free will, upon which I have made your destiny in life depend... You are free to be perverted into subhuman forms, but you are equally free to be reborn in higher divine forms through your own decision*" (Die Wurde des Menschen [Fribourg, Frankfurt, and Vienna: Pantheon Verlag, n.d.], 52; cf. H. de Lubac's commentary in Pico de la Mirandole (Paris, 1977).

[283] Pico di Mirandola, in Christoph Schönborn, *From Death to Life*, op. cit., p. 50.

[284] Ibid.

[285] Venerable Concepciòn, *To My Priests*, op. cit., p.158.

[286] Ibid., p.143.

[287] When the mystics speak of God uniting the soul's faculty of the will to himself, the other faculties, i.e., intellect and memory, are sublimated by virtue of this union as well.

[288] Of the many modern mystics that speak of the gift of Jesus' continuously eternal activity in the human creature, Jesus tells Luisa that she is the first creature conceived in original sin to receive this gift to inaugurate the "reign" of his will on earth. Luisa's works were the first of their kind to appear in print with the *imprimatur's* and *nihil obstat's* of Bishop Joseph Leo and St. Hannibal di Francia.

[289] May 24, 1902 the 10th Ferron child of Rose DeLima Matthieu and Jean Baptiste was born in a stable in St. Germain De Grantham, Quebec and baptized Marie Rose, "Little Rose." When 4 years old a boy her age carrying a cross asked her to help him carry his. The boy was the Jesus. So vivid was this first vision of Jesus that Little Rose kept calling him: "My Little Jesus." In early 1907 the Ferrons moved to Fall River, MA where a mystical illness finally confined her to bed. She could neither play nor go to school, except for a few weeks. Fr. Gauthier advised her parents: "Keep the flagellation wounds on her body secret, for people might think that they are a disease and your daughters may never find husbands." Gradually the crown of thorns, the flagellation marks and the five stigmata wounds of Christ became more visible. Every Friday Little Rose suffered the crucifixion with and for Jesus. Rheumatoid arthritis, opisthotonos and dislocated bones caused her to be tied tight to her bed of boards at her ankles, knees, thighs and chest, nailed to her cross! This was her bed of Jesus' sorrows in which she lived for many years, barely able to move her head, right arm and two fingers of her right hand. Her stomach regurgitated the food she tried to eat out of obedience. Sleeping only one hour a night she made religious articles with her teeth and two fingers, bilocated to those in need, and prayed in vision and ecstasy with her heavenly visitors, especially with Jesus, Mary and Joseph. Little Rose predicted her death seven years in advance. Many heard her repeat Jesus' words to her: "Seven years more and I will be with you forever." Seven years later little Rose died at the age of 33, the age of our Lord, on May 11, 1936 and was buried on May 15 in the Precious Blood Cemetery, Woonsocket, R.I. in the parish of her patroness, The Little Flower. Bishop Hickey begged her to offer her sufferings to stop the threat of Schism created by the French Sentinellists. The result? All 56 excommunicated Sentinellists submitted and returned to the Church! Many that had met Little Rose have publicly testified before the Church that she was "Always in pain, never complaining, always smiling and hiding her pain!" Although Little Rose was unable to write, her words were recorded in a journal by her spiritual director Fr. John Kowalska, Baptist Palm, S.J.

[290] Rom. 5:20.

[291] "It should be known that the Word, the Son of God… is hidden by *essence* and his presence in the innermost being of the soul. Individuals who want to find him should… enter within themselves in deepest recollection… God, then, is hidden in the soul, and there the good contemplative must seek him with love" ("Spiritual Canticle," John of the Cross, *The Collected Works*, op. cit., stanza 6, p.480).

[292] *Die Würde des Menschen* (Fribourg, Frankfurt, and Vienna: Pantheon Verlag, n.d.), 52; cf. H. de Lubac's commentary in *Pic de la Mirandole* (Paris, 1977).

[293] CCC, op. cit., 1305; 1546.

[294] St. Teresa of Avila, *The Interior Castle*, translated by the Benedictines of Stanbrook, (IL: Tan Books, 1997), p. 102.

[295] Thomas Dubay, *Fire Within*, (CO: Ignatius Press, 1989), pp. 85-86, 91.

[296] Ibid., p.105.

[297] St. Teresa of Avila, *The Interior Castle*, op. cit., pp. 272-73, 280.

[298] John of the Cross, "The Living Flame of Love," *The Collected Works*, op. cit., stanza, 1, 14-15, p.646.

[299] Ibid., "The Spiritual Canticle", stanza 39.

[300] "The Way of Perfection", St. Teresa of Avila (part 1, ch. 30), in *The Liturgy of the Hours* (NY: Catholic Book Pub. Co., 1975), vol. III, Wednesday of the 13th week, 2nd reading, pp. 431-432.

[301] Luisa Piccarreta, *Manuscripts*, op. cit., Dec. 6 1904.

[302] Ibid., May 9, 1907.

[303] Ibid., April 8, 1918.

[304] Ibid., Nov 26, 1921.

[305] Dina Bélanger, *The Autobiography*, op.cit., pp. 219, 227.

[306] Ibid., p.324, 333.

[307] Ibid., p. 214.

[308] Faustina Kowalska, *Diary*, op. cit., entry 1324.

[309] Ibid., entry 1393.

[310] Luisa Piccarreta, *Manuscripts*, op. cit., vol. I, undated; cf. also Dec 5, 1921.

[311] Ibid., October 25, 1903; July 18, 1926.

[312] Philipon, *Conchita*, op. cit., message of Sept. 22, 1927.

[313] Ibid., p.62. This new gift of mystical incarnation, far from demeaning the holiness of the state of spiritual marriage, affirms its nature of ongoing perfection. Fr. Thomas Dubay encounters a statement by the great mystical Doctor St. John of the Cross that may at first appear out of place. In addressing spiritual marriage, St. John states that *"this communication and manifestation of himself [God] to the soul... is the greatest possible in this life"* ("Living Flame of Love," John of the Cross, *The Collected Works*, stanza 3). Fr. Dubay then clarifies this expression by adding, *"one might think the story must be finished at this point. Not so. The saint goes on to explain that the person is within the divine splendors and is transformed in them"* ("Fire Within", John of the Cross, *The Collected Works* p.178). Furthermore, St. John, unlike Blessed Dina Bélanger, writes that while spiritual marriage confers on the soul a special transformation in this life, it is *"not in the open and manifest degree proper to the next life"* ("Spiritual Canticle", John of the Cross, *The Collected Works*, stanza 39, no. 4, p.623). When Blessed Dina and other contemporary mystics describe their transformation as proper to the next life, they are reaffirming a new "state," and a perfecting of the state of spiritual marriage.

[314] Hans Urs Von Balthasar, *Elizabeth of Dijon: An Interpretation of Her Spiritual Mission*,

(NY: Pantheon, 1956), p.106.

[315] Pope John Paul II's address to the Rogationist Fathers on the occasion of the centenary of the death of their Founder St. Hannibal di Francia, *arguably* favors this idea:

"The blessed founder (Hannibal)... saw in the 'rogate' the means God Himself provided to bring about *that new and divine holiness with which the Holy Spirit wishes to enrich the Church at the dawn of the third millennium, in order to make Christ the heart of the world*" (Pope John Paul II, *Letter on the Centenary of the Rogationist Fathers*).

The pontiff's words 'new and divine' holiness stem from the seer of La Salette, Melanie Calvat, to whom St. Hannibal di Francia was spiritual director. Melanie communicated to St. Hannibal a rule she said she had received from our Lady, to be called The Apostles of the Last Days, but Hannibal did not feel called to take upon himself this new rule of a new and divine holiness. In his letter to Fr. Jordan, St. Hannibal refers to the rule of Melanie and states that the seeds of a new and divine holiness were already contained in the "Rogationist spirituality."

It is noteworthy that the pope's expression 'new and divine' does not necessarily represent the gift of "Living in God's Divine Will". The expression 'new and divine' conveys the charism of Melanie's rule that is contained in the rule of the "Rogationist" fathers, which promotes a life of intercessory prayer for vocations and service within the Church to communicate 'new and divine' life to souls, especially through prayer for vocations, works of the apostolate and the administration of the sacraments of the living (the Eucharist, confirmation, marriage and holy orders) and of the dead (baptism, penance and sometimes extreme unction).

Luisa Piccarreta, on the other hand, does not use the expression 'new and divine' to describe the gift of 'Living in the Divine Will.' While the gift she describes of 'Living in the Divine Will' is indeed 'new', one ought not for that matter refer to it exclusively as a 'divine' holiness: The 'divine' holiness has *always* played an active role in the lives of the baptized, therefore, it is not 'new.' Rather, the new trait of Living in God's Will is the sublimation of the divine activity in the baptized through God's "continuously eternal" activity in the human creature (emphasis added). In short, "Living in the Divine Will" is not simply a divine holiness, it is an "eternal holiness." Thus Living in the Divine Will, as described by Luisa, is the creature's participation on earth in God's *"new and continuously eternal activity"* that the Blessed enjoy in heaven. It is heaven on earth internalized! The Church has always offered to the faithful a 'divine' sanctity, and in recent years it has received a greater outpouring of sanctity by virtue of God's gift of his 'new and continuously eternal activity' within the soul of the human creature.

[316] Hannibal di Francia was born in Messina, Italy, on July 5, 1851. He was of noble lineage, as his father Francis was a Knight of the Marquises, Papal Vice-Consul and Honorary Captain of the Navy, and his mother, Anna Toscano, belonged to the noble family of the Marquises of Montanaro. Hannibal was a very devout child who was spiritually guided by the Cistercian fathers. He subsequently developed a deep love for the Eucharist that he was allowed to receive communion daily, something exceptional in those days. At seventeen, he was in prayer before the Blessed Sacrament exposed

when he was given the "revelation of Rogate", that is, a revelation that vocations in the Church only come through prayer. Later, Hannibal came across Jesus' words in the gospel that captured the essence of his revelation: *"Beg the harvest master to send out laborers to gather his harvest"*. (Mt 9:38; Lk 10:2). These words would become the main source of inspiration for Hannibal's life.

Hannibal was ordained to the priesthood on December 8, 1869. As a young priest, Hannibal founded charitable institutions for the young, the poor, the elderly, for priests and nuns. The essence of these intuitions was prayer for vocations *(Rogate)*, which Hannibal understood to be an explicit order from Christ and an "infallible remedy" for the Church.

To carry out his ideals he founded two religious Congregations: the Daughters of Divine Zeal, founded in 1887, and ten years later, the Rogationist Fathers of the Sacred Heart of Jesus. To his men and women religious he entrusted the ideal of "Rogate" and, in addition to the three religious vows of poverty, chastity and obedience, he bound them by a fourth one: to pray daily for vocations. It is noteworthy that St. Hannibal never considered himself as the Founder of his two Congregations but only their initiator. The true Founder, he would insist, was Jesus in the Blessed Sacrament. He had held the priesthood in greatest esteem and strongly believed that only through the mission of many holy priests the world could be saved.

On June 1st, 1927, St. Hannibal died in Messina, and droves of people came to witness the funeral and began to say: "Let us go to see the sleeping saint". A few days before his death, Hannibal had a vision of the Blessed Virgin Mary who appeared to him as a reward for his tender devotion toward her and to assure him of her protection. St. Hannibal's writing make up 62 volumes in all. His religious institutions are today present in the five continents of the world.

[317] Letters of St. Hannibal to Luisa Piccarreta, *Collection of Letters Sent by St. Hannibal Di Francia to the Servant of God, Luisa Piccarreta* (Jacksonville 1997), letter n. 2.

[318] For a better understanding of the "beatific mode," I refer you to the section, The New Heavens and New Earth."

[319] Luisa Piccarreta, *Manuscripts*, op. cit., October 9, 1922.

[320] Faustina Kowalska, *Diary*, op. cit., entries 767, 768, 770.

[321] "There are those who without any fault do not know anything about Christ or his Church, yet who search for God with a sincere heart and, under the influence of grace, try to put into *effect* the will of God as known to them through *the dictate of conscience...* Nor does divine Providence deny the helps that are necessary for salvation to those who, through no fault of their own, have not yet attained to the express recognition of God yet who strive, not without divine grace, to lead *an upright life*. For whatever goodness and truth is found in them is considered by the church as a preparation for the gospel and *bestowed by him who enlightens everyone* that they may in the end have life" (*Lumen Gentium*, Vatican II, op. cit., 16).

[322] Nestle-Aland, op. cit., Heb 10:12.

[323] Jn. 1:1-3; Col 1:17; Heb 1:3; Phil 2:6-11.

[324] Col. 1:15; Rev 3:14.

[325] A.Hulsbisch, O.S.A., *God in Creation and Evolution*, translated by Martin Versfeld, (NY: Sheed and Ward, 1965), p.79

[326] Gutierrez, Rev. Juan, M.Sp.S., Cruz de Jesus: Concepción Cabrera de Armida, Vida Mystica E Itinerario Espiritual, Tomo I, 1998, p.479.

[327] Anne Catherine Emmerich was born into a poor and pious family in Flamschen bei Coesfeld, Westphalia, Germany on September 8, 1774. Despite resistance from her parents, Anne Catherine became a nun of the Augustinian Order at Dulmen. She had the use of reason from her birth and could understand liturgical Latin from her first time at Mass. Life in the convent was not easy for Anne Catherine. Some nuns looked down on her because of her poor health. But an accident in 1806 made it impossible for her to leave her room for the next six years.

At the end of 1811, the convent where she lived was suppressed, and Ann Catherine along with a few other sisters made arrangements to live in Dulmen. There she would frequently experience ecstasies and other mystic phenomena. Towards the end of 1812, she received the marks of Christ's Passion on her body. In her humility she attempted to hide these marks, but soon the sisters noticed the *stigmata* and brought it to the attention of their superior. An investigation followed, which concluded that the wounds were truly mystic phenomena and that Ann Catherine was indeed the recipient of many supernatural gifts.

During the last 12 years of her life, Anne Catherine was bedridden. During this time she neither ate any food except Holy Communion, nor had anything to drink except water, subsisting entirely on the Holy Eucharist. From 1802 until her death, she bore the wounds of the Crown of Thorns, and from 1812, the full stigmata of Our Lord, including a cross over her heart and the wound from the lance. Anne Catherine entered her eternal reward in Dulman on November 9, 1824, where her remains are preserved.

Anne Catherine Emmerich possessed the gift of reading hearts, and she beheld the realities of the next world as we see with the naked eye. She saw Eden and our first parents, angels and devils, Heaven, Purgatory and Hell. She witnessed in graphic detail the life of Our Lord and of the Blessed Mother, she beheld the Real Presence of Christ in the Eucharist and the grace of the Sacraments. All of these divine realities were as real to her as the material world, and her revelations make the hidden, supernatural world come alive.

In 2001 Ann Catherine Emmerich's practice of virtue was declared "heroic". She was beatified on October 3, 2004 by Pope John Paul II. Fernando Rojo Martínez, O.S.A., the Augustinian Postulator of Causes, oversees the progress of her cause for canonization.

[328] St. Joseph Marello, canonized by Pope John Paul II on November 25, 2001, was born in Turin on December 26, 1844. He spent his childhood in San Martino Alfieri near Asti, Italy and was very much devoted to the Virgin Mary to whom he attributed his vocation. He was ordained a priest in 1868. In 1878 he founded the Oblates of St. Joseph Congregation for which he proposed St. Joseph as the exemplar of intimate relationship with the divine Word and of "looking after Jesus." He participated in the

First Vatican Council and was instrumental in obtaining the solemn declaration of papal infallibility. His Eminence Gioacchino Pecci, later Pope Leo XIII, had occasion to appreciate the virtues and talents of the young priest who accompanied his bishop as secretary. Pope Leo XIII nominated Joseph Marello as Bishop of Acqui and he was consecrated in 1889. In his writings, St. Joseph Marello extols God's divine will and eternal activity as the center of every human action, without which, all undertakings, for however extraordinary they may seem, are useless and without merit. St. Marello was well known for his maxim: "Do ordinary things in an extraordinary way." Joseph Marello died on May 30, 1895.

[329] Therese Martin was born to Louis Martin and Zelie Guerin on January 2, 1873. At the age of 15, she entered the Carmelite convent at Lisieux, France. With the religious name of Sr. Therese of the Child Jesus and the Holy Face, she lived a hidden life of prayer, through sickness and darkness. She described her life as "a little way of spiritual childhood," that consisted "not in great deeds, but in great love." She died on September 30, 1897, at the age of 24. The inspiration of her life and her powerful presence from heaven touched so many people so quickly that she was solemnly canonized on May 17, 1925 by Pope Pius XI and acclaimed the "greatest saint of modern times."

[330] During the 11th videoconference sponsored by the Congregation for the Clergy, "Pneumatology from the Second Vatican Council to Our Times," many noted theologians were gathered from around the world to take part in the discussions on the gifts of the Holy Spirit. Among them Alfonso Carrasco Rouco, from the School of Theology at San Dámaso, Madrid, spoke of the relation between the Holy Spirit's gifts and the virtues:

"Thanks to *these gifts* a moral subject achieves his own and necessary form, not only because they *perfect his different virtues*, but also because, profoundly penetrating a person, they prepare him to receive a movement toward his ultimate goal that can only be self-generated, *that is greater than all moral and theological virtues*—although made more perfect by grace; *a movement that can only originate in the superior movement of the Spirit.*"

"Each Christian believer therefore receives the gifts of the Spirit, who bestows them forever, and *the only condition is to be in a state of grace*" (Vatican City, August 29, 2002, Zenit.org).

[331] Luisa Piccarreta, *Manuscripts*, op. cit., Dec. 22, 1920.

[332] Ibid., February 16, 1921.

[333] Ibid., June 15, 1922.

[334] Venerable Concepciòn, *To My Priests*, op. cit., p.158.

[335] Ibid., p.143.

[336] Dina Bélanger, *The Autobiography*, op. cit., p.216.

[337] Faustina Kowalska, *Diary*, op. cit., entry 145.

[338] Dina Bélanger, *The Autobiography*, op. cit., pp.188-189.

[339] Luisa Piccarreta, *Manuscripts*, op. cit., June 29, 1914.

[340] Venerable Concepciòn, *To My Priests*, op. cit., pp. 90, 92.

[341] Philipon, *Conchita*, op. cit., message of April 17, 1913.

[342] Vera Grita, *Tabernacoli Viventi*, op. cit., p.38.

[343] St. Catherine of Siena, *The Dialogue*, (Rockford, IL: Tan Books, 1907), *passim*.

[344] Anne Catherine Emmerich, *The Life of Christ*, Anne Catherine Emmerich, (Rockfort, IL: Tan Books, 1968), *passim*

[345] John of the Cross, *The Collected Works*, op. cit., "The Living Flame of Love," passim.

[346] Luisa Piccarreta, *Manuscripts*, op. cit., January 5, 1921.

[347] Ibid., June 15, 1922.

[348] Ibid., May 5, 1923.

[349] Ibid.

[350] Ibid., December 26, 1923.

[351] Venerable Concepciòn, *To My Priests*, op. cit., p. 206.

[352] Philipon, *Conchita*, op. cit., p.228.

[353] Sister Mary of the Holy Trinity (Luisa Jaques), was born in 1901 in Pretoria, Transvaal of French-Swiss Protestant parents. Her mother died giving birth to her, and her father was a protestant missionary. She grew up in Switzerland with two elder sisters who were assisted by their kind aunt. Her father's mission work presented her with trips to America, Africa, Italy and other countries. Much like St. Faustina, Sr. Mary was assured of her place in the convent through the inspired counsels of her spiritual confessor through whom Jesus spoke. She made the "vow of victim" for the reign of God's Will on earth, and also for the conversion of her own family. While Jesus obtained the latter in her lifetime in ways she did not expect, he promised an era where his will reigns in the souls of creatures. Sr. Mary possessed the mystical gift of "living in the Divine Will" and possessed Jesus' Real Presence 24/7 through the revelations she received in Jerusalem, where Jesus brought her to have her "hands, feet and heart pierced." These revelations contain the most enrapturing insights and sublime teachings on the love of neighbor, the value of simple living, interior silence, purity of intention and other virtues that enable one to "imitate Jesus' Eucharistic Life" and to "Live in the Divine Will". With the promise that Jesus, in her, would continue her work from heaven and the foreknowledge of her own death, Sr. Mary entered her eternal reward in 1942.

[354] *The Spiritual Legacy of Sister Mary of the Holy Trinity*, IL: Tan Books, 1981, p.322.

[355] Dina Bélanger, *The Autobiography*, op. cit., p. 305.

[356] Luisa Piccarreta, *Manuscripts*, op. cit., August 6, 1928.

[357] Ibid., July 8, 1933.

[358] Ibid., January 24, 1932.

[359] Walter Ciszek, *He Leadeth Me*, op. cit., pp.116-117.

[360] Colossians 1:24. The conciliar document on missionary activity affirms that Paul's "filling up" embraces all the trials, sufferings and calumnies that were thrust upon

him in his apostolic ministry and preaching of the gospel: "*So indeed did all the apostles journey in hope; by many trials and sufferings they filled up what was lacking in the sufferings of Christ, for the sake of his body, which is the church. Often too the blood of Christians has been a seed*" (Vatican II, op. cit., *Ad Gentes*, 5).

361 Faustina Kowalska, *Diary*, op. cit., entry 1641.

362 Luisa Piccarreta, Manuscripts, op. cit., Oct. 6, 1922.

363 Luisa refers to herself throughout this passage, intermittently exchanging "she" with "I." For the sake of consistency and clarity, the third person singular is applied throughout the quoted text.

364 Luisa Piccarreta, *Manuscripts*, op. cit., May 17, 1925.

365 Faustina Kowalska, *Diary*, op. cit., entry 1749.

366 "Man was created in God's image and was commanded to conquer the earth with all it contains and to rule the world in justice and holiness: he was to acknowledge God as maker of all things and *relate himself and the totality of creation to him*, so that through the dominion of all things by man the name of God would be majestic in all the earth... *When he works, not only does he transform matter and society, but he fulfills himself... Here then is the norm for human activity – to harmonize with authentic interests of the human race, in accordance with God's will and design*, and to enable men as individuals and as members of society to pursue and fulfill their *total* vocation" (*Gaudium et Spes*, Vatican II, op.cit., 34).

367 Romans 8:28.

368 Jesus tells Luisa: "When I came to earth I reunited the Divine Will with the human will. If a soul does not reject this bond, but rather surrenders itself to the mercy of my Divine Will and allows my Divine Will to *precede it, accompany it, and follow it*; if it allows its acts to be encompassed by my Will, then what happened to Me happens to that soul" (Luisa Piccarreta, *Manuscripts*, op. cit., June 15, 1922).

369 Ibid., Februrary 26, 1922.

370 Ibid., July 18, 1926.

371 Dina Bélanger, *The Autobiography*, op. cit., p. 343, June 14, 1928.

372 *The Spiritual Legacy of Sister Mary of the Holy Trinity*, op. cit., p.303.

373 Ez. 36:11.

374 The Liturgy of the Hours, vol. II, op. cit., p. 791.

375 *Padre Pio's Words of Hope*, Our Sunday Visitor Pub., Huntington, IN 1999, Meditation 89, p.111.

376 The Spirit can communicate the gift of living in the Divine Will in a soul that is in the state of grace and desires to do and receive all that which God asks of it and wishes to grant it.

377 St. Augustine's expression "entirely ignorant" signifies that the soul lacks even that "general knowledge" of which St John of the Cross writes, which is necessary in order for the soul to experience the Spirit's gifts.

[378] St. Augustine, Letter to Bishop Proba, Liturgy of the Hours, vol. IV, p.430.

[379] Denzinger, *Enchiridion Symbolorum, definitionum et declarationum*, op. cit., 4781, 4158.

[380] Ibid., 4131.

[381] Ibid., 4326.

[382] Ibid., 4141.

[383] Luisa Piccarreta, *Manuscripts*, op. cit., May 17, 1925.

[384] Ibid., October 4, 1906.

[385] Ibid., September 2, 1904; cf. also Ibid., May 4, 1925.

[386] During the 11th videoconference sponsored by the Congregation for the Clergy, "Pneumatology from the Second Vatican Council to Our Times," Alfonso Carrasco Rouco, from the School of Theology at San Dámaso, Madrid, spoke of the relation between the Holy Spirit's gifts and the virtues: *"Each Christian believer therefore receives the gifts of the Spirit, who bestows them forever, and the only condition is to be in a state of grace"* (Vatican City, August 29, 2002). Jesus tells Luisa: "So, I say to you as always, continue your journey in My Will, because the human will contains weaknesses, passions, and miseries. These are obstacles that prevent entry into the Eternal Will. *Mortal sins are like barricades erected between the human will and the Divine Will.* If My Fiat 'on earth as It is in Heaven' does not reign on earth, that is precisely what prevents entry into the Eternal Will" (April 20, 1923).

[387] Although *particular knowledge* of this new, eternal mode of holiness may not be present to one intellect as it is present to another, this need not impede the soul from experiencing or participating in the effects of God's eternal activity. This truth appears vividly in the writings of St. John of the Cross:

"You will say, "when the intellect does not understand particular things, the will is idle and does not love... because the will can only love what the intellect understands." This is true, especially in the natural operations and acts of the soul in which the will does not love except what the intellect understands distinctly. But in the contemplation we are discussing (by which God infuses himself into the soul), *particular knowledge as well as acts made by the soul are unnecessary.* The reason for this is that God in one act is communicating light and love together, which is loving supernatural knowledge. We can assert that this knowledge is like light that transmits heat, for that light also enkindles love. This light is general and dark to the intellect because it is contemplative knowledge, which is a ray of darkness for the intellect, as St. Dionysius teaches...

The love in the will is also general, without any clarity arising from particular understanding... *Yet sometimes in this delicate communication God wounds and communicates himself to one faculty more than to the other;* sometimes more knowledge is experienced than love, and at other times more love than knowledge; and likewise at times all knowledge is felt without any love, or all love is felt without any knowledge" ("The Living Flame of Love," Saint John of the Cross, *The Collected Works of St. John of the Cross*, (Washington, D.C.: ICS Publications Institute of Carmelite Studies, 1991).

Translated by Kieran Kavanaugh, O.C.D. and Otilio Rodriguez, O.C.D., stanza 49, p.693; cf. also Luisa Piccarreta, *Manuscripts*, op. cit., May 22, 1932).

[388] Luisa Piccarreta, *Manuscripts*, op. cit., June 10, 1920.

[389] Ibid., October 29, 1903. In the context of this message, Jesus' *allurements* are not intended as an effect of the reading of Luisa's volumes, but as infusions of light communicated directly by God to the soul's intellect.

[390] Ibid., August 13, 1933.

[391] Liliana Grita, *Vera of Jesus, Bride of Blood*, [translated by Don Paolo Glaentzer], Turin, Italy, 1998, p.8.

[392] Ibid.

[393] Luisa Piccarreta, *Manuscripts*, op. cit., June 10, 1920.

[394] Ibid., October 27, 1922.

[395] Ibid., November 11, 1922.

[396] Ibid., January 28, 1926.

[397] Philipon, *Conchita*, op. cit., p.33.

[398] Venerable Concepciòn, *To My Priests*, op. cit., pp.266-270.

[399] Letters from St. Hannibal, op. cit., letter n. 13.

[400] St. Padre Pio was born in Pietrelcina, Italy on May 25, 1887. He was baptized Francesco Forgione at Our Lady of Angels Church. From his youth Francesco helped his parents with their work in the fields, but, above all, he was the shepherd of the flock. When he felt the call to the priesthood, his father willingly agreed to pay for his studies and emigrated to America to obtain suitable work. At the age of fifteen Francesco entered the novitiate of the Capuchin Friars in Morcone, where on January 22, 1903 he assumed the clothing of Saint Francis and was called *Padre Pio* and, on August 10, 1910 he took was ordained a priest in the Cathedral of Benevento. On September 20, 1918, the five wounds of Our Lord's Passion appeared on his body, making him the first stigmatized priest in the history of Church. In his letters he writes of personal interior experiences that often culminated in the continuous identification of his will with the will of God.

On January 9, 1940, St. Pio set up a monumental work for the relief of the suffering. This work was carried out with the help of disciples and with the small spontaneous offerings of believers from all over the world. Padre Pio died in the odor of sanctity on the 23rd of September 1968, at 2 a.m., holding the Holy rosary in his hands and uttering the words: "Jesus!... Mary!". He was 81. On March 2, 1999, Pope John Paul II declared Padre Pio of Pietrelcina Blessed and on May 19, 2002 he declared him a Saint in St. Peter's Square.

[401] Padre Pio, Letters vol. I, Editions "Padre Pio da Pietrelcina", San Giovanni Rotondo, Italy, 1884, p. 137.

[402] Ibid., p.145, 147, 149.

[403] The Servant of God, Rev. Msgr. Michael Sopoćko (1888-1976), was the confessor and spiritual director prepared for St. Faustina by our Lord. He served her in that

capacity during the years she was assigned to the Vilnius Convent. The diocesan process towards his beatification was solemnly inaugurated on December 4, 1987. The funeral Mass of Rev. Msgr. Michael Sopoćko had as its main celebrant His Excellency Most Rev. Bishop Henry Gulbinowicz. With him 80 priests concelebrated and His Eminence, Stephen Cardinal Wyszinski , Primate of Poland, (with whom our present Holy Father, Pope John Paul II, had forged an intimate relationship), sent a telegram expressing his condolences.

[404] Faustina Kowalska, *Diary,* op. cit., entries, 86, 90.

[405] Ibid., entry 378.

[406] Ibid., entry 1598.

[407] Mother Teresa was born in Albanian on August 26, 1910 and received the name Agnes Gonxha Bojaxhiu. At the age of 18, she joined the religious Order of Our Lady of Loreto in Ireland. She received her spiritual training in Dublin, Ireland and Darjeeling, India. In 1931, Mother Teresa took the name of Teresa from the French nun Thérèse Martin, who was canonized in 1927 with the title St. Thérèse of Lisieux. In 1937, Mother Teresa took her vows. She taught for 20 years in Saint Mary's High School in Calcutta, India. On September 10, 1946, Mother Teresa received another call from God to serve the poorest of the poor who live in the streets. In 1948, Pope Pius XII granted Mother Teresa permission to leave her duties and as an independent nun she began to share her life with the poor, the sick and the hungry of Calcutta. She established the Congregation of the Missionaries of Charity. Her initial work consisted of teaching the children of the streets how to read. In 1950, Mother Teresa began to care for lepers. In 1965, Pope Paul VI put the Missionaries of Charity under the control of the Papacy and gave authorization to Mother Teresa to expand her Order to other countries. Centers have opened almost everywhere around the world to assist lepers, the elderly, the blind, and people living with AIDS. In her letters, she also speaks of the supremacy of God's will in all things and at all times, even in the most menial chores done with great love. Mother Teresa died as one of the most renowned champions of God's poor.

[408] An Hour With Mother Teresa of Calcutta, Anthony F. Chiffolo, Liguori Pub., MO, 2002, pp.12-13.

[409] Dina Bélanger, *The Autobiography,* op. cit., p. 354.

[410] *Eucharisticum Mysterium,* 1967, Pontificium Institutem Altioris Latinitatis (2012) n. 5.

[411] Luisa Piccarreta, *Manuscripts,* op. cit., November 13, 1915.

[412] Venerable Concepciòn, *To My Priests,* op. cit., p. 274.

[413] Faustina Kowalska, *Diary,* op. cit., entry 1489.

[414] Ibid., Entry 1393.

[415] Vera Grita, *Tabernacoli Viventi [Living Tabernacles],* op. cit. p.38.

[416] Ibid., pp.92, 93.

[417] Ibid., p.105.

[418] Luisa Piccarreta, *Manuscripts*, op. cit., Feb. 6, 1919.

[419] Philipon, *Conchita*, op. cit., p. 62.

[420] Dina Bélanger, *The Autobiography*, op. cit., p.333.

[421] An offering made by Marthe in 1939, as an renewal of her Act of Abandonment of 1925, echoes so closely that made by Padre Pio: *"Lord, I offer myself, I give myself again to You for all the souls in the world, for the sanctity of your beloved souls, the priests, especially for those whose sins I carry in my heart; that through me, Lord, by my prayer, by my love, by my sufferings, by my immolation, by any exterior actions I may have, that by my whole life their apostolate may be more effective, more fruitful, more holy and more divine."*

A woman of great courage and strength, with a deep love of Christ and the Church, Marthe Louise Robin was born on 13 March 1902 at Châteauneuf-de-Galaure, near Lyons in south-eastern France; she died there on 6 February 1981, aged 78, having been bedridden and almost totally paralyzed for more than half a century. She was widely loved and greatly revered, and her funeral in 1981 was attended by thousands of mourners, including six bishops and more than 200 priests.

Marthe Robin was a countrywoman ready always to listen and advise those who came to her for counsel. During her lifetime she had a deep devotion to Mary and strove to live a life of continuous union with God's divine will and communion with Jesus' internal sorrows. Despite losing her sight at the age of 38, she continued to meet with men and women at her bedside and deal with an unending flow of letters. In October 1930, she received the stigmata and each Friday thereafter underwent the most intense pains of Jesus' death on the Cross. In her prayers, Our Lord revealed a vision of a new era of holiness, the "Pentecost of love." God called her to help prepare for this Pentecost through the apostolate of consecrated lay men and women living together in communities of prayer and work. These communities would be called "Foyers de Lumière, de Charité et d'Amour" (Centers of Light, Charity and Love). She left a large number of influential spiritual writings, and many of her insights and instructions were written down by Père Georges Finet, her spiritual director and co-founder of the Foyers de Charité.

[422] *Marthe Robin*, vicaire general, Robert GLAS, Valence, 1986, P.17 [Clichés Office de Lisieux, Editions du Carmel de Lisieux, Lisieux].

[423] Grita, Liliana, *Vera of Jesus, Bride of Blood*, op. cit., p.8.

[424] Elizabeth Catez was born July 18, 1880 near Bourges, France. Her father was a captain in the French military. Baptized on the Feast of St. Mary Magdalene, a saint to whom Elizabeth would later become very devoted, her youthful spunk and strong will was guided by her mother toward the love of Christ. At the age of seven Elizabeth's father died. Four years later she received her first communion and she was confirmed. Elizabeth, her mother and her sister Marguerite lived in Dijon together until Elizabeth decided to enter Carmel.

Elizabeth entered Carmel in Dijon on August 2, 1901. She made her final vows on January 11, 1903. The following June Elizabeth learned that she had Addison's disease, a hormonal disorder which causes weight loss, muscle weakness, extreme fatigue, low blood pressure, and darkening of the skin. From 1903 and 1906, her painful episodes increased in frequency, and in 1906, Elizabeth was confined to the infirmary, never to leave it again. During the agony she endured, she was able to mystically enter Jesus' internal sorrows, such that her unity with the Trinity became more and more apparent as she offered her suffering to God. She was entirely consumed with the love of God and, shortly before her death, exclaimed, "I am going to light, to love, to life!" On November 9, 1906 her short religious life gave birth to the definitive reward of the eternal life that she had already begun to experience on earth. The Church established her feast day on November 8th.

[425] De Meester, Conrad, *Elizabeth of the Trinity, The Complete Works*, vol. 1, translated by sister Aletheia Kane, O.C.D., ICS Publications, Washington (1984) p.180.

[426] Faustina Kowalska, *Diary*, op. cit., entry 1826.

[427] Ibid., entry 1564.

[428] Ibid., entry 785.

[429] Ibid., entry 137.

[430] *Novo Millennio Inuente*, op. cit., 56.

[431] The *ad intra operatio* is the Latin expression that conveys God's internal operations. *Ad intra operatio* refers to the *immanent* Trinity, that is, to "God in himself." The *ad extra operatio*, on the other hand, is the Latin expression that conveys God's external operations. *Ad extra operatio* refers to the *economic* Trinity, that is, to the external reiteration of God's being through creation. The *ad extra operatio* consists solely of God's actions outside of himself in relation to his creation, or "God for us." This *ad extra operatio* makes it possible to affirm that God has truly revealed himself (*ad intra*) in his external works (*ad extra*). While God's *ad extra* operations constitute a true reiteration or revelation of himself, this revelation is *not* exhaustive of his intrinsic being.

Another important relationship between the concepts of *ad intra* and *ad extra* is that although the former has primacy over the latter, "the *whole Godhead* is present in whatever God does *ad extra*, or external to himself." This truth is known in theology as, *"Opera Trinitatis ad extra sunt indivisa"* (the external works of the Trinity are undivided).

[432] Luisa Piccarreta, *Manuscripts*, op. cit., June 29, 1914.

[433] Pio, Blessed Padre, Letters, Editions "Padre Pio da Pietrelcina", San Giovanni Rotondo, Italy, 1884, vol. II, pp.356-359.

[434] Monsignor Aldo Gregorio, *La venuta intermedia di Gesú*, Alone Editrice, Montefranco, Treni, 1994.

[435] Fr. Stefano Gobbi, *To the Priests, Our Lady's Beloved Sons*, The Marian Movement of Priests Pub., 2000, message of August 21, 1981.

[436] Mantaeu-Bonamy, *Immaculate Conception and the Holy Spirit*, op. cit., pp. 110, 117.

[437] I refer you to footnote 212.

[438] I refer you to St. Louis de Monfort's "second coming" in the footnotes of the chapter *Mary, Model of the Church's Holiness*, and the chapter *Magisterium and Millenarianism*.

Cf. also Heb 9:28: "So Christ, having been offered once to bear the sins of many, will come a *second* time, not to deal with sin, but to save those who are eagerly waiting for him."

[439] The terminology of approved mystics, seers and locutionists varies in *form*, not in *doctrine*. In fact, the accounts of the Blessed Virgin's life composed by St. Bridget of Sweden, Venerable Mary of Agreda and Anne Catherine Emmerich, appear to contradict one another on various points; nonetheless they are widely regarded as authentic revelations.

[440] Philipon, *Conchita*, op. cit., pp. 195-196.

[441] Dina Bélanger, *The Autobiography*, op. cit., pp. 324, 333.

[442] "It should be known that the Word, the Son of God... is hidden by *essence* and his presence in the innermost being of the soul. Individuals who want to find him should... enter within themselves in deepest recollection... God, then, is hidden in the soul, and there the good contemplative must seek him with love" *(The Collected Works of St. John of the Cross*, ICS Publications Institute of Carmelite Studies, Washington, D.C., 1991. Translated by Kieran Kavanuagh, O.C.D. and Otilio Rodriguez, O.C.D. p.480; Spiritual Canticle, stanza 6).

[443] Luisa Piccarreta, Manuscripts, op. cit., October 5, 1903. Cf. also July 18, 1926.

[444] Archbishop Luis Maria Martinez, The Unification With the Divine Will, op. cit., p.15.

[445] Dina Bélanger, *The Autobiography*, op. cit., p.346.

[446] Ibid., p.62.

[447] Venerable Concepciòn, *To My Priests*, op. cit., p. 210.

[448] The word *theandric* is from the Greek: God (θεός), and man (ἀνδρὸς) . This expression was first found in a letter of Pseudo-Dionysuis, and later defended by St. John Damascene. Since there are two distinct natures in Christ, there are also two series of operations, the one divine (to create, to conserve the being of creatures), the other human (to speak, to move around). But *the human nature*, subsisting in the person of the Word, *is sustained in being and operation*. Therefore, every human operation of Christ can be called also *divine* as proper to the Word, *which is the acting principle* not only of the divine activity, but also *of the human*" (*Catholic Dictionary of Dogmatic Theology*, Ibid., p.281). When we apply this theology to those souls who have lived in the eternal mode of God's eternal operation, their actions become *continuously divine and eternal*, for they have Christ as their acting principle who sustains, empowers, motivates and guides them.

[449] Heb. 9:14.

[450] Hans Urs Von Balthasar, *Elizabeth of Dijon*, op. cit., p.110-111.

[451] Venerable Concepciòn, *To My Priests*, op. cit., p.114.

[452] *Sermo 25*, 7-8: PL 46, 937-938, in "The Liturgy of the Hours", op. cit., vol. IV, p.1573.

[453] Luisa Piccarreta, *Manuscripts*, op. cit., November 26, 1921; April 20, 1923.

454 Ibid., Nov 26, 1921.

455 Ibid., Oct. 24, 1925.

456 Ibid., volume I, undated; cf. also Dec 5, 1921.

457 Ibid., October 5, 1903; July 18, 1926.

458 Dina Bélanger, *The Autobiography*, op .cit., pp. 219, 227, 235-236.

459 Luisa Piccarreta, *Manuscripts*, op. cit., January 8, 1919.

460 Cf. pp. 78, 122.

461 Luisa Piccarreta, *Manuscripts*, op. cit., May 9, 1907.

462 Ibid., March 14, 1926.

463 *The Spiritual Legacy of Sister Mary of the Holy Trinity*, op. cit., pp.197. Cf. also pp. 209-210, 213, 234, 239, 250, 294-295.

464 Ibid., p. 210.

465 Ibid., p. 213.

466 Ibid., p. 234.

467 Ibid., p. 239.

468 Ibid., pp. 294-295.

469 Luisa Piccarreta, *Manuscripts*, op. cit., October 6, 1922.

470 Dina Bélanger, *The Autobiography*, op. cit., pp. 219, 227.

471 Vatican II, op. cit., *Lumen Gentium*, 5, 40.

472 Vera Grita, *Tabernacoli Viventi*, op. cit., pp.127, 34.

473 *The Spiritual Legacy of Sister Mary of the Holy Trinity*, op. cit., pp. 217-218.

474 Eph. 4:11-13.

475 Catholic Dictionary of Dogmatic Theology, op. cit., p.208.

476 CCC, op. cit., 677.

477 Ibid., 1001.

478 Ibid., 1038.

479 Ibid., 1040. Eschatologists do not attempt to uncover the mysterious "day" or "hour" of the Lord's return. It is not the eschatologist's concern to develop a theology on the "end day" or "end hour," but a theology of the "End Times."

480 Ibid., 676.

481 John Paul II, *The Theology of the Body*, op. cit., p.317.

482 Adwinkler, R., *Death In The Secular City* (Grand Rapids. W.B. Eerdmans Pub. Co., 1974) p. 128.

483 Winklhofer, A., *The Coming of His Kingdom* (New York, Herder and Herder, 1963) p.164ff.

484 Mt. 24:40-42.

485 1 Thes. 4:16-17.

[486] Mt. 24:15-22.

[487] Is. 26:19.

[488] Rev. 20:12-13.

[489] Lactantius, *The Divine Institutes*, op. cit., vol. 7.

[490] CCC, op. cit., 1038.

[491] Ibid., 1040.

[492] Dn. 7:9-10.

[493] 2 Pt. 3:10.

[494] Rev. 20: 9-14.

[495] Ps. 97.

[496] Is. 34:4.

[497] 2 Pt. 3:5-13.

[498] Is. 65:17-18.

[499] Rev. 21:1-2.

[500] CCC, 1045, 1047.

[501] Lactantius, *The Divine Institutes*, op. cit., vol. 7.

[502] Denzinger, *Enchiridion Symbolorum*, definitionum et declarationum, op. cit., 1361.

[503] Vatican II, op. cit., *Lumen Gentium* 1, 48.

[504] A. Winklhofer, *The Coming of His Kingdom* (New York: Herder and Herder, 1963).

[505] Thomas Aquinas, *Quaestiones Disputatae* (Roma, Italy: Editrice Marietti, 1965), q. 5, art. 4, reply to objs. 11-12. Cf. also trans. by the English Dominican Fathers, On the Power of God, Westminster, Maryland: The Newman Press, 1952, reprint of 1932.

[506] Rom. 14:17.

[507] Rev. 20:11; 21:1-3. 22; 22:1-3.

[508] W.M. Smith, *The Biblical Doctrine of Heaven*, (Chicago: Moody Press, 1968).

[509] Rev. 21:22.

[510] Rev. 21:3; 22:4-5.

[511] Jn. 1:50, 51.

[512] Rev. 22:3.

[513] Martyr, *Dialogue with Trypho*, in *The Fathers of the Church*, op. cit., pp. 277-278.

[514] Tertullian, *Adversus Marcion, The Ante-Nicene Fathers*, op. cit., vol. 3, pp. 342-343.

[515] Lactantius, *The Divine Institutes*, op. cit., vol. 7, p. 211.

[516] Methodius, *The Symposium*, in "The Anti-Nicene Fathers,", The Newman Press, Westminster, MD, 1958, discourse 9, ch.3.

[517] Rev. 2:7.

[518] Rev. 22:2, 14.

[519] Is. 11:6-9.

[520] Is. 65:17-25.

[521] Irenaeus, *Adversus Haereses*, op. cit., Book V, 33.3.4, pp. 384-385.

[522] Lactantius, *The Divine Institutes*, op. cit., vol. 7.

[523] Is. 60:19-20.

[524] Rev. 21:23-24.

[525] Rev. 22:5.

[526] Rev. 21:23; 22:5.

[527] *Letter of Barnabas*, in "The Apostolic Fathers", op. cit., pp. 215-216.

[528] Is. 54:13.

[529] Jer. 31:33-34.

[530] Jn. 6:45.

[531] Heb. 8:11.

[532] CCC, 671.

[533] Mt. 28:19-20.

[534] 1 Cor. 11:26.

[535] *Letter of Barnabas*, in "The Apostolic Fathers", op. cit., p. 216.

[536] The Christian Faith in the Documents of the Catholic Church, op. cit., p. 949.

[537] On the Refutation of all Heresies, Saint Hippolytus, in *Liturgy of the Hours*, op. cit., p. 460.

[538] *Letter of Barnabas*, in "The Apostolic Fathers", op. cit., p. 210.

[539] Tertullian, *Adversus Marcion*, op. cit., vol. 3, pp. 342-343.

[540] The Christian Faith in the Documents of the Catholic Church, op. cit., 2312.

[541] Rev. 21:4.

[542] Luisa Piccarreta, *Manuscripts*, op. cit., February 16, 1921.

[543] St. Augustine, From a letter to bishop Proba; *Liturgy of the Hours*, op. cit., vol. IV, p.430.

[544] Letters of St. Hannibal to Luisa Piccarreta, op. cit., letter n. 2.

[545] Philipon, *Conchita*, op. cit., message of April 17, 1913.

[546] Vatican II, op. cit., *Lumen Gentium*, 25; CCC, 2034, 2039.

[547] Thomas Steven Molnar, *Utopia the Perennial Heresy* (NY: Sheed & Ward, 1967), p. 24.

[548] St. Augustine of Hippo, *De Civitate Dei*, op. cit., Bk. XX, Ch. 7.

[549] CCC, op. cit., 676. Cf. also Denzinger, op. cit., 3839 .

[550] Heinrich Denzinger, *Enchiridion Symbolorum*, definitionum et declarationum de rebus fidei et morum, cura di Peter Hünermann (Barcinone, Herder Pub., 1965) [ed. Dehoniane Bologna 1995]; Acta Apostolicae Sedis, Rome, 1944, ser. 2, vol. XI, n. 7, 3839.

[551] Heinrich Denzinger, *Enchiridion Symbolorum* (cura di Johannes B. Umberg, SJ, 1951), 423, One should not equate *spiritual millenarianism* with the "spiritual *blessings*" of the era of peace contained in the writings of the early Fathers and Doctors. As mentioned in the footnote under St. Justin Martyr, Tradition has upheld the spiritual interpretation of the era of peace. Conversely, *spiritual millenarianism* promotes the idea that Christ will return to and remain on earth before the General Judgment and visibly reign for literally 1,000 years. He would not, however, participate in immoderate carnal banquets. Hence the name *spiritual.*

[552] Heinrich Denzinger, *Enchiridion Symbolorum*, op. cit., ser. 2, vol. XI, n. 7, 3839.

[553] J. Neuner & J. Dupuis, *The Christian Faith in the Documents of the Catholic Church* (London, Harper Collins, 1995), 673.

[554] Paul Poupard, *Articolo sul Millenarianismo*, Il Grande Dizionario delle Religioni (Assisi, Italy: Cittadella Editrice, 1990), p. 1346 {in the original Italian: *"Il testo dell'Apocalisse mantiene una grandissima discrezione sulla felicità degli eletti durante il regno di mille anni. Mentre l'esegesi ebraica e millenarista 'stretta' descrive la felicità paradisiaca in modo fantastico"*}.

[555] Danielou, *A History of Early Christian Doctrine* pp. 377, 379. The 'risen saints' is an allusion to the allegory of the 20th Chapter of the Book of Revelation.

[556] E.J. Fortman, S.J., *Everlasting Life after Death* (NY: Alba House, 1976), pp.254-256.

[557] Catholic Dictionary of Dogmatic Theology, op. cit., pp.111-112.

[558] Jansenism was a heresy begun by Cornelius Jansenius (1585-1638). He held that human nature was intrinsically corrupted by original sin and that some men were, therefore, predestined to heaven, others to hell. Christ dies only for those predestined to heaven to whom the operations of grace are irresistible. Thus those already predestined to heaven are obliged to observe an extremely ascetical and rigorous moral code. Jansenism was condemned by Popes Urban VIII in 1642, Innocent X in 1653 and by Clement XI in 1713.

[559] Thomas Aquinas, *Quaestiones Disputatae*, op. cit., vol. II *De Potentia*, Q. 5, Art. 5, p. 140.

[560] Danielou, *A History of Early Christian Doctrine*, op. cit., pp. 377, 379.

[561] Denzinger, *Enchiridion Symbolorum*, definitionum et declarationum, ser. 2, Vol. XI, n. 7, 3839.

[562] Denzinger, *Enchiridion Symbolorum*, cura d Umburg, p. 423.

[563] Although Christ is immanent by grace in the soul of the human creature, he infinitely transcends the creature. Thus Christ, at one and the same time, may reign in the soul of the human creature and reign in the heavens through his personal and glorified presence.

[564] Ps. 57:6.

[565] Trese, *The Faith Explained*, op. cit.

[566] Faustina Kowalska, *Diary*, op. cit., entries 1789, 1796.

[567] Acta Apostolica Sedis, op. cit. [in the original Latin:*"Systema Millenarismi mitigati tuto doceri non posse"*].

568 Denzinger, *Enchiridion Symbolorum*, cura d Umburg,; Thomas Aquinas, *La Somma Teologica*, IV Sent. (Bologna: Studio Domenicano, 1985), d.43,q.1,a.3,qc.1; Robert Bellarmine *De Romano Pontefice*, 1.3, cap. 17, (Neapoli, apud Josephum Giuliano, 1856) [cf. *Enciclopedia Cattolica*, Città del Vaticano, Ente per l'Enciclopedia Cattolica e per il libro Cattolico, 1948, p. 1010]; Mt. 16:27: *"Filius hominis venturus est in gloria Patris sui cum Angelis, tunc reddet unicuique secundum opera sua"* [For the Son of man will come with his Angels in his Father's glory, and then he will repay everyone according to his conduct].

569 "The Last Judgment will come *when Christ returns in glory.* Only the Father... determines the moment of its coming. Then through his son Jesus Christ *he will pronounce the final word on all history"* (CCC, 1040);

"The Antichrist's deception already begins to take shape in the world every time the claim is made to realize within history *that messianic hope which can only be realized beyond history through the eschatological judgment"* (CCC, 676);

"The kingdom will be fulfilled, then, not by a historic triumph of the Church through the progressive ascendancy, but only by God's victory over the final unleashing of evil, which will cause his Bride to come down from heaven" (CCC, 677);

"Indeed, the [final] resurrection is closely associated with Christ's Parousia" (CCC, 1001).

"The resurrection of all the dead, 'of both the just and unjust', will precede the Last Judgment... Then Christ will come 'in his glory, and all the angels with him... Before him will be gathered all the nations, and he will separate them one from another" (CCC, 1038).

The renowned theologian Cardinal Jean Danielou, also places Christ's coming not before the symbolic 1,000 years of peace or before the end of time, but at the end of time:

"This truth is that of the Parousia, *Christ's return to this earth at the end of time* to establish his kingdom, a belief which was attacked by Marcion, and which Tertullian rightly defended against him. It implies no more than that there is to be a period of time, the duration of which is unknown to men, and which in the last days will cover the return of Christ, the resurrection of the saints, the general Judgment, and the inauguration of the New Creation" [emphasis added] (Danielou, *A History of Early Christian Doctrine*, op. cit., p. 377).

570 *New Catholic Encyclopedia*, Vol. VII, p. 2; cf. also Martyr, *Dialogue with Trypho*, pp. 277-278; Tertullian *Adversus Marcion*; Lactantius, The Divine Institutes.

571 Catholic Dictionary of Dogmatic Theology, op. cit., pp. 124-125.

572 Catholic Encyclopedia Revised, Nashville, TN, 1987, p. 387.

Printed by Amazon Italia Logistica S.r.l.
Torrazza Piemonte (TO), Italy

45104985R00181